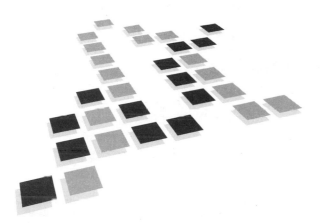

An SPSS Companion
to Political Analysis

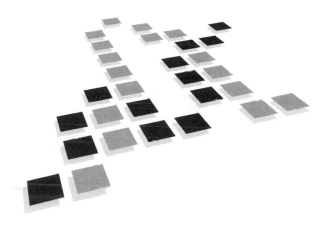

An SPSS Companion
to Political Analysis

Second Edition

Philip H. Pollock III
University of Central Florida

CQ PRESS

A Division of Congressional Quarterly Inc.
Washington, D.C.

CQ Press
1255 22nd Street, NW, Suite 400
Washington, DC 20037

Phone, 202-729-1900; toll-free, 1-866-427-7737 (1-866-4CQ-PRESS)

Web: www.cqpress.com

Credits: Datasets on the CD-ROM: GSS2002.sav and GSS2002student.sav: selected variables obtained from the 2002 General Social Survey, National Opinion Research Center, Chicago, and Inter-university Consortium for Political and Social Research (ICPSR), University of Michigan; NES2000.sav and NES2000student.sav: selected variables obtained from the 2000 National Election Study, Center for Political Studies and ICPSR, University of Michigan; States.sav: selected variables obtained from Gerald C. Wright, Indiana University. See Robert S. Erikson, Gerald C. Wright, and John P. McIver, *Statehouse Democracy* (Cambridge, U.K.: Cambridge University Press, 1993); World.sav: selected variables obtained from Mike Alvarez, José Antonio Cheibub, Fernando Limongi, and Adam Przeworski. See Mike Alvarez, José Antonio Cheibub, Fernando Limongi, and Adam Przeworski, *Democracy and Development: Political Institutions and Well-Being in the World, 1950–1990* (Cambridge, U.K.: Cambridge University Press, 2000). Additional World.sav variables obtained from Pippa Norris, www.pippanorris.com, John F. Kennedy School of Government, Harvard University, Cambridge, Mass. Screen-shot on page 193, "2003 Senate Voting Records," reprinted with the permission of Americans for Democratic Action, www.adaction.org/2003senatevr.htm.

Cover design: Malcolm McGaughy

∞ The paper used in this publication exceeds the requirements of the American National Standard for Information Sciences— Permanence of Paper for Printed Library Materials, ANSI Z39.48-1992.

Printed and bound in the United States of America

09   08   07   06   05   1   2   3   4   5

ISBN 1-56802-996-9

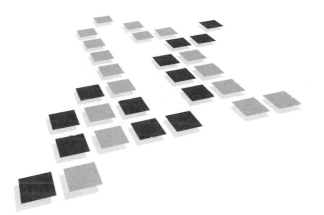

Contents

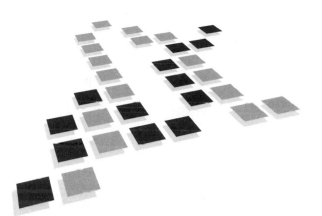

Tables and Figures

Tables

Figures

Preface

Ever since the bad old days of mainframe computing, I have tried to introduce my students to the joys of doing their own political analysis. After all, that's the best way to learn it. Students who appreciate the practical side of research are better prepared to contribute to in-class discussions of methodological concepts and problems than are students who do not. (A required research paper, in which students present their own data analysis, may provide additional encouragement.) Moreover, students often realize a salutary side benefit: Thanks to their excursions into the world of hands-on research, students develop a usable skill that they can hone as they continue their academic careers or pursue employment opportunities.

Although the days of punch cards and mainframe computing are (thankfully!) well behind us, the goal of combining substantive political research with computer analysis skills remains unchanged. During the time that SPSS has migrated to the server-based desktop, students' general level of computer sophistication (and their familiarity with the Windows operating system in particular) has increased dramatically. Interestingly, though, the supply of supplemental computer analysis texts—especially those that teach the essentials of political analysis with SPSS—has lagged behind demand. To be sure, over the past several years a number of all-in-one workbook-type publications have become available. These workbooks typically contain brief expositions of basic methods and permit students to use accompanying miniaturized versions of proprietary software to analyze datasets. My pedagogical experience with such self-contained workbooks has not been satisfactory. I have found that students do not learn a full complement of political analysis techniques, and their freedom to manipulate variables, explore patterns, and graph relationships is severely limited. More important, students do not build a working knowledge of SPSS, perhaps the most widely available data analysis package in academic and business environments.

This book instructs students in using SPSS for Windows to construct meaningful descriptions of variables and to perform substantive analysis of political relationships. The chapters cover all major topics in data analysis, from descriptive statistics to logistic regression. A final chapter describes several doable research projects, shows how to collect and code data, and lays out a framework for a well-organized research paper.

DATASETS

The CD-ROM that accompanies this book contains five datasets: selected variables from the 2002 General Social Survey (GSS) and the 2000 National Election Study (NES), as well as datasets on the 50 states, 114 countries of the world, and the partisanship, ideology, and voting behavior of members of the 2003 U.S. Senate. I wrote each chapter while sitting in front of a computer, using SPSS to analyze the datasets, describing each step, and pasting many screen-shots into the book. As a result, each chapter is written as a step-by-step tutorial, taking students through a series of guided examples in which they perform the analysis. The many figures allow students to check their work along the way.

This book contains 40 end-of-chapter exercises, which consumed the lion's share of the time I devoted to writing this book. All of the exercises are based on the datasets, and all are designed to give students opportunities to apply their new skills. I have tried to get beyond the workbook norm in which students simply run analyses and record the results. Rather, the exercises engage students in discovering the meaning of their findings and learning to interpret them.

Although I have assumed that students know how to handle files in Windows, I have also assumed that they have never heard of SPSS and have never used a computer to analyze data. After completing this book, students will have become competent SPSS users, and they will have learned a fair amount about substantive political science, too. Any student who has access to SPSS—the full version or the student version—can use this book. (The States.sav, World.sav, and senate2003.txt datasets are compatible with the student version. Compatible versions of the GSS and NES datasets are included on the CD-ROM. To perform logistic regression, covered in Chapter 10, students will need access to the full version of SPSS.)

DIFFERENT RELEASES OF SPSS

I wrote this book with SPSS 13.0, but I have made sure to accommodate readers who are using older versions. For many procedures—indeed, for all of the SPSS Analyze routines covered here—SPSS 13.0 runs the same as earlier releases. The major difference, which first appeared in 12.0, is SPSS Graph. (The Interactive graph subroutines remained unchanged.) The graphic output looks different, and the SPSS Chart Editor is completely new. Requesting, editing, and interpreting graphic output are important features of the book. Where appropriate, therefore, I have included separate chapter sections: one for 12.0 or later and one for 11.5 or earlier. On a related note, SPSS finally lifted the miserly eight-character restriction on the length of variable names beginning with 12.0 (at last!) and now generously permits variable names of up to 64 characters. Although I have retained the 11.5-compatible, eight-character naming convention in this book, readers using 12.0 or later may wish to give longer, more descriptive names to new variables they create.

CHAPTER ORGANIZATION

The introduction describes the datasets and shows students how to create their own copies of the data files. Chapter 1 introduces the SPSS Data Editor, discusses the output Viewer, and illustrates the print procedure. Chapter 2 covers central tendency and dispersion and guides students in using the Frequencies routine. Chapter 2 also shows how a frequency distribution, examined in conjunction with a bar chart or histogram, can enrich the description of a variable. In Chapter 3, which covers Crosstabs and Compare Means, students learn bivariate analysis and acquire the ability to tailor bar charts and line charts to depict relationships. Chapter 4 describes the main SPSS data transformation procedures, Recode and Compute. In Chapter 5 students use Crosstabs and Compare Means to obtain and interpret controlled comparisons. The chapter also discusses graphic support for controlled relationships. Chapter 6 uses One-Sample T Test and Independent-Samples T Test to demonstrate statistical significance for interval-level dependent variables, and Chapter 7 covers chi-square and measures of association for nominal and ordinal variables. In Chapter 8 students work through an extended guided example to learn Correlate (Bivariate) and Regression (Linear). Chapter 9 shows how to create dummy variables (essentially an application of Recode, which students learned in Chapter 4), perform dummy variable regression analysis, and model interaction in multiple regression. Chapter 10, new in this edition, covers binary logistic regression, including a discussion of how to present logistic regression results in terms of probabilities. Chapter 11 guides students as they collect, code, and analyze their own data. With the help of the text data file included with this book (the senate2003.txt dataset), students learn to use the Read Text Data function. This experience greatly enhances their ability to create and manipulate their own SPSS datasets.

These chapters are organized in the way that I normally teach my methods courses. I prefer to cover the logic of description and hypothesis testing before introducing inferential statistics and statistical significance. However, with a little rearranging of the chapters, this book will prove useful for instructors who do things differently. For example, after discussing cross-tabulation analysis (Chapter 3) and covering basic data transformations (Chapter 4), an instructor could assign the first part of Chapter 7, which covers chi-square and bivariate measures of association for categorical variables. Instructors who prefer using the regression approach to evaluating the statistical significance of mean differences might decide to skip Chapter 6 and move on to Chapters 8 and 9.

ACCOMPANYING CORE TEXT

Instructors will find that this book makes an effective supplement to any of a variety of methods textbooks. However, it is a particularly suitable companion to my own core text, *The Essentials of Political Analysis*. The textbook's eight substantive chapters cover basic and intermediate methodological issues and ideas: measurement, explanations and hypotheses, univariate statistics and bivariate analysis, controlled relationships, sampling and inference, statistical significance, correlation and linear regression, and logistic regression.

Each chapter also includes end-of-chapter exercises. Students can read the textbook chapters, do the exercises, and then work through the guided examples and exercises in *An SPSS Companion to Political Analysis*. The idea is to get students in front of the computer, experiencing political research firsthand, fairly early in the academic term. An instructor's solutions manual, available on CD-ROM and free to adopters, provides solutions for all the textbook and workbook exercises.

ACKNOWLEDGMENTS

The constructive criticism generated by the first edition of this book has, I hope, resulted in an improved second edition. There were three recurring suggestions in the anonymous reviews: include more exercises, include more exercises using the comparative politics dataset (World.sav), and provide better step-by-step annotation for screen-shots. Accordingly, I have increased the number of exercises by nearly a third—to 40, up from 31 in the first edition—and I have more than doubled the number using World.sav, from 4 to 9. All the screen-shots are new, and I have added numbered step-by-step instructions for many SPSS procedures. Many thanks to the anonymous reviewers for pointing me in the right direction on these improvements. I am grateful to University of Central Florida colleagues Bruce Wilson and Kerstin Hamann for suggesting ideas for exercises on comparative politics, and to Terri Susan Fine for pointing out key errors in the first edition. I offer special thanks to Pete Furia of Wake Forest University and William Claggett of Florida State University for sharing their SPSS know-how with me.

I also thank the academic reviewers of the first edition for their helpful comments and useful suggestions: Cal Clark of Auburn University, Ross Burkhart of Boise State University, and Lori Weber of California State University at Chico. I am especially grateful to Brian Schaffner of American University, whose meticulous review and constructive insights greatly improved this book. Any remaining errors, however, are mine.

I gratefully acknowledge the encouragement and professionalism of everyone associated with CQ Press: Charisse Kiino, acquisitions editor; Colleen Ganey, assistant editor; Steve Pazdan, managing editor; Amy Marks, copy editor; and Joan Gossett, production editor. Thanks, too, to everyone who worked on the first edition and helped get this project off the ground: Charisse Kiino; Michelle Tupper, development editor; Christopher Karlsten, copy editor; and Lorna Notsch, production editor.

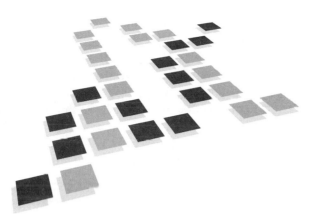

Getting Started

To get started with this book you will need
- Access to a Microsoft Windows–based computer
- The CD-ROM that accompanies this workbook
- One formatted 1.44-MB floppy disk or other portable media

As you have learned about political research and explored techniques of political analysis, you have studied many examples of other people's work. You may have read textbook chapters that present frequency distributions, or you may have pondered research articles that use cross-tabulation, correlation, or regression analysis to investigate interesting relationships between variables. As valuable as these learning experiences are, they can be enhanced greatly by performing political analysis firsthand—handling and modifying social science datasets, learning to use data analysis computer software, obtaining your own descriptive statistics for variables, setting up the appropriate analysis for interesting relationships, and running the analysis and interpreting your results.

This book is designed to guide you as you learn these valuable practical skills. In this volume you will gain a working knowledge of SPSS, a data analysis package used widely in academic institutions and business environments. SPSS has been in use for many years, and it contains a great variety of statistical analysis routines—from basic descriptive statistics to sophisticated predictive modeling. It is extraordinarily user friendly. In fact, although this book assumes that you have practical knowledge of the Windows operating system and that you know how to perform elemental file-handling tasks, it also assumes that you have never heard of SPSS and that you have never used a computer to analyze data of any kind. By the time you complete the guided examples and the exercises in this book, you will be well on your way to becoming an SPSS aficionado. The skills you learn will be durable, and they will serve you well as you continue your educational career or enter the business world.

This book's chapters are written in tutorial fashion. Each chapter contains several guided examples, and each includes exercises at the end. You will read each chapter while sitting in front of a computer, doing the analysis described in the guided examples, analyzing the datasets that accompany this text. Each data analysis procedure is described in step-by-step fashion, and the book has many figures that show you what your computer screen should look like as you perform the procedures. Thus the guided examples allow you to develop your skills and to become comfortable with SPSS. The end-of-chapter exercises allow you to apply your new skills to different substantive problems.

In Chapter 1 you will learn how to navigate the SPSS Data Editor, and you will learn how to print and save the output that your analyses generate. Chapter 2 demonstrates how to obtain and interpret frequency distributions. In Chapter 3 you will explore and apply cross-tabulation analysis and mean comparison analysis. Chapter 4 covers basic data transformations in SPSS—recoding variables and computing new variables that you will want to add to your datasets. In Chapter 5 you will learn to make controlled comparisons using SPSS, examining and interpreting the relationship between a dependent variable and an independent variable, controlling for a third variable. In Chapter 6 you will use SPSS to obtain the information you need to establish the boundaries of random sampling error and to assess the statistical significance of an empirical relationship. In Chapter 7 you will learn how tests of significance and measures of association add statistical support to your cross-tabulation analyses. Chapter 8 introduces the SPSS procedures for performing correlation and regression analyses, and Chapter 9 shows how to use SPSS to model and estimate complex relationships. Chapter 10 describes how to perform logistic regression, a technique that has gained widespread use in political research. Finally, Chapter 11 considers some of the challenges you might face in finding and collecting your own data, and offers some suggestions on how best to organize and present your original research.

Before you get started on Chapter 1, some necessary file-handling chores are required. The remainder of this introduction describes the book's datasets in more detail, and it guides you in getting them into ready-to-analyze form.

COPYING THE DATASETS TO FLOPPY DISK OR OTHER PORTABLE MEDIA

The datasets you will analyze in this book are contained on the accompanying CD-ROM. As you work your way through this book, you will modify these datasets—recoding some variables, computing new variables, and otherwise tailoring the datasets to suit your purposes. You will need to make your own personal copies of the datasets and store them on a floppy disk, removable USB drive, or ZIP disk. Here we will describe how to copy the datasets onto a floppy. Follow these steps:

1. On a blank, formatted 1.44-MB floppy disk, write your name and this label: "Datasets."
2. Insert the floppy disk into your computer's floppy drive.
3. Insert the CD-ROM that came with this book into your computer's CD drive.
4. On the computer's desktop, double-click the My Computer icon.
5. Double-click the icon representing the CD-ROM drive. This will show you the CD's datasets. (See Figure I-1.)
6. Click Edit → Select All. This selects all the datasets on the CD.
7. Now place the cursor on any selected file and *right*-click. Move the cursor to Send To → 3½ Floppy, as shown in Figure I-2, and click.
8. After the datasets have been copied to the floppy disk, remove the disk and the CD-ROM and put them in a safe place.

HOW TO HANDLE THE DATASETS

This book was written in just the manner in which you will probably read it—by sitting at a computer in a college or university lab and using a licensed release of SPSS to analyze the data. (You may have purchased SPSS Student Version. This situation is discussed below.) When you begin each chapter's guided examples, or when you do the exercises, you will want to insert the Datasets disk you just created into the lab computer's floppy drive. SPSS will read the data from the floppy. (Chapter 1 covers this operation in detail.) If you make any changes to a dataset, you can save the newly modified dataset directly to the floppy. Alternatively, your lab's administrator may permit you to work on datasets that have been copied to the lab computer's desktop or to a folder designated for such a purpose. If this is the case, you would begin each chapter's guided examples by inserting the Datasets floppy into the computer's drive. You would then open My Computer and double-click on the floppy drive icon, revealing the datasets. You could then copy the datasets you wish to analyze onto the desktop by dragging it from the floppy and dropping it on the desktop or into the appropriate folder. In any case, if you have modified a dataset during a data analysis session, it is important that you copy the dataset to the Datasets disk—and take the disk with you! (A comforting thought: The original datasets are still safely stored on the CD-ROM.)

CONTENTS OF THE DATASETS

Five different datasets are included with this book:

1. GSS2002.sav. This dataset includes selected variables from the 2002 General Social Survey, a random of sample of 2,765 adults aged 18 years or older, conducted by the National Opinion Research Center and made available through the Inter-university Consortium for Political and Social Research (ICPSR) at the University of Michigan.[1] Some of the scales contained in GSS2002.sav were constructed by the author. These constructed variables are described in the appendix (Table A-1).

Figure I–1 Datasets on the CD–ROM

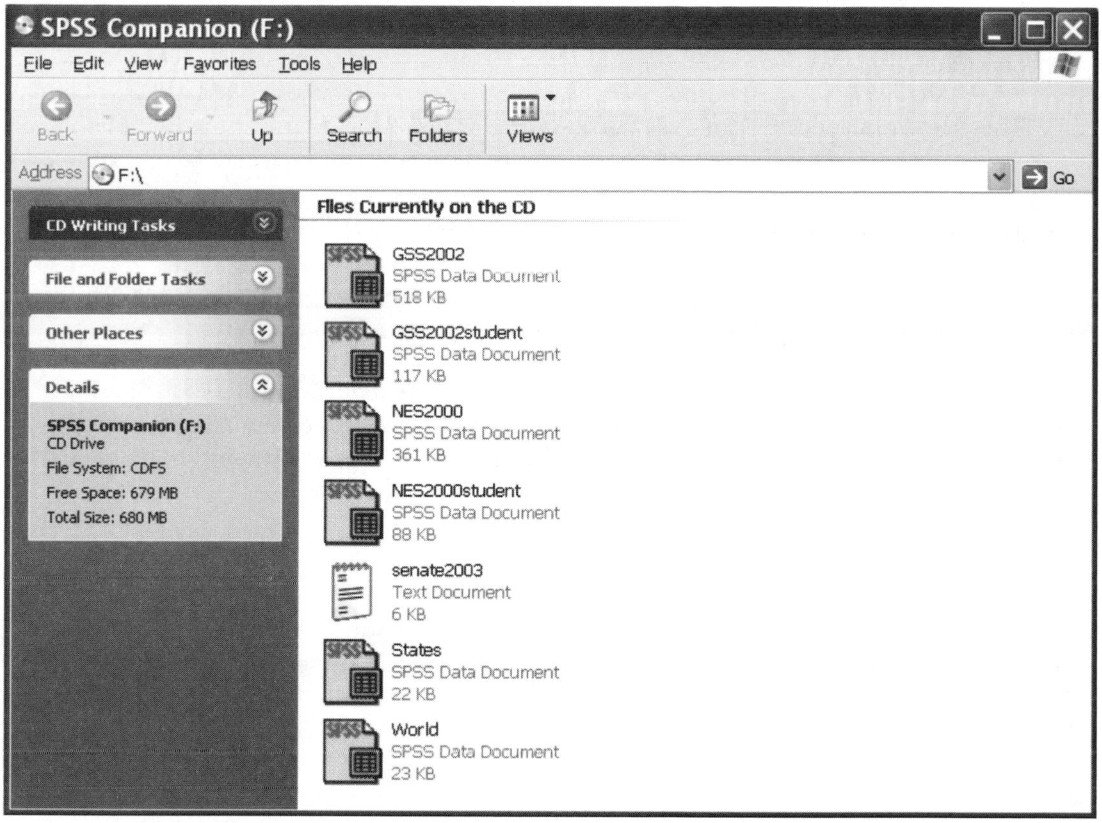

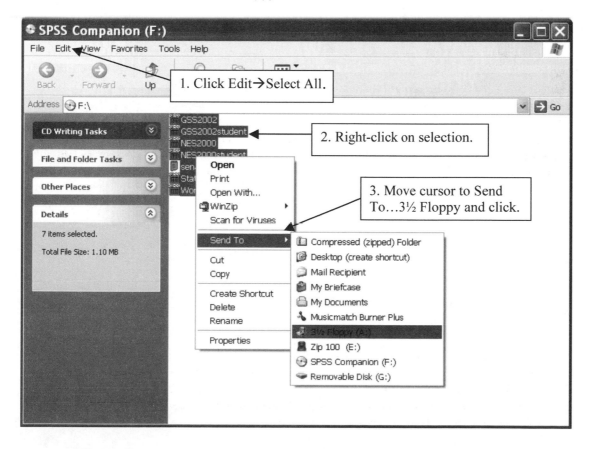

Figure I–2 Copying Datasets to the Floppy Drive

2. NES2000.sav. This dataset includes selected variables from the 2000 National Election Study, a random sample of 1,807 citizens of voting age, conducted by the University of Michigan's Institute for Social Research and made available through ICPSR.[2]

3. States.sav. This dataset includes variables on each of the 50 states. Most of these variables were compiled by the author. A complete description of States.sav is found in the appendix (Table A-2).

4. World.sav. This dataset includes variables on 114 countries of the world. Many of the variables in World.sav were compiled by Mike Alvarez, José Antonio Cheibub, Fernando Limongi, and Adam Przeworski and made available for download at Professor Cheibub's Internet site.[3] Many were compiled by Pippa Norris, John F. Kennedy School of Government, Harvard University, and made available through her Internet site.[4] A complete description of World.sav appears in the appendix (Table A-3).

5. senate2003.txt. This dataset, compiled by the author, includes information on each member of the 2003 U.S. Senate. You won't use senate2003.txt until Chapter 11.

This book was written for any SPSS user who is running SPSS 12.0 (or later) or SPSS 11.5 or earlier. Most of the time, SPSS commands and procedures are the same, no matter which version you are using. Sometimes (particularly for editing graphics) the procedures will be different for earlier and later releases of SPSS. In these instances, this book contains separate sections, one for readers who are using 12.0 or later and one for readers who are using 11.5 or earlier.

A NOTE TO USERS OF SPSS STUDENT VERSION

You may have purchased SPSS Student Version and installed it on your personal computer. This book was written with you in mind. You will be able to work through all the guided examples and do all the exercises.[5] When you analyze States.sav, World.sav, or senate2003.txt, you will obtain results that are identical in every respect to those obtained by non–Student Version users. There is one way, however, in which your use of this book will differ from that of non–Student Version users. SPSS Student Version will analyze only datasets having 1,500 or fewer cases and 50 or fewer variables. Because NES2000.sav and GSS2002.sav exceed these limits, you will not be able to analyze the data in these files using SPSS Student Version. However, this book's CD-ROM contains two datasets that you will be able to analyze: NES2000student.sav and GSS2002student.sav. These datasets are based on the "big" version datasets, and they meet SPSS Student Version's restrictions on the number of cases and the number of variables.

Whenever an example or exercise instructs the reader to open NES2000.sav or GSS2002.sav, you will instead open NES2000student.sav or GSS2002student.sav. Therefore, the five datasets you will be using in this book are

1. NES2000student.sav
2. GSS2002student.sav
3. States.sav
4. World.sav
5. senate2003.txt

Because you installed SPSS Student Version on your personal computer, you will want to copy these files to your computer's hard drive. A final note: Although each of these datasets contains all the variables you will need to work the examples and do the exercises, the figures presented in this book were created using the non–Student Version datasets. So when a figure or table deals with NES2000.sav or GSS2002.sav, the results you see on your screen will be somewhat different from those discussed in this book. Your results will be close to those depicted, but they will not be identical.

NOTES

1. GSS2002.sav was created from the General Social Survey 1972–2002 Cumulative Data File. James A. Davis, Tom W. Smith, and Peter V. Marsden, *General Social Surveys, 1972–2002* (Chicago, Ill.: National Opinion Research Center [producer], 2003; Storrs, Conn.: Roper Center for Public Opinion Research, University of Connecticut/Ann Arbor, Mich.: Inter-university Consortium for Political and Social Research [distributors], 2003).
2. Principal investigators: Nancy Burns, Donald R. Kinder, Steven J. Rosenstone, Virginia Sapiro, and the National Election Studies.
3. www.ssc.upenn.edu/~cheibub/data/.
4. www.pippanorris.com.
5. For Chapter 10, which covers logistic regression, you will need access to the full version of SPSS. The student version does not permit the user to perform logistic regression.

1

Introduction to SPSS

Suppose you were hired by a telephone-polling firm to interview a large number of respondents. Your job is to find out and record three characteristics of each person you interview: the region of the country where the respondent lives, how liberal or conservative the respondent claims to be, and the respondent's age. The natural human tendency would be to record these attributes in words. For example, you might describe a respondent this way: "Respondent #1 lives in the North Central United States, is 'conservative,' and is forty-nine years old." This would be a good thumbnail description, easily interpreted by another person. To SPSS, though, it would make no sense at all. Whereas people excel at recognizing and manipulating words, SPSS excels at recognizing and manipulating numbers. This is why researchers devise a *coding system*, a set of numeric identifiers for the different values of a variable. For one of the above variables, age, a coding scheme would be straightforward: Simply record the respondent's age in number of years, 49. In recording information about region and liberalism-conservatism, however, a different set of rules is needed. For example, the National Election Study (NES) applies these codes for region and liberalism-conservatism:

Variable	Response	Code
Region	Northeast	1
	North Central	2
	South	3
	West	4
Liberalism-Conservatism	Strong liberal	1
	Liberal	2
	Slightly liberal	3
	Moderate	4
	Slightly conservative	5
	Conservative	6
	Strong conservative	7

Thus the narrative profile "lives in the North Central United States, is 'conservative,' and is forty-nine years old" becomes "2 6 49" to SPSS. SPSS doesn't really care what the numbers stand for. As long as SPSS has numeric data, it will crunch the numbers—telling you the mode of the region codes, for example, or the median of liberalism-conservatism codes, or the mean age of all respondents. It is important, therefore, to provide SPSS with labels for each code so that the software's analytic work makes sense to the user. Accordingly, the SPSS Data Editor has two "views." The Data View shows the codes that SPSS recognizes and

Figure 1-1 SPSS Data Editor: Data View

	caseid	region	libcon7	age	attent	clintpre	gorepre	gbushpre	hillary
1	1	2	6	49	3	0	65	60	4
2	2	2	3	35	5	50	50	50	5
3	3	2	5	57	3	75	80	60	9
4	4	1	5	63	1	70	55	55	6
5	5	1	6	40	1	50	40	80	
6	6	1	1	77	3	90	80	70	8
7	7	1	4	43	3	50	50	60	3
8	8	1	3	47	1	90	95	10	9
9	9	1	2	26	3	70	60	60	7
10	10	2	2	48	1	90	95	30	8
11	11	1	3	41	3	60	60	55	7
12	12	1	3	41	3	90	85	30	5
13	13	2	5	37	3	75	50	50	7
14	14	2	2	18	5	75	60	50	5
15	15	2	4	70	1	50	70	40	99
16	16	4	7	31	3	0	25	90	2
17	17	4	5	18	1	50	50	40	4
18	18	3	3	22	3	95	90	20	9
19	19	3	.	60	3	100	100	70	99
20	20	3	6	44	3	50	50	75	

analyzes. The Variable View, among other useful features, shows the word labels that the researcher has assigned to the numeric codes.

THE SPSS DATA EDITOR

Let's open the 2000 National Election Study dataset and see how this works.[1] Insert into the computer's floppy drive the Datasets disk that you created in the introduction. If you copied the datasets onto a USB drive or other media, insert your portable storage device into the appropriate drive of the computer. Double-click the My Computer icon on the desktop and then double-click the icon representing your computer's drive where the datasets are stored. Double-click the NES2000.sav icon. (Alternatively, you may want to open NES2000.sav after you have copied it onto the desktop. SPSS will run faster if the dataset is located on the computer's hard drive.) SPSS opens the data file and displays the Data Editor (Figure 1-1). Notice the two tabs at the bottom of the window: Data View and Variable View. Let's look at the Data View first. (Make sure the Data View tab is clicked.) This shows how all the cases are organized for analysis. Information for each case occupies a separate row. The variables, given brief no-nonsense names, appear along the columns of the editor. Because we are familiar with a few of the codes, we can tell that the first case (code 1 on caseid) is from the North Central region (code 2 for region), is a self-described "conservative" (code 6 on libcon7), and is forty-nine years of age. To paint a more complete word-portrait of this respondent, however, we need to see how all the variables are coded. To reveal this information, click the Variable View tab (Figure 1-2). This view shows complete information on the meaning and measurement of each variable in the dataset. (You can adjust the width of a column by clicking, holding, and dragging the column border.)

The most frequently used variable information is contained in Name, Label, Values, and Missing. Name is the brief descriptor recognized by SPSS when it does analysis. If you are running SPSS 11.5 or earlier, SPSS restricts names to eight characters or fewer, and it requires them to begin with a letter (not a number). Plus, names may not contain any special characters, such as dashes or commas, although underscores are

Figure 1–2 SPSS Data Editor: Variable View

	Name	Type	Width	Decimals	Label	Values	Missing
1	caseid	Numeric	4	0	Case ID	None	None
2	region	Numeric	1	0	Census region of intervie	{1, Northea	None
3	libcon7	Numeric	1	0	Self placement lib-con sc	{1, 1. Strong li	None
4	age	Numeric	2	0	Respondent age	{0, 00. NA}...	0
5	attent	Numeric	1	0	Attention R paid to campa	{1, 1. Very mu	None
6	clintpre	Numeric	3	0	Pre:Thermometer Bill Clin	{997, 997. DO	997, 998
7	gorepre	Numeric	3	0	Pre:Thermometer Al Gore	{99	
8	gbushpre	Numeric	3	0	Pre:Thermometer George	{99	
9	hillary	Numeric	3	0	Pre:Thermometer Hillary	{99	
10	demtherm	Numeric	3	0	C2a. Thermometer Dem P	{99	
11	envir	Numeric	3	0	D2t. Thermometer enviro	{99	
12	feminist	Numeric	3	0	Thermometer feminists	{997, 997. DO	997, 998
13	military	Numeric	3	0	Post:Thermometer militar	{997, 997. DO	997, 998
14	abortion	Numeric	1	0	Abortion scale	{1, 1. Never p	None
15	attent2	Numeric	8	0	Campaign interest	{1, High}...	None
16	cohort3	Numeric	1	0	Year born:3 categories	{1, 1949 or be	None
17	crime	Numeric	1	0	How reduce crime?	{1, 1. Address	None
18	deathpen	Numeric	1	0	Death penalty	{1, 1. Favor st	None
19	drive	Numeric	3	0	How many miles R drives	{997, 997. 997	997
20	educ3	Numeric	3	0	Education: 3 categories	{1, 1. Less tha	None
21	egalit3	Numeric	8	0	We have pushed equal rig	{1, 1. Agree}...	None
22	envreas3	Numeric	8	0	Environmental regulation	{1. Tougher r	None

NES2000.sav - SPSS Data Editor

Widen the Label column by pinching here and dragging to the right.

okay. For SPSS 12.0 or later, SPSS permits names of up to 64 characters, although the other naming restrictions remain. (To ensure that all versions of SPSS are accommodated, this book's datasets follow the 11.5 conventions.)

Regardless of the SPSS version you are using, you are encouraged to make good use of Label, a much longer descriptor (up to 256 characters are allowed in all versions of SPSS), for each variable name. For example, when SPSS analyzes the variable attent, it will look in the Variable View for a label. If it finds one, then it will label the results of its analysis by using Label instead of Name. So attent shows up as "Attention R paid to campaigns"—much more user friendly. Just as Label attaches a wordier description to Name, Values attaches word labels to the numeric variable codes. Consider libcon7, which, according to Label, measures "Self-placement lib-con scale." Click the mouse anywhere in the Values cell and then click the gray button that appears. A Value Labels window pops up, revealing the labels that SPSS will attach to the numeric codes of libcon7 (Figure 1-3). Unless you instruct it to do otherwise, SPSS will apply these labels to its analysis of libcon7. (Click the Cancel button in the Value Labels window to return to the Variable View.)

Finally, a word about Missing: Sometimes a dataset does not have complete information for some variables on a number of cases. In coding the data, researchers typically give a special numeric code to these missing values. In coding age, for example, the NES coders entered a value of "0" for respondents who did not reveal their ages. To ensure that SPSS does not treat "0" as a valid code for age, coders defined "0" as missing, to be excluded from any analysis of age. Similarly, people who did not know who Hillary Clinton is (see the variable named hillary and labeled "Pre:Thermometer Hillary Clinton") or who did not know where to rate her were coded 997 or 998 on this variable. These two codes were then defined as missing.[2]

A WORKBOOK CONVENTION: SETTING OPTIONS FOR VARIABLE LISTS

Now you have a feel for the number-oriented side and the word-oriented side of SPSS. Before looking at how SPSS produces and handles output, there is one more thing to do. In the main menu bar of the Data

Figure 1–3 Value Labels Box

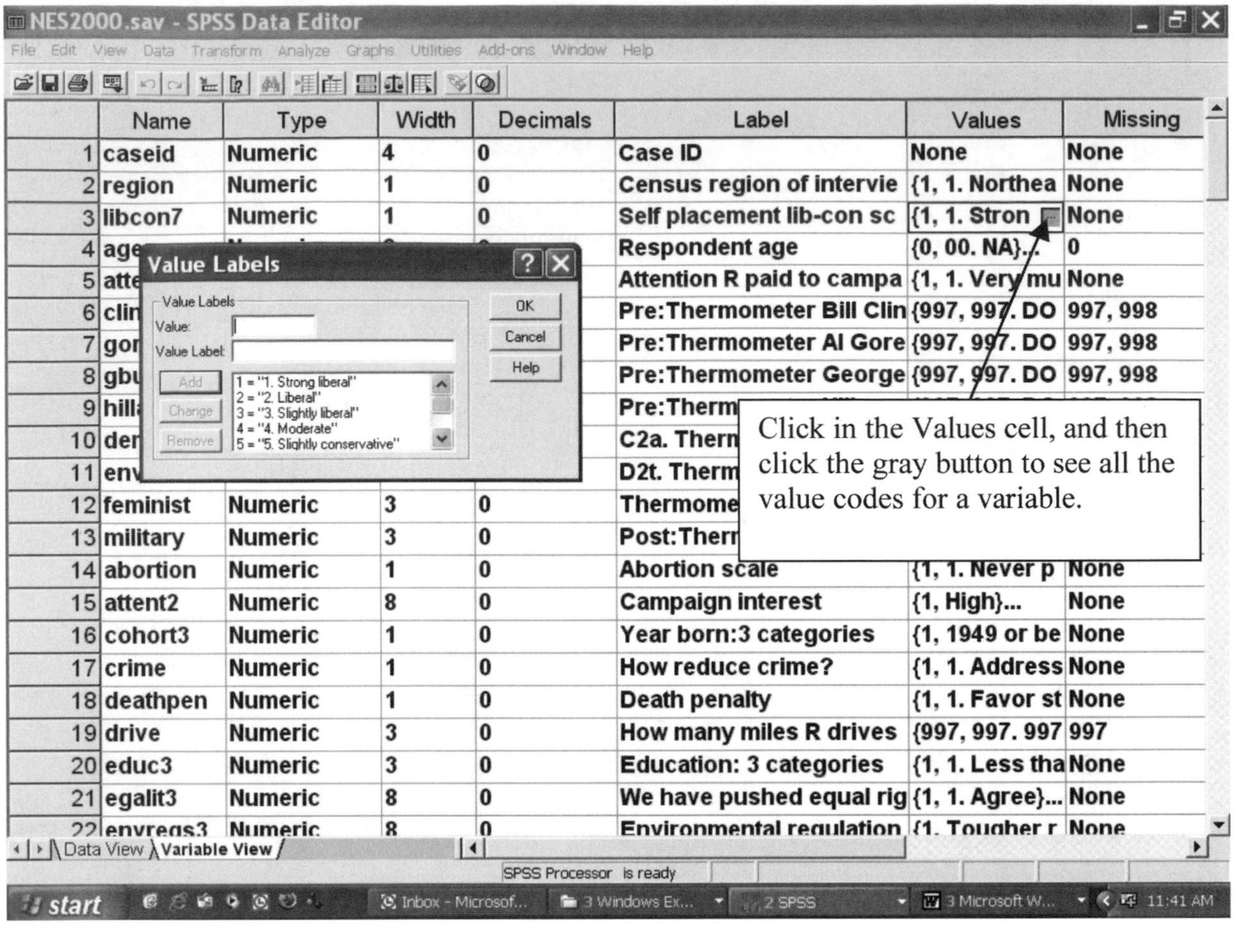

Editor, click Edit → Options. Make sure that the General tab is clicked. (See Figure 1-4.) As you can see, SPSS allows the user to tailor the software in many areas of function and appearance. The radio buttons in the Variable Lists area, for example, determine the mode (variable labels or variable names) and order (alphabetical order or the order in which they appear in the file) in which SPSS will display variables that the user is about to analyze. After gaining experience with SPSS, you will settle on your own preferences, but for now we need to ensure that all the examples in this workbook correspond to what you see on your screen.

If the radio button Display names *and* the radio button Alphabetical were already selected when you opened the Options menu, you are set to go. Click Cancel. If, however, Display names and/or Alphabetical were not already selected when you opened the Options menu, select them (as in Figure 1-4). Click Apply. Click OK, returning to the Data Editor.

THE SPSS VIEWER

Let's run through a quick analysis and see how SPSS handles variables and output. On the main menu bar, click Analyze → Descriptive Statistics → Frequencies. The Frequencies window appears (Figure 1-5). There are two panels. On the right is the (currently empty) Variable(s) panel. This is the panel where you enter the variables you want SPSS to analyze. On the left you see the names of all the variables in NES2000.sav in alphabetical order, just as you specified in the Options menu. Although the names are not terribly informative, complete coding information is just a (right) mouse click away. Put the mouse pointer on the first variable, abortion, and right-click. Then click on Variable Information. As shown in Figure 1-6, SPSS retrieves and displays the label (Abortion scale), name (abortion), measurement (ordinal level), and, most usefully, the value labels for the numeric codes. (To see all the codes, click the drop-down arrow in the Variable Information box.) Respondents who believe abortion should never be permitted are coded 1, those who

Figure 1–4 Setting Options for Variable Lists

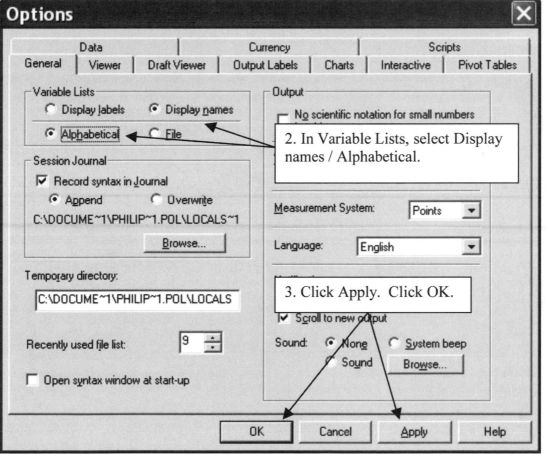

think abortion should be permitted under specific circumstances (rape, incest, health of the mother) are coded 2, and so on.

Return the mouse to the Frequencies window and click abortion into the Variable(s) panel. (Click on abortion and then click the black arrow between the panels.) Click OK. SPSS runs the analysis and displays the results in the SPSS Viewer (Figure 1-7). The SPSS Viewer has two panes. In the Outline pane, SPSS keeps a running log of the analyses you are performing. The Outline pane references each element in the Contents pane, which reports the results of your analyses. In this book we are interested exclusively in the Contents pane. Hide the Outline pane by first placing the cursor on the Pane divider. Click and hold the left button of the mouse and then move the Pane divider over to the left-hand border of the SPSS Viewer. The SPSS

Figure 1–5 Frequencies Window

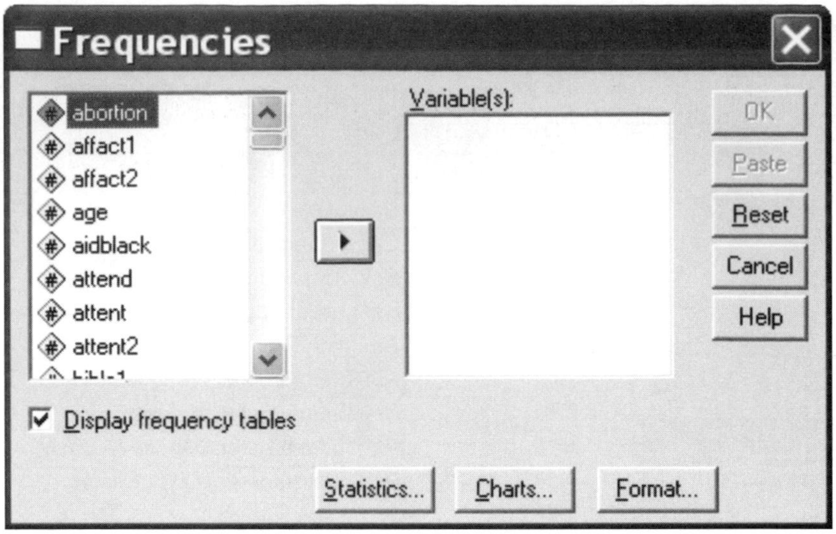

Figure 1–6 Retrieving Coding Information

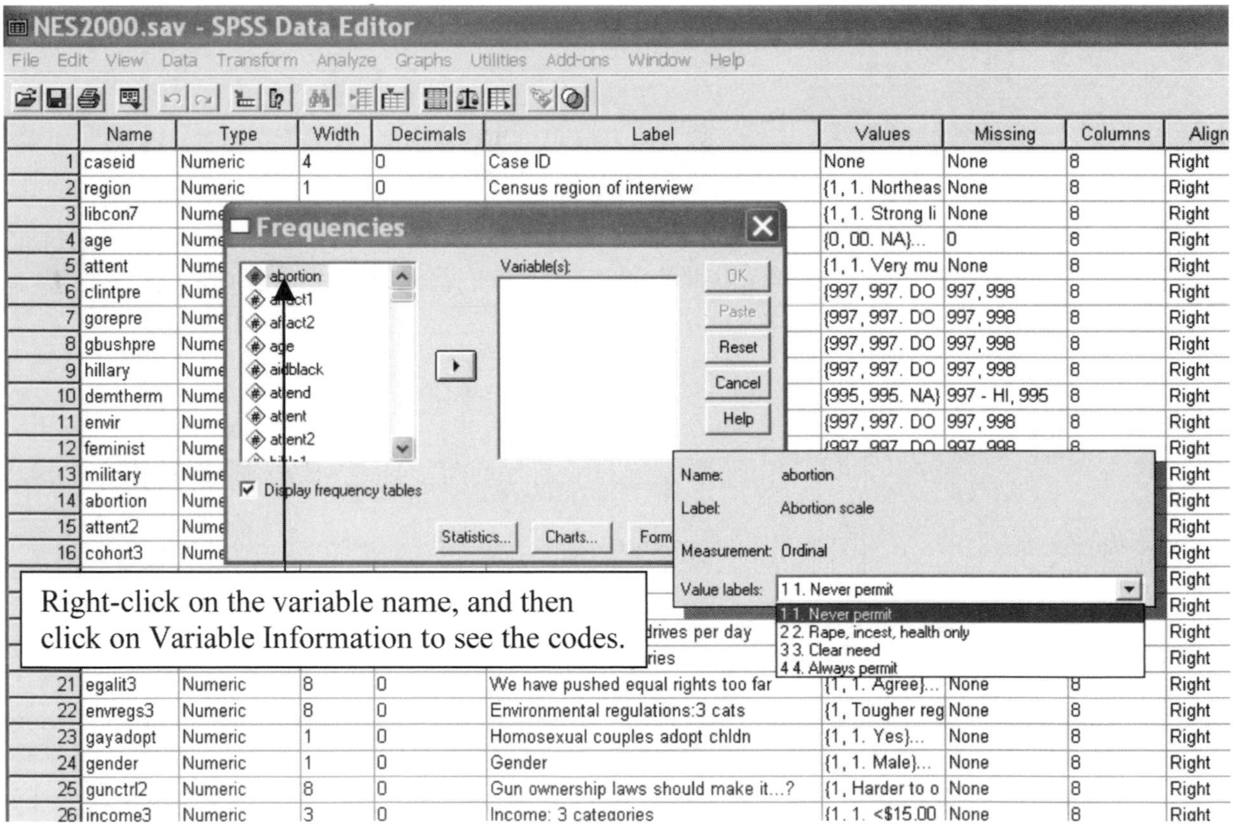

Viewer should now look like Figure 1-8. The output for abortion shows you the frequency distribution for all valid responses, with value codes nicely labeled. In Chapter 2 we discuss frequency analysis in more detail. Our immediate purpose is to become familiar with SPSS output.

Here are some key facts about the SPSS Viewer. First, the SPSS Viewer is a separate file, created by you during your analysis of the data. It is completely distinct from the data file. Whereas SPSS data files all have the file extension *.sav, SPSS Viewer files have the file extension *.spo. The output can be saved, under a name that you choose, and then reopened later. Second, the output from each succeeding analysis does not

Figure 1–7   SPSS Viewer: Outline Pane and Contents Pane

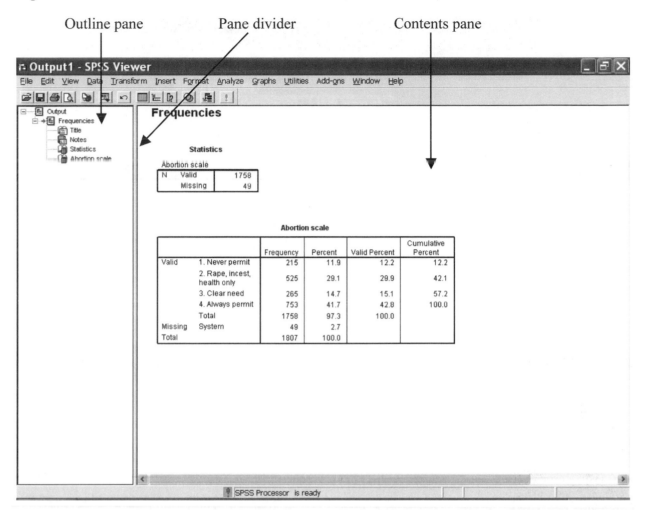

Figure 1–8   SPSS Viewer: Hidden Outline Pane

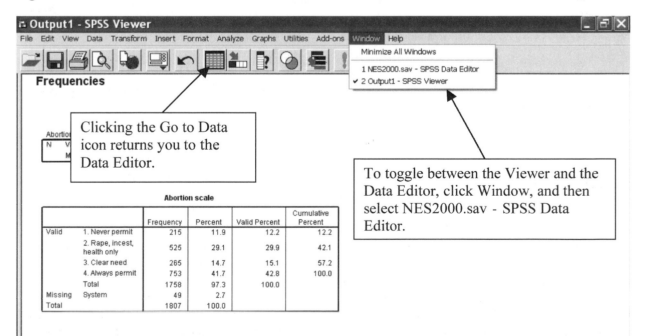

Figure 1–9 Selecting Output for Printing

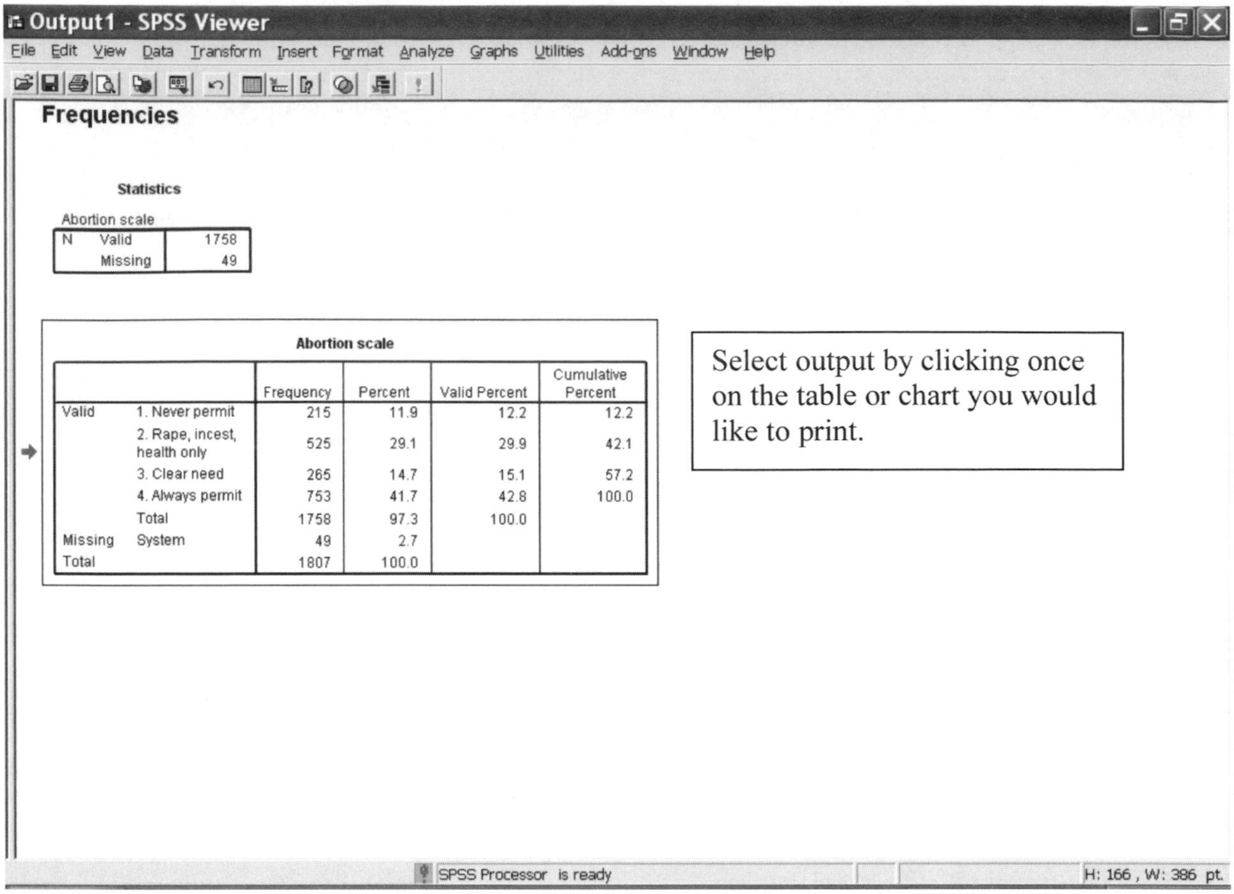

overwrite the file. Rather, it appends new results to the SPSS Viewer file. If you were to run another analysis for a different variable, SPSS would dump the results in the SPSS Viewer below the abortion analysis you just performed. Third, there are a number of ways to toggle between the SPSS Viewer and the Data Editor. (See Figure 1-8.) Clicking the "Go to Data" icon on the toolbar takes you to the Data Editor. Clicking Window on the main menu bar and checking "NES2000.sav - SPSS Data Editor" also returns you to the Data Editor. Clicking Window on the main menu bar in the Data Editor and checking "Output1 - SPSS Viewer" sends you to your output file. Finally, you may select any part of the output file, print it, or copy and paste it into a word processing program. Many of the exercises in this workbook will ask you to print the results of your SPSS analyses, so let's cover the print procedure.

Selecting and Printing Output

Printing the desired results in SPSS requires, first, that you select the output or portion of output you want to print. A quick and easy way to select a single table or chart is to place the cursor anywhere on the desired object and click once. Let's say you want to print the abortion frequency distribution. Place the cursor on the frequency table and click. A red arrow appears in the left-hand margin next to the table (Figure 1-9). Now click the printer icon on the SPSS Viewer menu bar. The printer window opens. In the printer window's Print range panel, the radio button next to Selection should already be clicked. Clicking OK would send the abortion frequency table to the printer. To select more than one table or graph, hold down the Control key (Ctrl) while selecting the desired output with the mouse. Thus, if you wanted to print the abortion frequency table and the statistics table, first click on one of the desired tables. While holding down the Ctrl key, click on the other table. SPSS will select both tables.

Saving an Output File

The output in the SPSS Viewer is your work product, and the output file belongs to you. Before continuing, let's save the work you have done. To save your output to a 3½-inch diskette, you would first insert a diskette into the computer's floppy drive.[3] In the SPSS Viewer, click File → Save. (Alternatively, click the save file icon on the main menu bar.) Select the floppy drive (probably A:). Invent a file name (but preserve the .spo extension), such as "chap1.spo," and click Save. SPSS saves all of the information in SPSS Viewer to the file chap1.spo on the floppy drive. Saving your output protects your work. Plus, the .spo file can always be reopened later. Suppose you are in the middle of a series of SPSS analyses and you want to stop and return later. You can save the .spo file, as described here, and exit SPSS. When you return, you start SPSS and load a data file (like NES2000.sav) into the Data Editor. In the main menu bar of the Data Editor, you click File → Open → Output, find your .spo file on the floppy drive, and open it. Then you can pick up where you left off.

NOTES

1. If you are using SPSS Student Version, you will open NES2000student.sav.
2. These are examples of user-defined missing values. The author has set most of the variables in the datasets you will be using in this book to *system missing*. A system missing code appears as a dot (.) in the Data View. These codes are treated automatically as missing by SPSS.
3. You may save your output to your Datasets floppy. The space available on the diskette will accommodate the output generated in this chapter. However, you will be creating a lot of output as you work through this book, so you will probably want to obtain a separate diskette and label it "Output Files." In succeeding chapters you could save your output to this separate disk.

2

Descriptive Statistics

Analyzing descriptive statistics is the most basic—and sometimes the most informative—form of analysis you will do. Descriptive statistics reveal two attributes of a variable: its typical value (central tendency) and its spread (degree of dispersion or variation). The precision with which we can describe central tendency for any given variable depends on the variable's level of measurement. For nominal-level variables we can identify the *mode*, the most common value of the variable. For ordinal-level variables, those whose categories can be ranked, we can find the mode and the *median*—the value of the variable that divides the cases into two equal-size groups. For interval-level variables, we can obtain the mode, median, and arithmetic *mean*, the sum of all values divided by the number of cases.

Finding a variable's central tendency is ordinarily a straightforward exercise. Simply read the computer output and report the numbers. Describing a variable's degree of dispersion or variation, however, often requires informed judgment.[1] Here is a general rule that applies to any variable at any level of measurement: A variable has no dispersion if all the cases—states, countries, people, or whatever—fall into the same value of the variable. Using ordinary language, we might describe such a variable as "homogeneous." A variable has maximum dispersion if the cases are spread evenly across all values of the variable. The number of cases in one category equals the number of cases in every other category. In this circumstance, we would describe the variable as "heterogeneous."

INTERPRETING MEASURES OF CENTRAL TENDENCY AND VARIATION

Central tendency and variation work together in providing a complete description of any variable. Some variables have an easily identified typical value and show little dispersion. For example, suppose you were to ask a large number of U.S. citizens what sort of economic system they believe to be the best: capitalism, communism, or socialism. What would be the modal response, the economic system preferred by most people? Capitalism. Would there be a great deal of dispersion, with large numbers of people choosing the alternatives, communism or socialism? Probably not. In other instances, however, you may find that one value of a variable has a more tenuous grasp on the label *typical*. And the variable may exhibit more dispersion, with the cases spread out more evenly across the variable's other values. For example, suppose a large sample of voting-age adults were asked, in the weeks preceding a presidential election, how interested they are in the campaign: very interested, somewhat interested, or not very interested. Among your own acquaintances you probably know a number of people who fit into each category. So even if one category, such as "somewhat interested," is the median, many people will likely be found at the extremes of "very interested" and "not very interested." This would be an instance in which the amount of dispersion in a variable—its degree of spread—is essential to understanding and describing it.

These and other points are best understood by working through some guided examples. For the analyses that follow, you will analyze GSS2002.sav. Open the dataset by double-clicking the GSS2002.sav icon.[2] In the Data Editor, click Edit → Options and then click on the General tab. Just as you did with NES2000.sav in

Figure 2–1   Obtaining Frequencies and a Bar Chart (nominal variable)

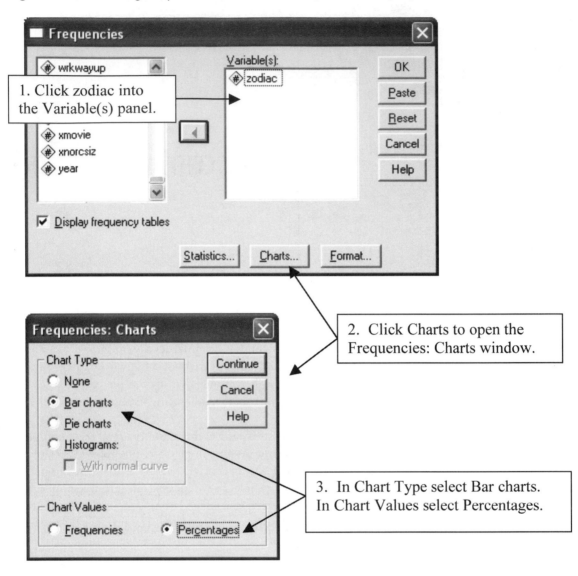

Chapter 1, make sure that the radio buttons in the Variable Lists area are set for Display names and Alphabetical. (If these options are already set, click Cancel. If they are not set, select them, click Apply, and then click OK. Now you are ready to go.)

DESCRIBING NOMINAL VARIABLES

First, you will obtain a frequency distribution and bar chart for a nominal-level variable, zodiac, which records respondents' astrological signs. In the Data Editor, click Analyze → Descriptive Statistics → Frequencies. Scroll down to the bottom of the left-hand list until you find zodiac. Click zodiac into the Variable(s) panel. At the bottom of the Frequencies window, click the Charts button (Figure 2-1). The Frequencies: Charts window appears. In Chart Type select Bar charts. In Chart Values select Percentages. Click Continue, which returns you to the main Frequencies window. Click OK. SPSS runs the analysis.

SPSS has produced two items of interest in the SPSS Viewer: a frequency distribution of respondents' astrological signs and a bar chart of the same information. Examine the frequency distribution (Figure 2-2). The value labels for each astrological code appear in the left-most column, with Aries occupying the top row of numbers and Pisces the bottom row. There are four numeric columns: Frequency, Percent, Valid Percent, and Cumulative Percent. What does each column mean? The Frequency column shows raw frequencies, the actual number of respondents having each zodiac sign. Percent is the percentage of *all* respondents, including missing cases, in each category of the variable. Ordinarily, the Percent column can be ignored, because

Figure 2–2 Frequencies Output (nominal variable)

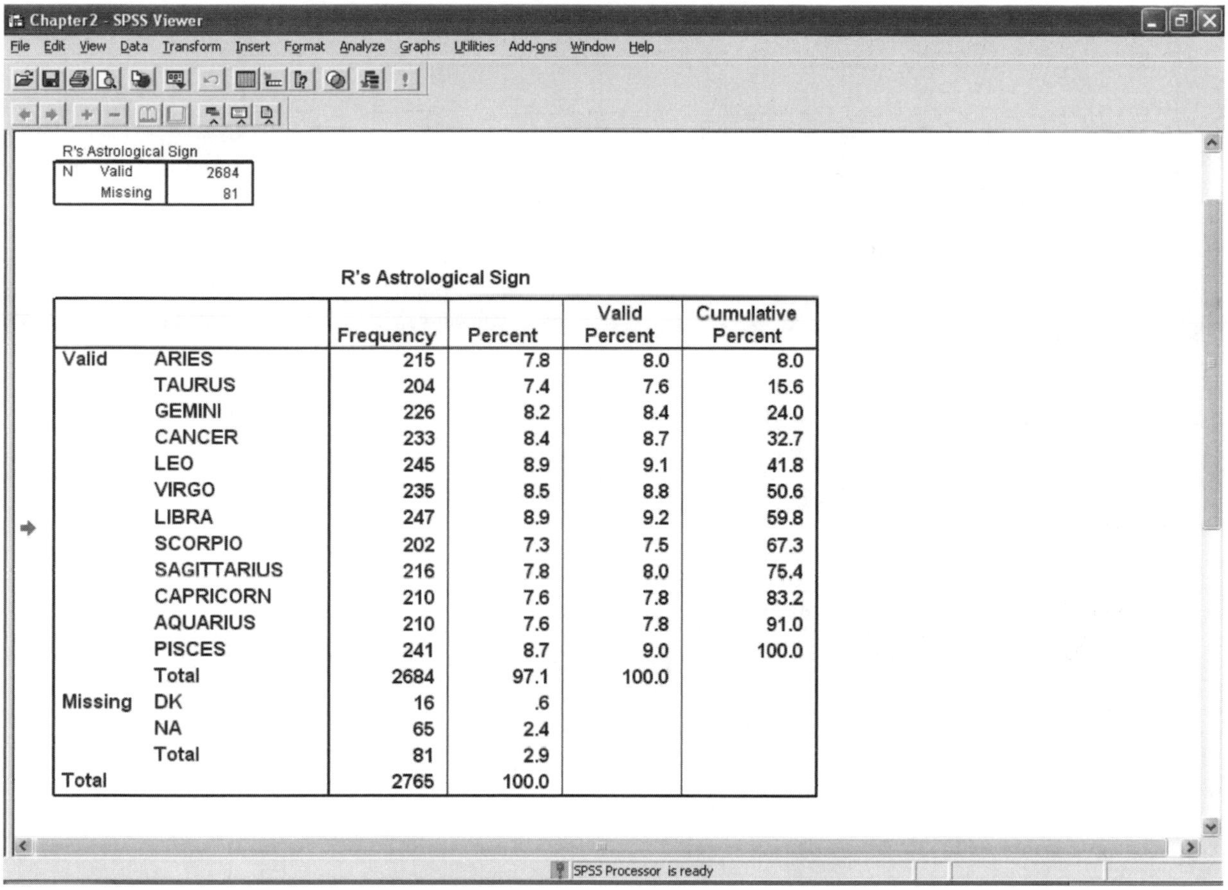

R's Astrological Sign

N	Valid	2684
	Missing	81

R's Astrological Sign

		Frequency	Percent	Valid Percent	Cumulative Percent
Valid	ARIES	215	7.8	8.0	8.0
	TAURUS	204	7.4	7.6	15.6
	GEMINI	226	8.2	8.4	24.0
	CANCER	233	8.4	8.7	32.7
	LEO	245	8.9	9.1	41.8
	VIRGO	235	8.5	8.8	50.6
	LIBRA	247	8.9	9.2	59.8
	SCORPIO	202	7.3	7.5	67.3
	SAGITTARIUS	216	7.8	8.0	75.4
	CAPRICORN	210	7.6	7.8	83.2
	AQUARIUS	210	7.6	7.8	91.0
	PISCES	241	8.7	9.0	100.0
	Total	2684	97.1	100.0	
Missing	DK	16	.6		
	NA	65	2.4		
	Total	81	2.9		
Total		2765	100.0		

we generally are not interested in including missing cases in our description of a variable. Valid Percent is the column to focus on. Valid Percent tells us the percentage of nonmissing responses in each value of zodiac. Finally, Cumulative Percent reports the percentage of cases that fall in *or below* each value of the variable. For ordinal or interval variables, as we will see, the Cumulative Percent column can provide valuable clues about how a variable is distributed. But for nominal variables, which cannot be ranked, the Cumulative Percent column provides no information of value.

Now consider the Valid Percent column more closely. Scroll between the frequency distribution and the bar chart, which depicts the zodiac variable in graphic form (Figure 2-3). What is the mode, the most common astrological sign? For nominal variables, the answer to this question is (almost) always an easy call: Simply find the value with the highest percentage of responses. Libra is the mode. Does this variable have little dispersion or a lot of dispersion? Again study the Valid Percent column and the bar chart. Apply the following rule: A variable has no dispersion if the cases are concentrated in one value of the variable; a variable has maximum dispersion if the cases are spread evenly across all values of the variable. Are most of the cases concentrated in Libra, or are there many cases in each value of zodiac? Because respondents show great heterogeneity in astrological signs, we would conclude that zodiac has a high level of dispersion.

DESCRIBING ORDINAL VARIABLES

Next, you will analyze and describe two ordinal-level variables, one of which has little variation and the other of which is more spread out. Along the top menu bar of the SPSS Viewer, click Analyze → Descriptive Statistics → Frequencies. SPSS "remembers" the preceding analysis, so zodiac is still in the Variable(s) list. Click zodiac back into the left-hand list. Scroll through the list until you find these variables: helppoor and helpsick. Each of these is a 5-point ordinal scale. Helppoor asks respondents to place themselves on a scale between 1 ("The government should take action to help poor people") and 5 ("People should help themselves"). Helpsick, using a similar 5-point scale, asks respondents about government responsibility or

Figure 2–3 Bar Chart (nominal variable)

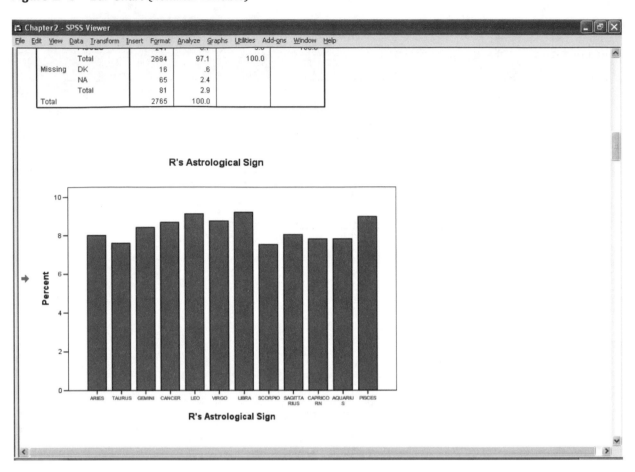

individual responsibility for medical care. Click helppoor and helpsick into the Variable(s) list. SPSS retained your earlier settings for Charts, so accompanying bar charts will appear in the SPSS Viewer. Click OK.

SPSS runs the analysis for each variable and produces two frequency distributions, one for helppoor and one for helpsick, followed by two bar charts of the same information. First, let's focus on helppoor. To get a feel for this variable, scroll back and forth between the frequency distribution (Figure 2-4) and the bar chart (Figure 2-5). How would you describe the central tendency and dispersion of this variable? Because it is an ordinal variable, we can report both its mode and its median. Its mode, clearly enough, is the response "Agree with both." What about the median? This is where the Cumulative Percent column of the frequency distribution comes into play. *The median for any ordinal (or interval) variable is the category below which 50 percent of the cases lie.* Is the first category, "Government action," the median? No, because this code contains fewer than half the cases. How about the next higher category? No again, because the Cumulative Percent column still has not reached 50 percent. The median occurs in the "Agree with both" category.

Does helppoor have a high or low degree of dispersion? The dispersion of an ordinal variable can be evaluated in two complementary ways. The first way is to take a close look at the bar graph. If helppoor had a high level of variation, the bars would have roughly equal heights, much like the zodiac variable that you analyzed earlier. If helppoor had no dispersion, then all the cases would fall into one category—there would be only one bar showing in the graphic. Another way to evaluate variation is to compare the mode and the median. If the mode and the median fall in the same category, then the variable has lower dispersion than if the mode and the median fall in different values of the variable. You sometimes have to exercise judgment in determining variation, but it seems clear that helppoor is a variable with a fairly low degree of dispersion. The fence-straddling response, "Agree with both," is prominent in the bar graph. What is more, both the mode and the median are within this response category.

Now turn your attention to the frequency distribution for helpsick (see Figure 2-4) and the accompanying bar chart (Figure 2-6). What is the mode? Again, the most common response is "Agree with both." So "Agree with both" is the mode. Use the Cumulative Percent column to find the median. Is the first value, "Govt should

Figure 2–4   Frequencies Output (ordinal variables)

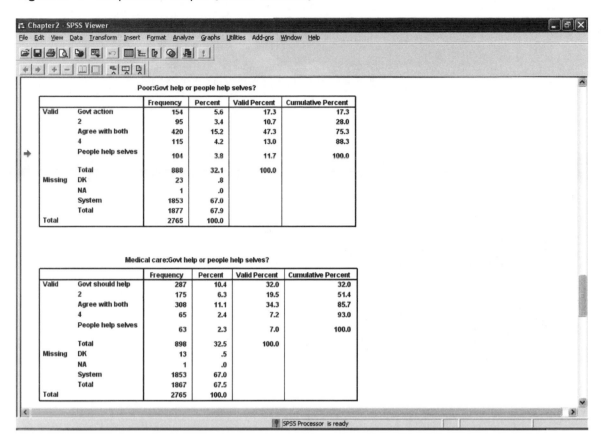

Figure 2–5   Bar Chart (ordinal variable with low dispersion)

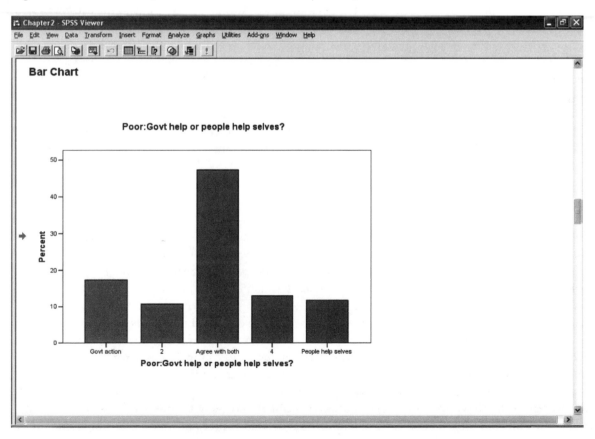

Figure 2–6 Bar Chart (ordinal variable with high dispersion)

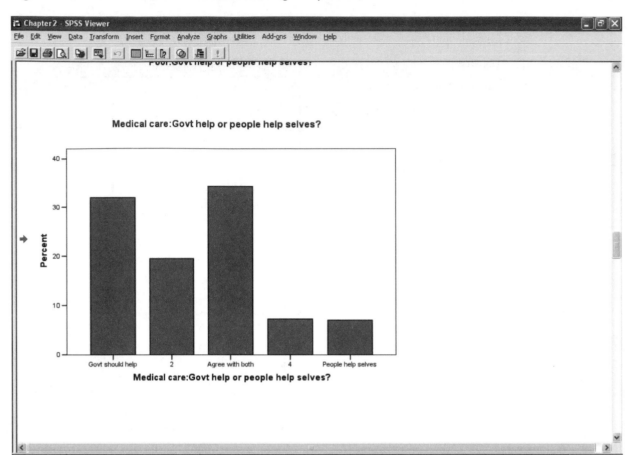

help," the median? No, this value contains fewer than half the cases. Now go up one value to the category labeled "2" on the 5-point ordinal scale. Is this the median? Yes, it is. According to the Cumulative Percent column, 51.4 percent of the cases fall in or below this value. So "Agree with both" is the mode, but the median falls within response category 2, which lies a bit more toward the "Govt should help" side of the variable.

Which variable, helppoor or helpsick, has higher variation? Notice that, unlike helppoor, respondents' values on helpsick are more spread out, with sizeable numbers of cases falling in the first two categories. Indeed, "Govt should help," favored by 32 percent of respondents, is a close rival to "Agree with both" in popularity. And, unlike helppoor, helpsick's mode and median are different, providing a useful field mark of higher variation. Thus one would have to conclude that helpsick has more variation—greater dispersion—than helppoor.

DESCRIBING INTERVAL VARIABLES

Let's now turn to the descriptive analysis of interval-level variables using SPSS. An interval-level variable represents the most precise level of measurement. Unlike nominal variables, whose values stand for categories, and ordinal variables, whose values can be ranked, the values of an interval variable *tell you the exact quantity of the characteristic being measured*. For example, age qualifies as an interval-level variable because its values impart each respondent's age in years.

Because interval variables have the most precision, they can be described more completely than can nominal or ordinal variables. For any interval-level variable, we can report its mode, median, and arithmetic average, or *mean*. In addition to these measures of central tendency, we can make more sophisticated judgments about variation. Specifically, one can determine if an interval-level distribution is *skewed*. What is skewness, and how do you know it when you see it?

Skewness refers to the symmetry of a distribution. If a distribution is not skewed, the cases tend to cluster symmetrically around the mean of the distribution, and they taper off evenly for values above and below

Figure 2–7 Frequencies: Statistics Window (modified)

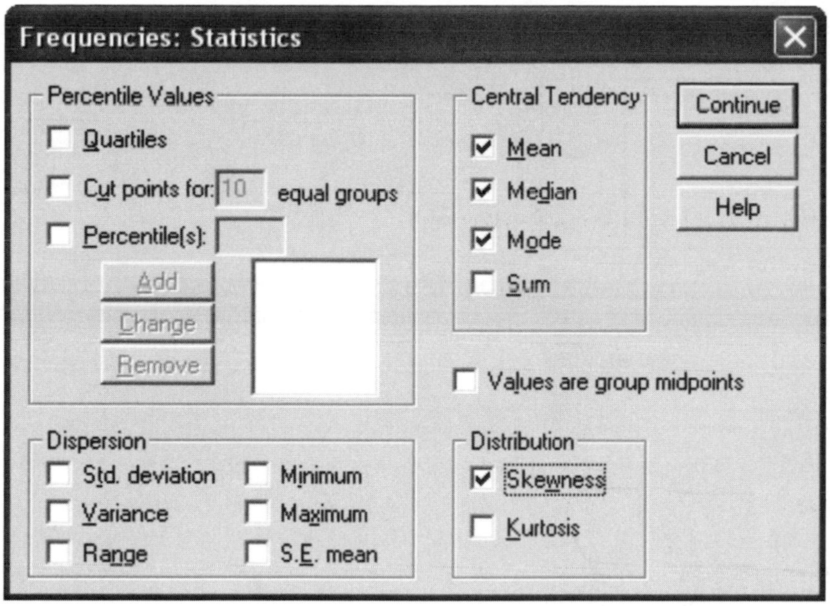

the mean. If a distribution is skewed, by contrast, one tail of the distribution is longer and skinnier than the other tail. Distributions in which some cases occupy the higher values of an interval variable—distributions with a skinnier right-hand tail—are said to have a *positive skew*. By the same token, if the distribution has some cases at the extreme lower end—the distribution has a skinnier left-hand tail—then the distribution has a *negative skew*. Skewness has a predictable effect on the mean. A positive skew tends to "pull" the mean upward; a negative skew pulls it downward. However, skewness has less effect on the median. Because the median reports the middle-most value of a distribution, it is not tugged upward or downward by extreme values. *For badly skewed distributions, it is a good practice to use the median instead of the mean in describing central tendency.*

A step-by-step analysis of a GSS2002.sav variable, age, will clarify these points. Click Analyze → Descriptive Statistics → Frequencies. If helppoor and helpsick are still in the Variable(s) list, click them back into the left-hand list. Click age into the Variable(s) list. Click the Charts button. Make sure that Bar charts (under Chart Type) and Percentages (under Chart Values) are selected. Click Continue, which returns you to the main Frequencies window.

So far, this procedure is the same as in your analysis of zodiac, helppoor, and helpsick. When running a frequencies analysis of an interval-level variable, however, you need to do two additional things. One of these is a must-do. The other is a may-want-to-do. The must-do: Click the Statistics button at the bottom of the Frequencies window. The Frequencies: Statistics window appears. In the Central Tendency panel, click the boxes next to Mean, Median, and Mode. In the Distribution panel, click Skewness. The Frequencies: Statistics window should look like Figure 2-7. Click Continue, returning to the main Frequencies window. The may want to do: *Un*click the box next to Display frequency tables, appearing at the foot of the left-hand list.[3] Click OK.

SPSS runs the analysis of age and dumps the requested statistics and bar chart into the SPSS Viewer (Figure 2-8). Most of the entries in the Statistics table are familiar to you: valid number of cases (N); number of missing cases; and mean, median, and mode. SPSS has reported values for skewness and for something called standard error of skewness that are as precise as they are mysterious. What do these numbers mean? Though their statistical properties need not concern us, the basics are useful to know. When a distribution is perfectly symmetrical—no skew—it has skewness equal to 0. If the distribution has a skinnier right-hand tail—positive skew—then skewness will be a positive number. A skinnier left-hand tail, logically enough, returns a negative number for skewness. Just about all distributions will have some degree of skewness. How much is too much? That's where the standard error of skewness comes into play. Follow this simple rule: Divide skewness by its standard error. If the result has a magnitude (absolute value) of greater than 2, then the distribution is significantly skewed, and you should use the median as the best measure of

Figure 2–8 Statistics and Bar Chart (interval variable)

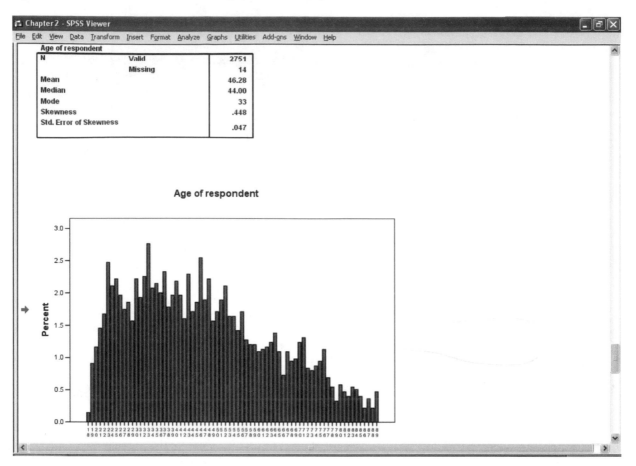

central tendency. If you divide skewness by its standard error and get a number whose magnitude is 2 or less, the distribution is not significantly skewed. In this case, use the mean as the best measure of central tendency.

The age variable plainly has a positive skew. Compare the mean age with the median age. Recall that a positive skew pulls the mean upward. Remember also that the mean is susceptible to skewness, and the median less so. Is the skewness more than twice its standard error? Yes, and then some. Obviously, a number of cases in the upper reaches of this variable have pulled the mean off the exact 50-50 center of the distribution.

The bar chart confirms this suspicion. Notice the large group of respondents in the heart of the distribution, between about 30 and 48 years of age. Another sizable clump occurs in the older age range, between about 64 and 78 years. This older group has the effect of pulling the mean upward. In this situation the median should be used to describe the central tendency of the distribution.[4]

CHOOSING GRAPHIC DISPLAYS: BAR CHARTS OR HISTOGRAMS?

All of the guided examples thus far have used bar charts for graphic support. For nominal and ordinal variables, a bar chart should always be your choice. For interval variables, however, you may want to ask SPSS to produce a histogram instead. What is the difference between a bar chart and a histogram? When do we prefer one to the other? A bar chart displays each value of a variable and shows you the percentage (alternatively, the raw number) of cases that fall into each category. A histogram is similar, but instead of displaying each discrete value, it collapses categories into ranges (called bins), resulting in a compact display. Histograms are sometimes more readable and elegant than bar charts. Most of the time a histogram will work just as well as a bar chart in summarizing an interval-level variable. For interval variables with a large number of values, a histogram is the graphic of choice. (Remember: For nominal or ordinal variables, you always want a bar chart.)

Write a few sentences explaining your reasoning. _____

_____

_____

_____

C. Print the output from this exercise.

That concludes the exercises for this chapter. Before exiting SPSS, be sure to save your output file.

NOTES

1. In this chapter we use the terms *dispersion*, *variation*, and *spread* interchangeably.
2. If you are using *SPSS Student Version*, open GSS2002student.sav.
3. For interval-level variables that have a large number of categories, as does age, a frequency distribution can run to several output pages and is not very informative. Unclicking the Display frequency tables box suppresses the frequency distribution. A general guide: If the interval-level variable you are analyzing has 15 or fewer categories, go ahead and obtain the frequency distribution. If it has more than 15 categories, suppress the frequency distribution.
4. For demographic variables that are skewed, median values rather than means are often used to give a clearer picture of central tendency. One hears or reads reports, for example, of median family income or the median price of homes in an area.
5. See http://www.ipu.org/english/home.htm.

3

Making Comparisons

All hypothesis testing in political research follows a common logic of comparison. The researcher separates subjects into categories of the independent variable and then compares these groups on the dependent variable. For example, suppose I think that gender (independent variable) affects opinions about gun control (dependent variable) and that women are less likely than men to oppose gun control. I would divide subjects into two groups on the basis of gender, women and men, and then compare the percentage of women who oppose gun control with the percentage of men who oppose gun control. Similarly, if I hypothesize that Republicans have higher incomes than do Democrats, I would divide subjects into partisanship groups (independent variable), Republicans and Democrats, and compare the average income (dependent variable) of Republicans with that of Democrats.

Although the logic of comparison is the always the same, the appropriate method depends on the level of measurement of the independent and dependent variables. In this chapter you will learn how to use SPSS to address two common hypothesis-testing situations: those in which both the independent and the dependent variables are categorical (nominal or ordinal) and those in which the independent variable is categorical and the dependent variable is interval level. You will also learn to add visual support to your hypothesis testing by creating and editing bar charts and line charts.

USING CROSSTABS

Cross-tabulations are the workhorse vehicles for testing hypotheses for categorical variables. When setting up a cross-tabulation, you must observe the following three rules. First, put the independent variable on the columns and the dependent variable on the rows. Second, always obtain percentages of the independent variable, not the dependent variable. Third, test the hypothesis by comparing the percentages of subjects who fall into the same category of the dependent variable.

Consider this hypothesis: In comparing individuals, those who have lower levels of education will pay less attention to political campaigns than will those who have higher levels of education. NES2000.sav contains the variable attent, which measures respondents' levels of interest in the presidential campaign: very much, somewhat, or not much interested. This will serve as the dependent variable. Another variable, educ3, categorizes respondents into three levels of education: less than high school, high school, or more than high school. This is the independent variable.

Open NES2000.sav, and let's test the hypothesis. In the SPSS Data Editor, click Analyze → Descriptive Statistics → Crosstabs. The SPSS Crosstabs window appears (Figure 3-1), sporting four panels. For now, focus on the two upper right-hand panels: Row(s) and Column(s). (The oddly labeled Layer 1 of 1 panel comes into play in Chapter 5.) This is where we apply the first rule for a properly constructed cross-tabulation: The independent variable defines the columns, and the dependent variable defines the rows. Because attent is the dependent variable, click it into the Row(s) panel. Find educ3 in the left-hand variable list and click it into the Column(s) panel.

Figure 3–1 Crosstabs Window

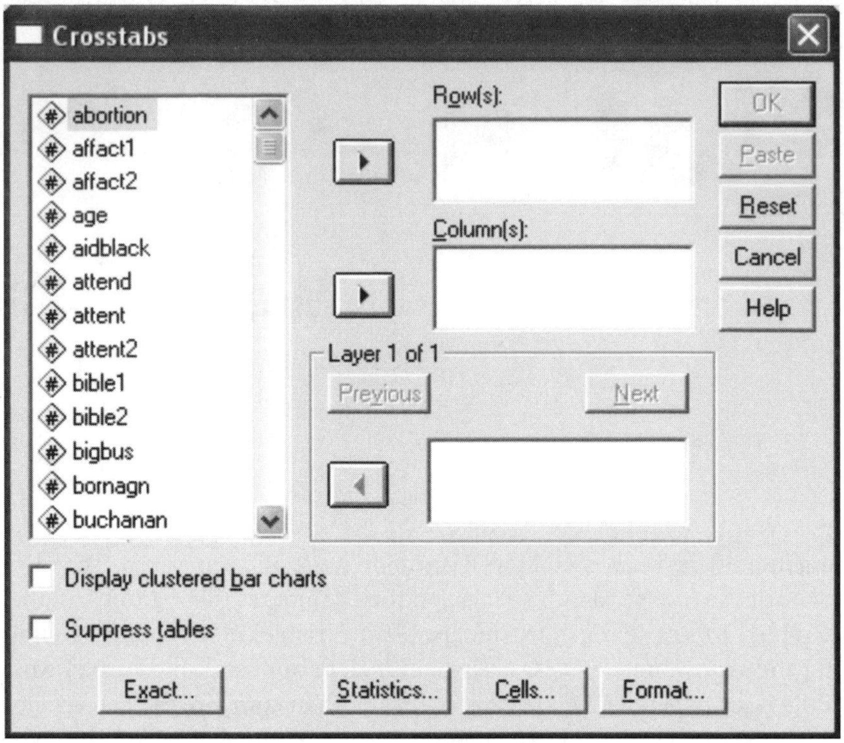

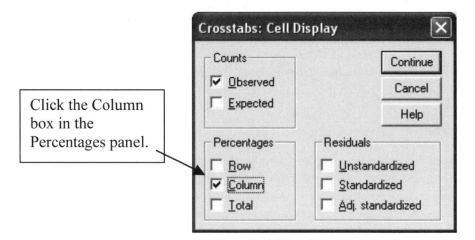

Figure 3–2 Crosstabs: Cell Display Window (modified)

Now for the second rule of cross-tab construction: Always obtain percentages of the independent variable. At the bottom of the Crosstabs window, click the Cells button. SPSS displays the available options for Counts, Percentages, and Residuals (Figure 3-2). Left to its own defaults, SPSS will produce a cross-tabulation showing only the number of cases ("observed" counts) in each cell of the table. That's fine. But to follow the second rule we also want column percentages—the percentage of each category of the independent variable falling into each category of the dependent variable. Click the Column box in the Percentages panel. Click Continue, which returns you to the SPSS Crosstabs window. That's all there is to it. Click OK.

SPSS runs the analysis and displays the results in the SPSS Viewer: a case processing summary followed by the requested cross-tabulation (Figure 3-3). Scroll down so that you can view the cross-tabulation in its entirety. By convention, SPSS identifies its Crosstabs output with the label of the dependent variable, followed by an asterisk (*), and then the label of the independent variable. In fact, when SPSS runs Crosstabs, it produces a set of side-by-side frequency distributions of the dependent variable—one for each category of the

Figure 3–3 Crosstabs Output

Chapter 3 - SPSS Viewer

File Edit View Data Transform Insert Format Analyze Graphs Utilities Add-ons Window Help

Crosstabs

Case Processing Summary

	Cases					
	Valid		Missing		Total	
	N	Percent	N	Percent	N	Percent
Attention R paid to campaigns * Education: 3 categories	1800	99.6%	7	.4%	1807	100.0%

Attention R paid to campaigns * Education: 3 categories Crosstabulation

			Education: 3 categories			
			1. Less than HS	2. HS	3. More than HS	Total
Attention R paid to campaigns	1. Very much interested	Count	31	107	385	523
		% within Education: 3 categories	17.2%	20.6%	35.0%	29.1%
	3. Somewhat interested	Count	86	259	540	885
		% within Education: 3 categories	47.8%	49.9%	49.0%	49.2%
	5. Not much interested	Count	63	153	176	392
		% within Education: 3 categories	35.0%	29.5%	16.0%	21.8%
Total		Count	180	519	1101	1800
		% within Education: 3 categories	100.0%	100.0%	100.0%	100.0%

independent variable—plus an overall frequency distribution for all analyzed cases. Accordingly, the table has four columns of numbers: one for respondents with less than high school, one for those with a high school education, one for those with more than high school, and a total column showing the distribution of all cases across the dependent variable. And, as requested, each cell shows the number (count) and column percentage.

What do you think? Does the cross-tabulation fit the hypothesis? The third rule of cross-tabulation analysis is easily applied. Focusing on the "very much interested" value of the dependent variable ("Attention R paid to campaigns"), we see a clear pattern in the hypothesized direction. A comparison of respondents in the "Less than HS" column with those in the "HS" column reveals an increase in the "very much interested" percentage. A comparison of the "HS" and "More than HS" columns reveals yet another boost in campaign interest. Yes, the analysis supports the hypothesis.

USING COMPARE MEANS

We now turn to another common hypothesis-testing situation: when the independent variable is categorical and the dependent variable is interval level. The logic of comparison still applies—divide cases on the independent variable and compare values of the dependent variable—but the method is different. Instead of comparing percentages, we now compare means.

To illustrate, let's say that you are interested in explaining this dependent variable: attitudes toward Hillary Clinton. Why do some people have positive feelings toward her whereas others harbor negative feelings? Here is a plausible idea: Partisanship (independent variable) will have a strong effect on attitudes toward Hillary Clinton (dependent variable). The hypothesis: In comparing individuals, those who are Democrats will have more favorable attitudes toward Hillary Clinton than will those who are Republicans.

NES2000.sav contains hillary, a 100-point feeling thermometer. Each respondent was asked to rate Ms. Clinton on this scale, from 0 (cold or negative) to 100 (warm or positive). This is the dependent variable. NES2000.sav also has partyid7, which measures partisanship in seven ordinal categories, from Strong

Figure 3–4 Means Window

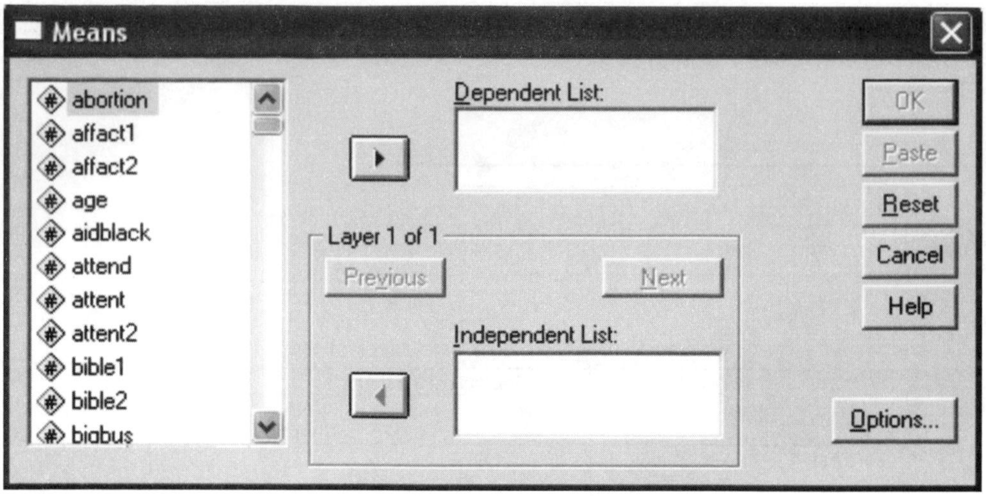

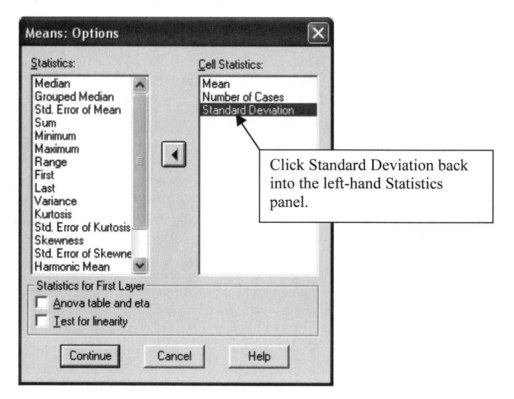

Figure 3–5 Means: Options Window

Democrat (coded 0) to Strong Republican (coded 6). (The intervening codes capture gradations between these poles: Weak Democrat, Independent-Democrat, Independent, Independent-Republican, and Weak Republican.) This is the independent variable. If the hypothesis is correct, we should find that Strong Democrats have the highest mean scores on hillary and that mean scores decline systematically across categories of partyid7, hitting bottom among respondents who are strong Republicans. Is this what happens?

Click Analyze → Compare Means → Means. The SPSS Means window pops into view (Figure 3-4). Scroll down the left-hand variable list until you find hillary, and then click it into the Dependent List panel. Now scroll to partyid7 and click it into the Independent List panel. In the bottom right-hand corner of the Means window, click Options. The Means: Options window (shown in Figure 3-5) permits you to select desired statistics from the left-hand Statistics panel and click them into the right-hand Cell Statistics panel. Alternatively, you can remove statistics from Cell Statistics by clicking them back into the left-hand panel.

Figure 3-6 Mean Comparison Output

| Chapter 3 - SPSS Viewer |
| File Edit View Data Transform Insert Format Analyze Graphs Utilities Add-ons Window Help |

Means

Case Processing Summary

	Cases					
	Included		Excluded		Total	
	N	Percent	N	Percent	N	Percent
Pre:Thermometer Hillary Clinton * Party ID	1750	96.8%	57	3.2%	1807	100.0%

Report

Pre:Thermometer Hillary Clinton

Party ID	Mean	N
0. Strong Democrat	77.07	342
1. Weak Democrat	62.93	270
2. Independent-Dem	61.61	264
3. Independent	48.21	200
4. Independent-Rep	34.45	230
5. Weak Republican	38.99	212
6. Strong Republican	21.03	232
Total	51.61	1750

Unless instructed otherwise, SPSS will always report the mean, number of cases, and standard deviation of the dependent variable for each category of the independent variable. Because at present we are not interested in obtaining the standard deviation, select it with the mouse and click it back into the left-hand Statistics panel. Our mean comparison table will report only the mean value of hillary and the number of cases for each category of partyid7. Click Continue, returning to the Means window. Click OK.

Compared with cross-tabulations, mean comparison tables are the soul of simplicity. Figure 3-6 displays the mean comparison output obtained from this analysis. The bottom table bears the generic title "Report," and the label of the dependent variable, "Pre:Thermometer Hillary Clinton," appears along the top of the table.[1] The label for the independent variable, "Party ID," defines the left-most column, which shows all seven categories, from Strong Democrat at the top to Strong Republican at the bottom. Beside each category, SPSS has calculated the mean of hillary and reported the number of respondents falling into each value of partisanship. (The bottom row, "Total," gives the mean for the whole sample.)

Among Strong Democrats the mean for hillary is pretty high—about 77 degrees. Does the mean decline as attachment to the Democratic Party weakens and identification with the Republican Party strengthens? Well, the mean drops sharply among Weak Democrats (who average about 63 degrees), shows a not-so-precipitous drop among Independent-Democratic leaners (about 62), and then continues to decline predictably, with a noticeable "hiccup" between Independent-Republican leaners and Weak Republicans. Strong Republicans, who average close to 21 degrees on the thermometer, have the chilliest response to Ms. Clinton. On the whole, then, the data support the hypothesis.[2]

VISUALIZING RELATIONSHIPS WITH SPSS GRAPH

We have already seen that bar charts and histograms can be a great help in describing the central tendency and dispersion of a *single* variable. SPSS graphic procedures are also handy for illustrating relationships *between* variables. It will come as no surprise that SPSS supports a large array of graphic styles. Most of the

Figure 3–7 Line Chart Shell: Mean Values of Hillary Clinton Thermometer, by Party Identification

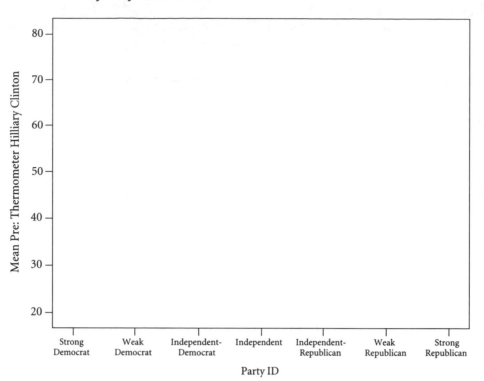

relationships that you will be investigating, however, can be illustrated nicely with one of these types: a bar chart or a line chart. A bar chart is useful for summarizing the relationship between two categorical variables. It is the graphic companion of cross-tabulation analysis. A line chart adds clarity to the relationship between a categorical independent variable and an interval-level dependent variable. It is the graphic companion of mean comparison analysis. Because you just performed a mean comparison analysis, we cover line charts first.

To get an idea of how SPSS produces a line chart, let's begin by creating one of our own, using the results from the hillary-partyid7 example. Turn your attention to Figure 3-7, an empty graphic "shell." The horizontal axis, called the *category axis*, displays values of the independent variable, party ID. Each partisanship category is represented by a hash mark, from Strong Democrat on the left to Strong Republican on the right. The vertical axis, called the *summary axis*, represents mean values of the dependent variable, Hillary Clinton thermometer ratings. Now, with a pen or pencil, make a dot directly above each category of the independent variable, recording the mean of hillary for each partisan category. Above the Strong Democrat hash mark, for example, place a dot at 77 on the summary axis. Go to the right along the category axis until you reach the hash mark for Weak Democrat and make a dot directly above the hash mark, at about 63. Do the same for the remaining partisan groups, placing a dot vertically above each hash mark at the mean value of hillary. (Refer to your output or use the mean values in Figure 3-6. Don't worry about being precise. Just get the dots close to the mean values.) Using a straight edge, connect the dots. Voilà! You've created a line chart for the relationship, a visual summary that is easy to interpret and present.

Using Line Chart

Now let's get SPSS to do the work for us. Click Graphs → Line. The SPSS Line Charts window opens (Figure 3-8). Make sure that the icon next to "Simple" is clicked and that the radio button next to "Summaries for groups of cases" is selected.[3] Click Define. The Define Simple Line window appears (Figure 3-9). The two top-most boxes—the (currently grayed out) Variable box in the Line Represents panel and the Category Axis box—are where we tailor the line chart to our specifications. (With SPSS 13.0, the Define Simple Line window offers two additional boxes in the Panel by area, one labeled "Rows" and one labeled "Columns," as shown in Figure 3-9. For our purposes in this book, these boxes may be safely ignored.)

Figure 3–8 Line Charts Window (default)

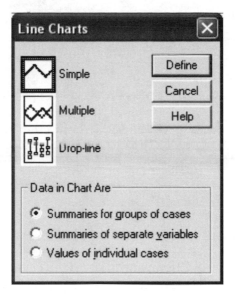

Figure 3–9 Define Simple Line Window (default)

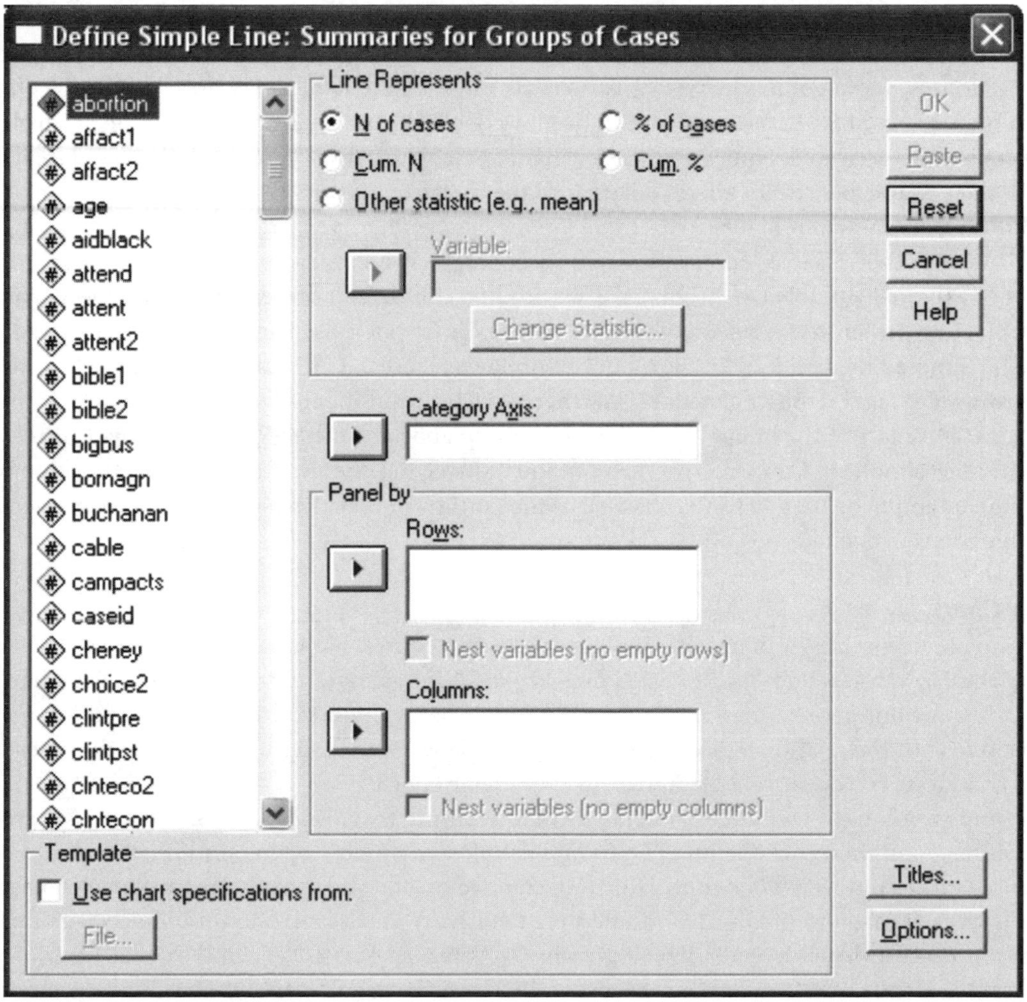

Figure 3–10 Define Simple Line Window (modified)

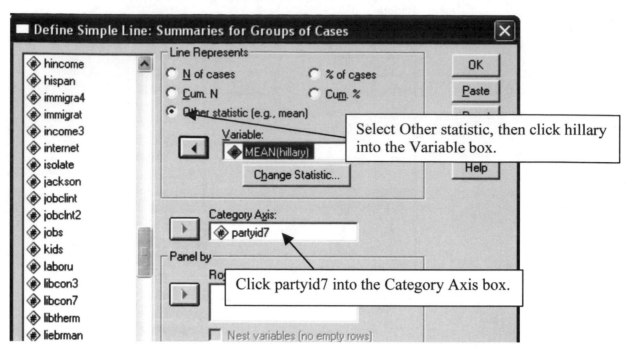

Note: In SPSS 12.0 or earlier, the Other statistic radio button is labeled "Other summary function," and Change Statistic is labeled "Change Summary."

We know that we want partyid7 to define the horizontal category axis. Scroll down to partyid7 and click it into the Category Axis box. We also want to graph the mean values of hillary for each category of partyid7. To do this, we've got to give SPSS instructions.[4] In the Line Represents panel, select the Other statistic radio button. (In SPSS 12.0 or earlier, this button is labeled "Other summary function.") The box beneath "Variable" is activated. Now scroll the left-hand variable list until you find hillary, and then click hillary into the Variable box. SPSS moves hillary into the Variable box and gives it the designation "MEAN(hillary)," as shown in Figure 3-10. In SPSS Line Chart, whenever you request Other statistic and click a variable into the Variable box (as we have just done), SPSS assumes that you want to graph the mean values of the requested variable (as, in this case, we do).[5] So this default serves our current needs. If you are using SPSS 11.5 or earlier, you need to follow one more step: Click Options in the lower right-hand corner of the Define Simple Line window. In the Options window (Figure 3-11), make sure that the box next to "Display groups defined by missing values" is *unchecked*. Click Continue. All set. Click OK.

Finally! A line chart of the hillary-partyid7 relationship appears in the SPSS Viewer (Figure 3-12). Line charts are at once simple and informative. You can immediately see the negative linear relationship between the independent and dependent variables as well as the curious similarities between the independent leaners and weak partisans of each party.

Using Bar Chart

Now that you are becoming familiar with SPSS graphing procedures, Bar Chart will require only an abbreviated treatment. However, we do need to dwell on a key difference between Line Chart and Bar Chart. Also, we will take a short but necessary excursion into the SPSS Chart Editor. In this guided example, you will obtain a bar chart of the relationship you analyzed earlier between campaign interest (the dependent variable attent) and level of education (the independent variable educ3).

Click Graphs → Bar. In the SPSS Bar Charts window, ensure that Simple *and* Summaries for groups of cases are selected, and then click Define. The Define Simple Bar window opens, and it is identical to the Define Simple Line window in every detail. As a substantive matter, we want to depict the percentage of respondents in each category of educ3 who said they were "very much interested" in the 2000 campaigns. Because educ3 is the independent variable, it goes in the Category Axis box. (Scroll to educ3 and click it over.) So far this is the same as before. At this point, however, the peculiarities of Bar Chart require that we refamiliarize ourselves with specific coding information about the dependent variable, attent.

Figure 3–11   Line Charts Options Window

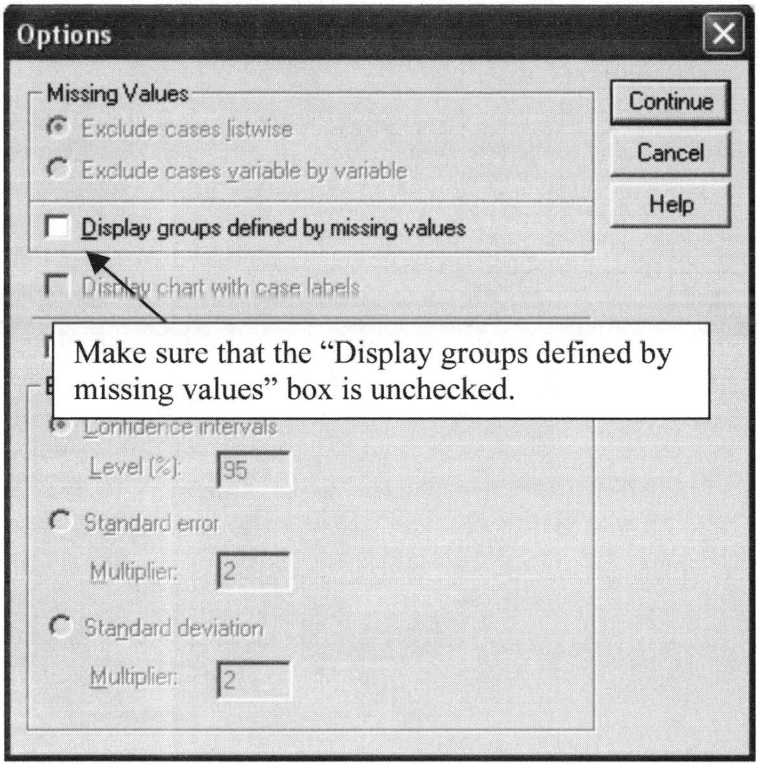

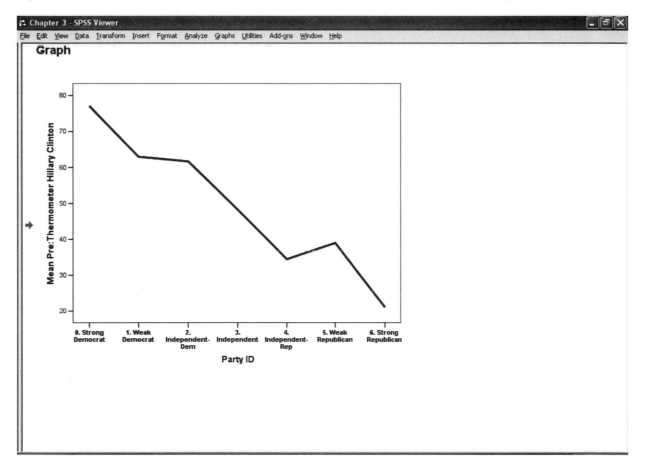

Figure 3–12   Line Chart Output: Mean Values of Hillary Clinton Thermometer, by Party Identification

Figure 3–13 Reviewing Numeric Codes

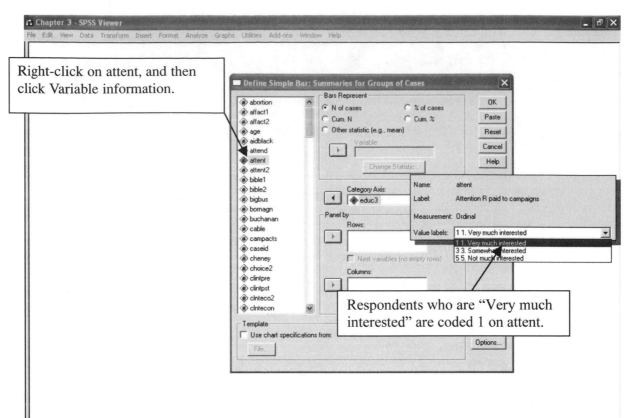

Scroll down the left-hand variable list until you find attent, place the cursor pointer on it, and then *right*-click. Click on Variable Information and review the numeric codes. Respondents saying that they were "very much interested" are coded 1, those "somewhat interested" are coded 3, and the "not much interested" are coded 5 (Figure 3-13). Commit this fact to short-term memory: Respondents who are "very much interested" are coded 1 on the dependent variable, attent.

Now return to the Bars Represent panel. Select the Other statistic radio button, and click attent into the Variable box. The designation "MEAN(attent)" appears in the Variable box, as shown in Figure 3-14. Just as it did in Line Chart, SPSS assumes that we are after the mean of attent. This default is fine for mean comparisons, but in this case it won't do. Click the Change Statistic button.[6] (In SPSS 12.0 or earlier, this button is labeled "Change Summary.")

The truly spellbinding Statistic window presents itself (Figure 3-15). The radio button for the default, Mean of values, is currently selected. However, we are interested in obtaining the percentage of cases in code 1 ("Very much interested") on attent. How do we get SPSS to cooperate with this request? Click the radio button at the bottom on the left, the one labeled "Percentage inside." The two boxes, one labeled "Low" and the other labeled "High," go active. Our request is specific and restrictive: We want the percentage of respondents in code 1 only. Expressed in terms that SPSS can understand, we want the percentage of cases "inside" a coded value of 1 (on the low side) and a coded value of 1 (on the high side). Click the cursor in the Low box and type a 1. Click the cursor in the High box and type a 1.[7] The Statistic window should now look like Figure 3-16. Click Continue, returning to the Define Simple Bar window. Click Options and make sure that the Display groups defined by missing values box is unchecked. Click Continue. The Define Simple Bar window should now look like Figure 3-17. Click OK.

All of your point-and-click drudgery has paid off. SPSS displays a bar chart of the relationship between education and campaign interest (Figure 3-18). The horizontal axis is nicely labeled, and the heights of the bars clearly depict the positive pattern: As education level increases, so does the percentage of respondents who are "very much interested" in the campaign. At least *we* know what the bars represent, because we did the analysis. An interested observer (such as your instructor), however, might do a double-take at the title

Figure 3–14 Define Simple Bar Window (default)

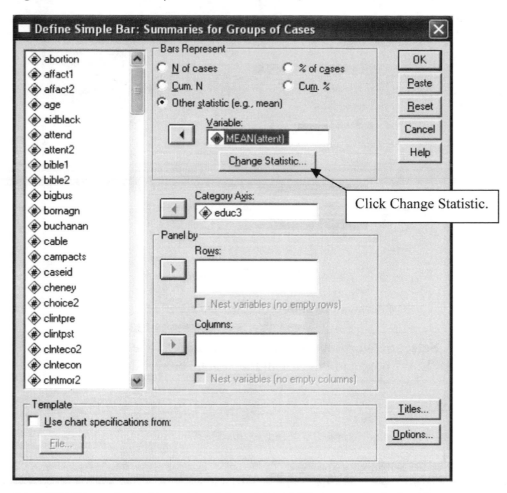

Note: In SPSS 12.0 or earlier, the Other statistic radio button is labeled "Other summary function," and Change Statistic is labeled "Change Summary"

Figure 3–15 Statistic Window (default)

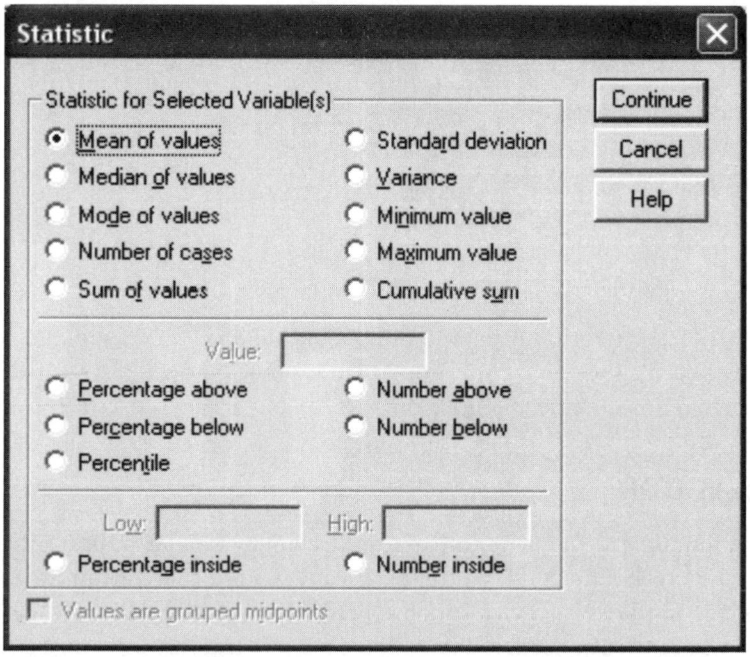

Note: In SPSS 12.0 or earlier, the Statistic window is the Sumary Function window.

Figure 3–16   Statistic Window (modified)

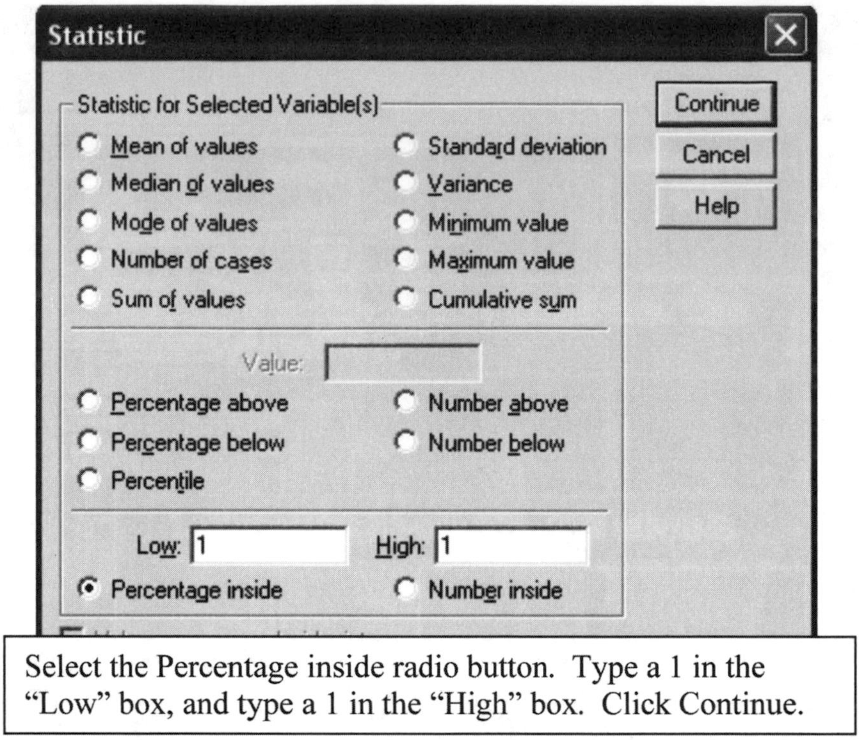

Select the Percentage inside radio button. Type a 1 in the "Low" box, and type a 1 in the "High" box. Click Continue.

Figure 3–17   Define Simple Bar Window (modified)

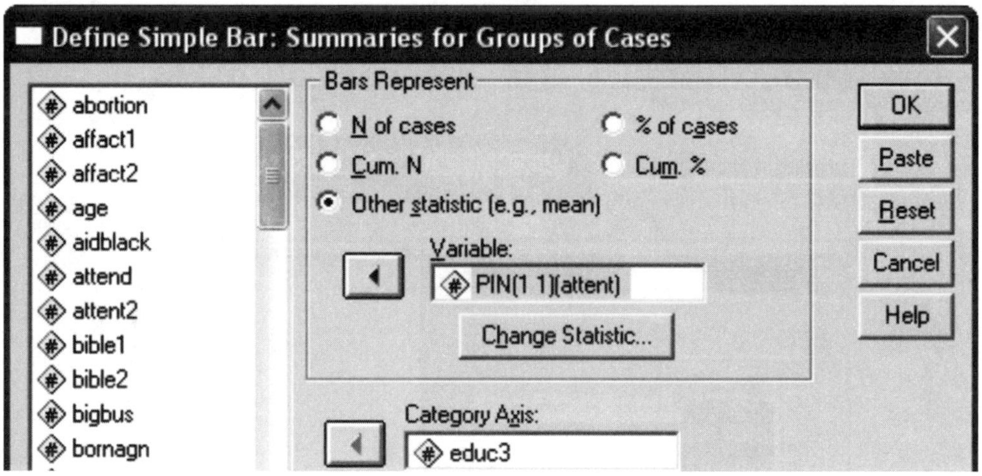

on the vertical axis, "% in(1,1) Attention R paid to campaigns." SPSS is very literal. We asked it to graph the percentages of people between code 1 and code 1 on attent, so that is how SPSS has titled the axis. This chart is not ready for prime time. We need to give the vertical axis a more descriptive title.

USING THE CHART EDITOR

SPSS permits the user to modify the content and appearance of any tabular or graphic object it produces in the SPSS Viewer. The user invokes the SPSS Editor, makes any desired changes, and then returns to the SPSS Viewer. The changes made in the SPSS Chart Editor are recorded automatically in the SPSS Viewer. In this section we describe how to retitle the vertical axis of the bar chart you just created. First we illustrate how to use the Chart Editor in SPSS 12.0 or later. Then we cover SPSS 11.5 or earlier.

Figure 3–18 Bar Chart Output

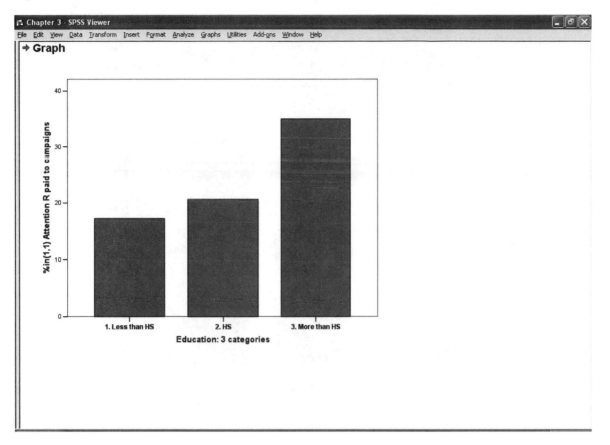

SPSS 12.0 or Later

In the SPSS Viewer, place the cursor anywhere on the bar chart and double-click. SPSS opens the Chart Editor (Figure 3-19). As with any editing software, the SPSS Chart Editor recognizes separate elements within an object. It recognizes some elements as text. These elements include the axis titles and the value labels for the categories of educ3. It recognizes other elements as graphic, such as the bars in the bar chart. The icons on the menu toolbar are mostly set up to edit graphic elements. You could select the bars in the chart (by clicking on one of them) and then use the menu toolbar to modify their appearance. For example, after selecting the bars, you could click the Properties Window icon—the multi-colored button that looks like a file folder—and change the color and spacing of the bars. You are encouraged to explore and experiment. Our immediate goal, however, is simpler. We want to edit a text element: the title on the vertical axis.

Place the cursor anywhere on the title "% in(1,1) Attention R paid to campaigns" and single-click. SPSS selects the axis title. With the cursor still placed on the title, single-click again. SPSS moves the text into editing mode inside the chart (Figure 3-20). Delete the current text: % in(1,1) Attention R paid to campaigns. In its place type the title "Percent 'Very interested' in campaign." Close the SPSS Chart Editor by clicking the X-button in the upper right-hand corner (or by clicking File → Close on the menu bar). This returns you to the SPSS Viewer, where you will find a newly modified bar chart of the attent-educ3 relationship.

SPSS 11.5 or Earlier

In the SPSS Viewer, place the cursor anywhere on the bar chart and double-click. SPSS opens the Chart Editor (Figure 3-21). As with any editing software, the SPSS Chart Editor recognizes separate elements within an object. It recognizes some elements as text. These elements include the axis titles and the value labels for the categories of educ3. It recognizes other elements as graphic, such as the bars in the bar chart. The icons on the menu toolbar are mostly set up to edit graphic elements. You could select the bars in the chart (by clicking on one of them) and then use the menu toolbar to modify their appearance. The "crayon" icon, for example, would let you change the color of the bars, and the icon with two yellow bars would allow you to label the bars with the percentage of cases in each category. You are encouraged to explore and experiment. Our immediate goal, however, is simpler. We want to edit a text element: the title on the vertical axis.

Figure 3–19 Chart Editor (SPSS 12.0 or later)

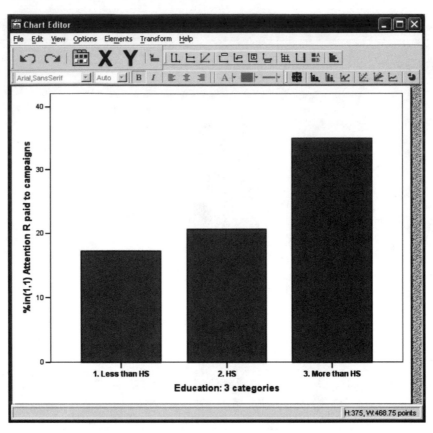

Figure 3–20 Bar Chart Axis Title Ready for Editing

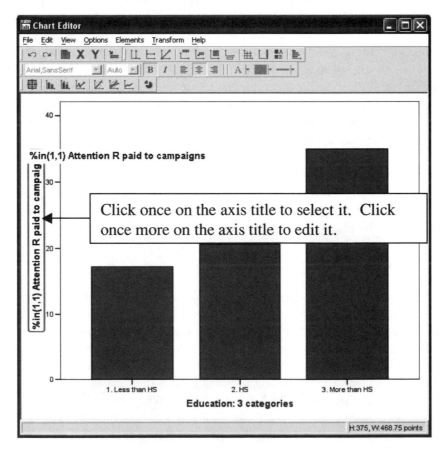

C. NES2000.sav contains partyid3, which measures respondents' partisanship by three categories: Democrat, independent, and Republican. Another variable, timing, measures how soon before the election respondents made up their minds. Using Graphs → Bar, obtain a bar chart of the timing-partyid3 relationship. Put the independent variable, partyid3, on the category axis. In the left-hand variable list, find timing. Right-click on timing and review the numeric codes. Respondents who decided "4–2 wks before" election day are coded 4 on timing, and respondents who made up their minds "right before or on" election day are coded 5 on timing. You want to create a bar chart that depicts the percentages of Democrats, independents, and Republicans who made up their minds 4 weeks before the election or later. In the Bars Represent panel, click Other statistic, and then click timing into the Variable box. Click Change Statistic. Click the Percentage inside radio button. Type a 4 in the Low box. Type a 5 in the High box. Click Continue. (If you are running SPSS 11.5 or earlier: In Options, make sure that Display groups defined by missing values is unchecked.) Click OK. SPSS will produce a bar chart showing the percentage of each partisan group deciding late (4 weeks before the election or later) in the campaign.

Based on this bar chart, would you say that the hypothesis is correct or incorrect (check one)?

❏ The hypothesis appears to be correct.   ❏ The hypothesis appears to be incorrect.

D. Using the Chart Editor, give the vertical axis a more descriptive title. Print the bar chart you created.

5. Why do some people hold more traditional views about the role of women in society and politics whereas others take a less traditional stance? General ideological orientations, liberalism versus conservatism, may play an important role in shaping individuals' opinions on this cultural question. Thus it seems plausible to suggest that ideology (independent variable) will affect opinions about appropriate female roles (dependent variable). The hypothesis: In comparing individuals, liberals will be more likely than conservatives to approve of nontraditional female roles.

GSS2002.sav contains fem_role, a scale that measures opinions about the appropriate role of women. You analyzed this variable in Chapter 2. Recall that fem_role ranges from 0 (women "domestic") to 12 (women in "work, politics"). So higher scores denote less traditional beliefs. This is the dependent variable. GSS2002.sav also has polviews, a 7-point ordinal scale measuring ideology. Scores on polviews can range from 0 ("extremely liberal") to 6 ("extremely conservative"). This is the independent variable.

A. According to the hypothesis, as the values of polviews increase, from 0 through 6, mean values of fem_role should (circle one)

Decrease   Neither decrease nor increase   Increase

B. Test the hypothesis using Compare Means → Means. Click fem_role into the Dependent List panel. Click polviews into the Independent List panel. In Options, remove Standard Deviation by selecting it with the mouse and clicking it back into the left-hand Statistics list. Run the analysis and write the results in the table that follows.

Female role: Children, home, politics

Ideological self ID	Mean	N
Extremely liberal		
Liberal		
Slightly liberal		
Moderate		
Slightly conservative		
Conservative		
Extremely conservative		
Total		

C. Do the results support the hypothesis? Write a few sentences explaining your reasoning. _____

_____

_____

_____

D. Using Graphs → Line, obtain a line chart of this relationship. In the Define Simple Line window, click polviews into the Category Axis box. In the Line Represents panel, select the Other statistic radio button, and then click fem_role into the Variable box. Print the line chart you created.

6. Here are two common media fixtures in our lives: newspapers and television. Are people who consume the printed word also avid consumers of broadcast media? Or is it an either-or proposition, with newspaper readers being less likely than newspaper nonreaders to watch television? There isn't much theory to rely on here, so let's test an exploratory hypothesis: In comparing individuals, people who read newspapers more often will spend more hours watching television than will those who read newspapers less often.

A. In this hypothesis, the dependent variable is _____, and the

independent variable is _____.

B. According to this hypothesis, if one compares people who frequently read a newspaper with people who infrequently read a newspaper (check one),

❑ the mean number of hours spent watching television will be higher among newspaper readers than among the nonreaders.

❑ the mean number of hours spent watching television will be lower among newspaper readers than among the nonreaders.

C. Using GSS2002.sav, test this hypothesis with Compare Means → Means. GSS2002.sav contains these variables: tvhours and news. The variable tvhours measures the number of hours the respondent watches television each day. And the news variable measures how frequently the respondent reads a newspaper during the week. Lower values on news denote less frequent newspaper reading, and higher values on news denote more frequent newspaper reading. Run the appropriate mean comparison analysis and record your results in the table that follows. Write the value labels of the independent variable in the left-most column. Record the mean values of the dependent variable in the column labeled "Mean" and the number of cases in the column labeled "N."

Values of independent variable	Mean	N
Total		

D. Would you say that your analysis supports the hypothesis or does not support the hypothesis? Check the appropriate box and complete the statement:

❑ The analysis supports the hypothesis because _____

_____.

❑ The analysis does not support the hypothesis because _____

_____.

E. Obtain a line chart of this relationship using Graphs → Line. (If you are running SPSS 11.5 or earlier: In Options, make sure that the Display groups defined by missing values box is unchecked.) Print the line chart you created.

7. Where are unions stronger? Where are they weaker? Consider the following two claims:

Claim 1: States in the northeastern United States are more likely to have unionized workforces than are states in the South.

Claim 2: States in the Midwest and West have levels of unionization more similar to those in the South than to those in the Northeast.

A. States.sav contains union, the percentage of each state's workforce who are union members. Another variable, region, is a four-category census classification of the states. Run a mean comparison analysis. Record your results in the table that follows.

Percentage of workers who are union members

Census region	Mean	N
Northeast		
Midwest		
South		
West		
Total		50

B. Based on your analysis, would you say that Claim 1 is correct or incorrect? How do you know? Check the appropriate box and complete the following sentence.

❑ Claim 1 is correct, because _____

_____.

❑ Claim 1 is incorrect, because _____

_____.

C. Based on your analysis, would you say that Claim 2 is correct or incorrect? How do you know? Check the appropriate box and complete the following sentence.

❑ Claim 2 is correct, because _____

_____.

❑ Claim 2 is incorrect, because _____

_____.

8. Two policy researchers are trying to figure out why seat belt usage varies across states.

Policy researcher 1: "I think seat belt usage depends on education. A less-educated populace will be less aware of the safety benefits associated with seat belts and will be less prone to use them. A more-educated citizenry, by contrast, will be more likely to buckle up. So as state education levels go up, so will seat belt usage."

Policy researcher 2: "I disagree. I don't know why belt usage varies across states, but I'm sure that education has nothing to do with it. If you compare lower-education states with states having higher levels of education, you'll find no differences in seat belt usage."

Imagine a line chart of the relationship between education and seat belt use. The horizontal axis measures state education levels in four ordinal categories: low, medium-low, medium-high, and high. The vertical axis records the mean percentage of drivers who use a seat belt: Higher values denote higher usage. Now consider line charts X, Y, and Z, which follow.

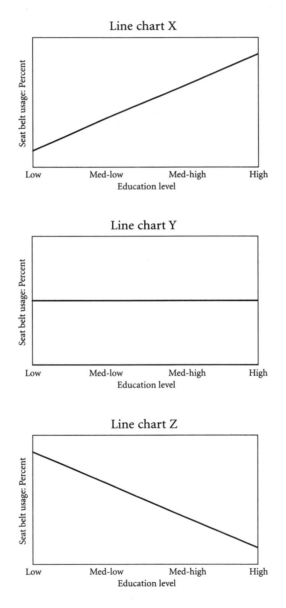

A. If policy researcher 1 were correct, which line chart would most accurately depict the relationship between states' education levels and seat belt usage (circle one)?

Line chart X   Line chart Y   Line chart Z

Freedom House democ rating reversed 2003–2004

% of democracies in region: 3 cats	Mean	N
Total		

C. Using Graphs → Line, obtain a line chart of the relationship between fh03rev and dem_oth3. Print the line chart you created.

D. Examine the mean comparison table and the line chart. Which of the following statements are supported by your analysis (check all that apply)?

❑ Countries in regions having fewer democracies are more likely to be democratic than are countries in regions having more democracies.

❑ The relationship between the independent and dependent variables is positive.

❑ The democratic diffusion hypothesis is incorrect.

❑ Countries in regions having fewer democracies are less likely to be democratic than are countries in regions having more democracies.

❑ The relationship between the independent and dependent variables is negative.

That concludes the exercises for this chapter. Before exiting SPSS, be sure to save your output file.

NOTES

1. Respondents in the National Election Study are asked some of the same questions before and after an election. The "Pre" in the labels of the NES2000.sav variables tells the researcher that the variables were measured in the preelection wave of the survey. A variable with "Post" in its label was part of the postelection wave.
2. Interestingly, Weak Democrats and Independent-Democrats often hold similar opinions and attitudes, as do Weak Republicans and Independent-Republicans. Your future analyses of NES2000.sav may uncover more examples of these similarities.
3. Because we are graphing one relationship, we want a single line. And because we are comparing groups of partisans, we want SPSS to display a summary measure, the mean, for each group.
4. Unless we modify the Line Represents panel to suit our analysis, SPSS will produce a line chart for the number of cases (N of cases) in each category of partyid7.
5. Of course, you will encounter situations in which you do not want mean values. Later in this chapter we review the procedure for Change Statistic.
6. The Change Statistic button will not be available unless the variable in the Variable box is highlighted. A variable is highlighted automatically when you click it into the Variable box. If you are experimenting and lose the highlighting, simply click directly on the variable in the Variable box. This restores the highlighting.
7. The same result can be achieved by clicking the Percentage below radio button and typing a 3 in the Value box. Because code 1 is the only value of attent lower than 3, SPSS will return the percentage of respondents having code 1 on attent.
8. The variable who00_2 is confined to voters who cast ballots for either Gore or Bush. Another variable in NES2000.sav, who00, records voters' choices among Gore, Bush, Buchanan, and Nader.
9. In raw form, the Freedom House scale ranges from 1 (most democratic) to 7 (least democratic). The "rev" part of fh03rev communicates that the Freedom House scale has been reverse-coded so that higher scores denote higher levels of democracy.

4

Transforming Variables in SPSS

Political researchers sometimes must modify the variables they want to analyze. Generally speaking, such *variable transformations* become necessary or desirable in two common situations. Often a researcher wants to collapse a variable, combining its values or codes into a smaller number of useful categories. The researcher can do so in SPSS through the Recode transformation feature. In other situations a dataset may contain several variables that provide similar measures of the same concept. In these instances the researcher may want to combine the codes of different variables, creating a new and more precise measure. The SPSS Compute transformation feature is designed for this task.

In this chapter you will learn how to use the Recode and Compute commands. The chapter contains three guided examples. In the first example, you will recode a variable in NES2000.sav. In the second and third examples, you will use GSS2002.sav to recode a variable and compute a variable. The variables you modify or create in this chapter (and in this chapter's exercises) will become permanent variables in the datasets. After you complete each guided example, be sure to save the dataset.

USING RECODE

With SPSS Recode, you can manipulate any variable at any level of measurement—nominal, ordinal, or interval. But you should exercise vigilance and care. Three guidelines are worth following. First, before using Recode, you must obtain a frequency distribution of the variable you intend to manipulate. Second, after using Recode, it is important to check your work. Third, if you create a new variable using Recode, you should properly label the new variable and its values. Open NES2000.sav, and let's work through the first example.

Recoding a Variable in NES2000.sav

NES2000.sav contains marital, a demographic variable that measures marital status in six categories:

Marital Status	Code
Married	1
Widowed	2
Divorced	3
Separated	4
Never married	5
Partnered, not married	6

An SPSS Frequencies analysis of marital produced the following distribution:

Code and marital status	Frequency	Percent	Valid percent
1. Married	935	51.7	52.1
2. Widowed	168	9.3	9.4
3. Divorced	238	13.2	13.3
4. Separated	55	3.0	3.1
5. Never married	348	19.3	19.4
6. Partnered, not married	49	2.7	2.7
Valid total	1793	99.2	100.0
System missing	14	.8	
Total	1807	100.0	

Now, think about research questions for which the researcher might want to make fine distinctions among people—comparing, for example, the 238 divorced individuals with the 348 individuals who never married. Much of the time, however, you might be after a simpler comparison—the 52.1 percent of the valid cases who are married (code 1) and the remaining 47.9 percent of the sample who are unmarried (codes 2 through 6). How would you collapse the codes of marital into two categories and still preserve the potentially useful values of the original variable?

In the SPSS Data Editor, Click Transform and place the cursor on Recode. SPSS presents two options: Into Same Variables and Into Different Variables. Which one to choose? When the user recodes a variable into the same variable, SPSS replaces the original codes with the new codes. The original information is lost. When the user recodes a variable into a different variable, SPSS uses the original codes to create a new variable. The original variable is retained. In some situations (discussed later) you will want to pick Into Same Variables. Most of the time, however, you should use the second option, Into Different Variables.

Click Into Different Variables. The Recode into Different Variables window opens (Figure 4-1). Scroll down the left-hand variable list and find marital. Click marital into the Input Variable → Output Variable box. SPSS puts marital into the box, with this designation: "marital → ?" This is SPSS-speak for "What do you want to name the new variable you are creating from marital?" Click in the Name box and type "married" (without quotation marks). Let's take this opportunity to give the new variable, married, a descriptive

Figure 4–1 Recode into Different Variables Window

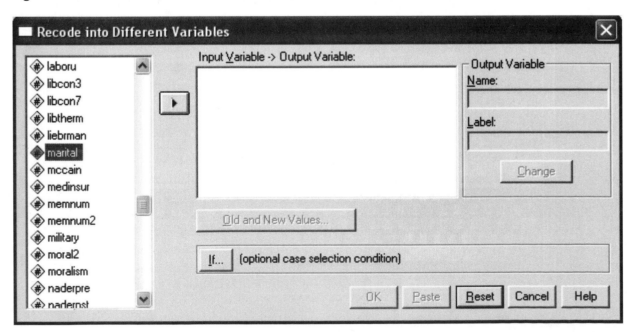

Figure 4–2   Recoding a Nominal-level Variable

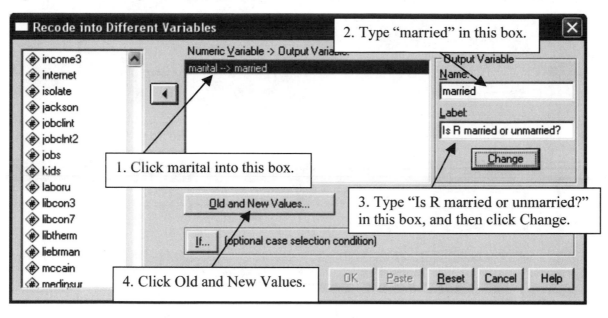

label. Click in the Label box and type "Is R married or unmarried?" Click the Change button. The Recode into Different Variables window should now look like Figure 4-2.

Now let's do the recoding. Click Old and New Values. The Recode into Different Variables: Old and New Values window pops up (Figure 4-3). There are two main panels. In the left-hand, Old Value panel, we will tell SPSS how to combine the original codes for marital. In the right-hand, New Value panel, we will assign codes for the new variable, which we have named married.

How do we want things to end up? Let's say that we want the new variable, married, to have two codes: code 1 for married respondents and code 0 for unmarried respondents. Plus we need to make sure that any respondents who have missing values on marital also have missing values on married. So we need to instruct SPSS to follow this recoding protocol:

Marital status	Old value (marital)	New value (married)
Married	1	1
Widowed	2	0
Divorced	3	0
Separated	4	0
Never married	5	0
Partnered, not married	6	0
	Missing	Missing

Make sure that the top radio button in the Old Value panel is selected (the default), click the cursor in the box next to "Value," and type "1." Move the cursor directly across to the right-hand New Value panel, make sure the top radio button is selected (again, the default setting), and type "1" in the Value box. Click the Add button. In the Old → New box, SPSS records your instruction with "1 → 1," meaning "All respondents coded 1 on marital will be coded 1 on married." Now return to the left-hand Old Value panel and select the Range radio button. The two boxes beneath "Range" are activated. In the left-hand Range box, type "2." In the right-hand Range box, type "6." Move the cursor to the New Value panel and type "0" in the Value box. Click Add. SPSS responds, "2 thru 6 → 0," letting you know that all respondents coded 2, 3, 4, 5, or 6 on marital will be coded 0 on married. One last loose end: In the Old Value panel, click the radio button next to "System- or user-missing." In the New Value panel, click the radio button next to "System-missing." Click Add. SPSS records your instruction as "MISSING → SYSMIS," meaning that any respondents having missing values on marital will be assigned missing values on married. The Recode into Different Variables: Old

Figure 4–3 Recode into Different Variables: Old and New Values Window

Recode into Different Variables: Old and New Values

Old Value
- ⊙ Value:
- ○ System-missing
- ○ System- or user-missing
- ○ Range: [ ] through [ ]
- ○ Range: Lowest through [ ]
- ○ Range: [ ] through highest
- ○ All other values

New Value
- ⊙ Value: [ ]   ○ System-missing
- ○ Copy old value(s)

Old --> New:

Add
Change
Remove

☐ Output variables are strings Width: 8
☐ Convert numeric strings to numbers ('5'->5)

Continue   Cancel   Help

and New Values window should now look like Figure 4-4. Click Continue, returning to the main Recode into Different Variables window. Click OK. SPSS runs the recode and returns you to the Data Editor.

Did the recode work correctly? This is where the check-your-work guideline takes effect. It is a good idea to run Frequencies on a newly created variable to ensure that you did things right. Figure 4-5 shows the frequency distribution for married. The frequency table displays the label for our newly minted variable. More important, the valid percentages check out: 47.9 percent coded 0 and 52.1 percent coded 1. The recode worked as planned. However, we have not completed our work. Notice how SPSS expresses our numeric codes: 0 shows up as ".00" and 1 as "1.00." We need to change these codes back to 0 and 1. Also note that the numeric codes do not have the appropriate labels, "unmarried" and "married." To complete the recoding process, one more step is required.

In the SPSS Data Editor, make sure that the Variable View tab is clicked. Scroll down to the bottom of the Data Editor, where you will find married (Figure 4-6). (SPSS always puts newly created variables on the bottom row of the Variable View.) Click in the Decimals cell, which shows "2," and change this value to "0." Next, click in the Values cell (which currently says "None"), and then click on the gray button that appears. The Value Labels window presents itself. In the box next to "Value," type "0." In the box next to "Value Label," type "unmarried." Click Add. Repeat the process for code 1, typing "1" in the Value box and "married" in the Value Label box. Click Add. Click OK. Looks good.

Figure 4–4 Collapsing a Nominal-level Variable into Categories

Recode into Different Variables: Old and New Values

Old Value
- ○ Value: [ ]
- ○ System-missing
- ⊙ System- or user-missing
- ○ Range: [ ] through [ ]
- ○ Range: Lowest through [ ]
- ○ Range: [ ] through highest
- ○ All other values

New Value
- ○ Value: [ ]   ⊙ System-missing
- ○ Copy old value(s)

Old --> New:

Add
Change
Remove

1 --> 1
MISSING --> SYSMIS
2 thru 6 --> 0

☐ Output variables are strings Width: 8
☐ Convert numeric strings to numbers ('5'->5)

Continue   Cancel   Help

Figure 4–5 Frequencies Output for a Collapsed Nominal Variable

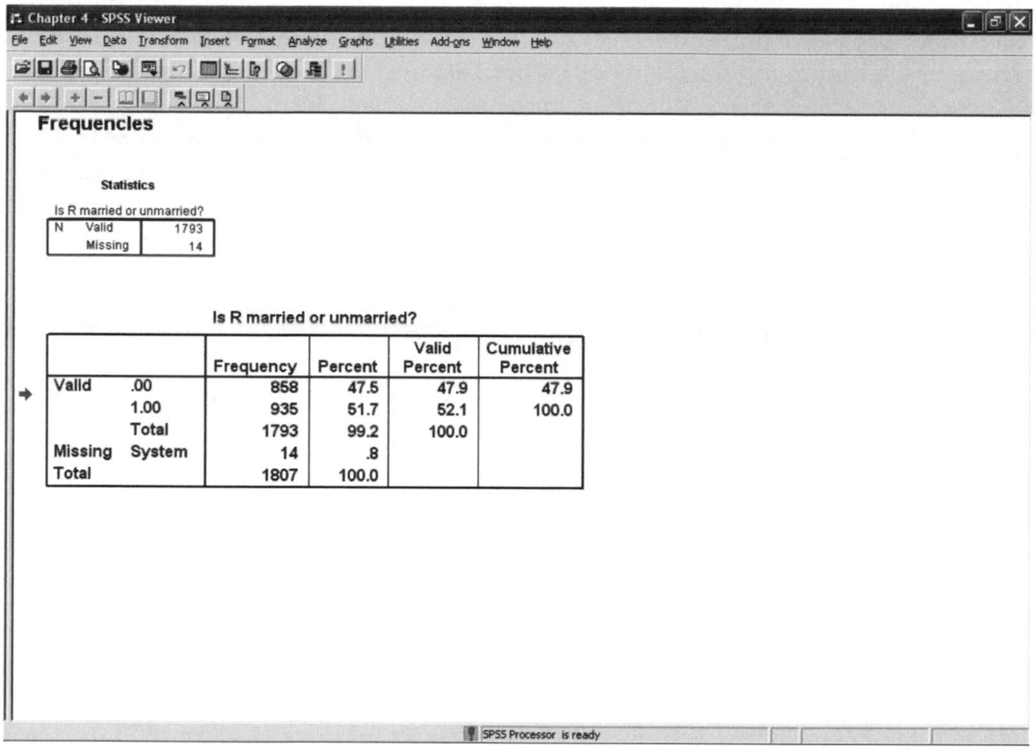

Figure 4–6 Assigning Value Labels to a Recoded Variable

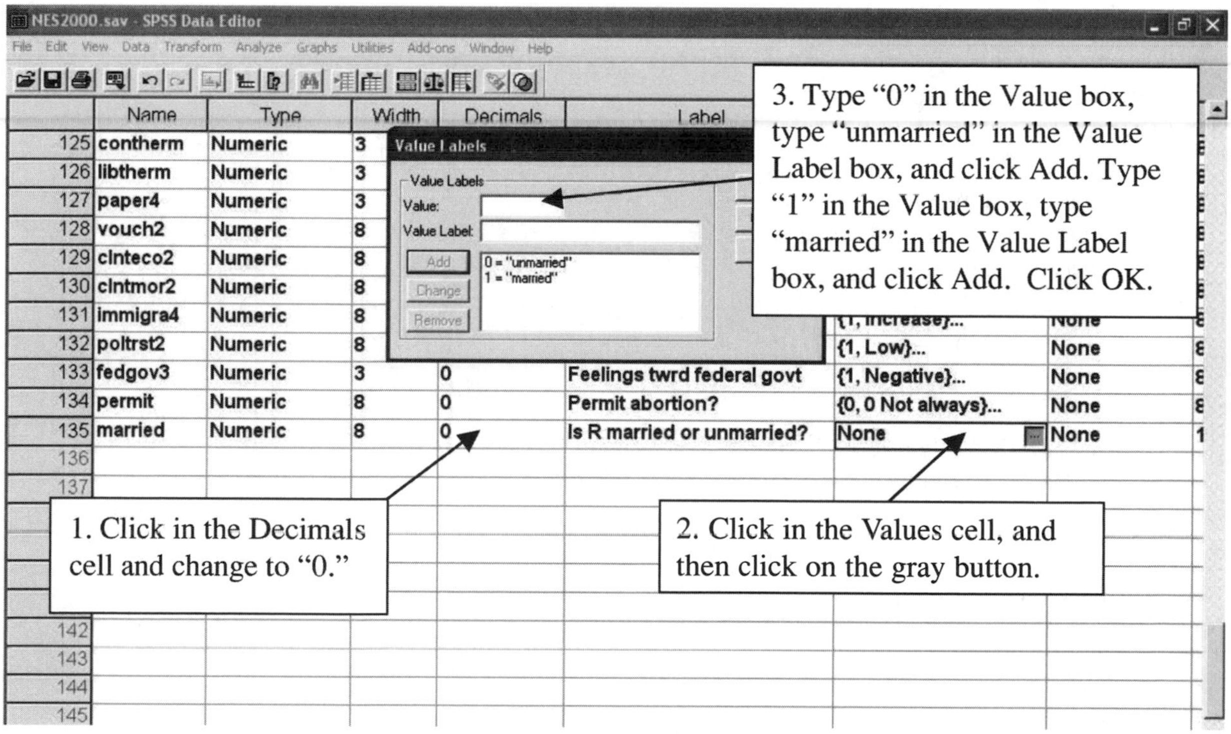

You have just invested your time in recoding an original variable into a new variable and, in the process, made NES2000.sav better and more useable. Before going on to the next example, make sure you save the dataset.

Recoding a Variable in GSS2002.sav

Collapsing the values of a categorical variable, as you have just done, is perhaps the most common use of the Recode transformation feature. The original variable may be nominal level, such as marital. Or it may be ordinal level. For example, it might make sense to collapse four response categories such as "strongly agree," "agree," "disagree," and "strongly disagree" into two, "agree" and "disagree." At other times the original variable is interval level, such as age or income. In such cases the researcher would use Recode to create a new variable having, say, three or four ordinal-level categories. Let's pursue this route, using GSS2002.sav.

GSS2002.sav contains the variable cohort, which records the year of birth for each respondent. Our goal here is to collapse cohort into three theoretically useful categories: respondents born before 1950, those born between 1950 and 1965, and those born after 1965. How do we proceed? First, of course, we need a frequency distribution for cohort. Click Analyze → Descriptive statistics → Frequencies, click cohort into the Variable(s) list, and run the analysis. (In the main Frequencies window, make sure the Display frequency tables box is checked.) The frequency distribution is a real monster:

Year of birth

		Frequency	Percent	Valid percent	Cumulative percent
Valid	1913	13	.5	.5	.5
	1914	6	.2	.2	.7
	1915	10	.4	.4	1.1
	1916	6	.2	.2	1.3
	1917	11	.4	.4	1.7
	1918	14	.5	.5	2.2
	1919	15	.5	.5	2.7
	1920	11	.4	.4	3.1
	1921	13	.5	.5	3.6
	1922	16	.6	.6	4.2
	1923	9	.3	.3	4.5
	1924	15	.5	.5	5.1
	1925	19	.7	.7	5.7
	1926	31	1.1	1.1	6.9
	1927	26	.9	.9	7.8
	1928	24	.9	.9	8.7
	1929	22	.8	.8	9.5
	1930	23	.8	.8	10.3
	1931	36	1.3	1.3	11.6
	1932	34	1.2	1.2	12.9
	1933	27	1.0	1.0	13.8
	1934	26	.9	.9	14.8
	1935	30	1.1	1.1	15.9
	1936	20	.7	.7	16.6
	1937	30	1.1	1.1	17.7
	1938	38	1.4	1.4	19.1
	1939	34	1.2	1.2	20.3
	1940	32	1.2	1.2	21.5
	1941	31	1.1	1.1	22.6
	1942	30	1.1	1.1	23.7
	1943	33	1.2	1.2	24.9
	1944	33	1.2	1.2	26.1
	1945	35	1.3	1.3	27.4
	1946	47	1.7	1.7	29.1
	1947	39	1.4	1.4	30.5
	1948	45	1.6	1.6	32.1
	1949	45	1.6	1.6	33.8
	1950	58	2.1	2.1	35.9
	1951	52	1.9	1.9	37.8
	1952	47	1.7	1.7	39.5

Year of birth—*continued*

		Frequency	Percent	Valid percent	Cumulative percent
	1953	43	1.6	1.6	41.0
	1954	61	2.2	2.2	43.3
	1955	52	1.9	1.9	45.1
	1956	70	2.5	2.5	47.7
	1957	51	1.8	1.9	49.5
	1958	47	1.7	1.7	51.3
	1959	63	2.3	2.3	53.5
	1960	44	1.6	1.6	55.1
	1961	54	2.0	2.0	57.1
	1962	60	2.2	2.2	59.3
	1963	54	2.0	2.0	61.3
	1964	49	1.8	1.8	63.0
	1965	64	2.3	2.3	65.4
	1966	55	2.0	2.0	67.4
	1967	59	2.1	2.1	69.5
	1968	57	2.1	2.1	71.6
	1969	76	2.7	2.8	74.3
	1970	62	2.2	2.3	76.6
	1971	53	1.9	1.9	78.5
	1972	61	2.2	2.2	80.7
	1973	43	1.6	1.6	82.3
	1974	51	1.8	1.9	84.2
	1975	48	1.7	1.7	85.9
	1976	54	2.0	2.0	87.9
	1977	61	2.2	2.2	90.1
	1978	58	2.1	2.1	92.2
	1979	68	2.5	2.5	94.7
	1980	46	1.7	1.7	96.3
	1981	40	1.4	1.5	97.8
	1982	32	1.2	1.2	98.9
	1983	25	.9	.9	99.9
	1984	4	.1	.1	100.0
	Total	2751	99.5	100.0	
Missing	NA	14	.5		
Total		2765	100.0		

Let's use this distribution to get an idea of what the recoded variable should look like. To do this, focus on the "Cumulative percent" column. What percentage of the sample falls into the oldest category—born before 1950? That's easy: 33.8 percent. What percentage of the sample falls *in or below* the middle category, people born between 1950 and 1965? Well, 65.4 percent of the sample was born in 1965 or earlier, so 65.4 percent of the sample should fall into the first two categories of the recoded variable. These two numbers, 33.8 percent and 65.4 percent, will help us to verify that our recode was performed properly.

Now do the recode. Click Transform → Recode → Into Different Variables. Click cohort into the Input Variable → Output Variable box. Type "cohort3" in the Name box. Type "Year born: 3 categories" in the Label box and click Change (Figure 4-7). Click Old and New Values. Let's first create the oldest category for cohort3. In the Old Value panel, select the radio button next to "Range: Lowest through"; doing so activates the box. Type "1949" in the box. In the New Value panel, type "1" in the Value box and click Add. SPSS translates the instruction as "Lowest thru 1949 → 1," lumping all respondents between the lowest value of cohort (1909) and a value of 1949 on cohort into code 1 of the new variable, cohort3. In the Old Value panel, select the Range button and type "1950" in the left-hand box and "1965" in the right-hand box. Type

Figure 4–7 Recoding an Interval-level Variable

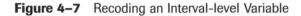

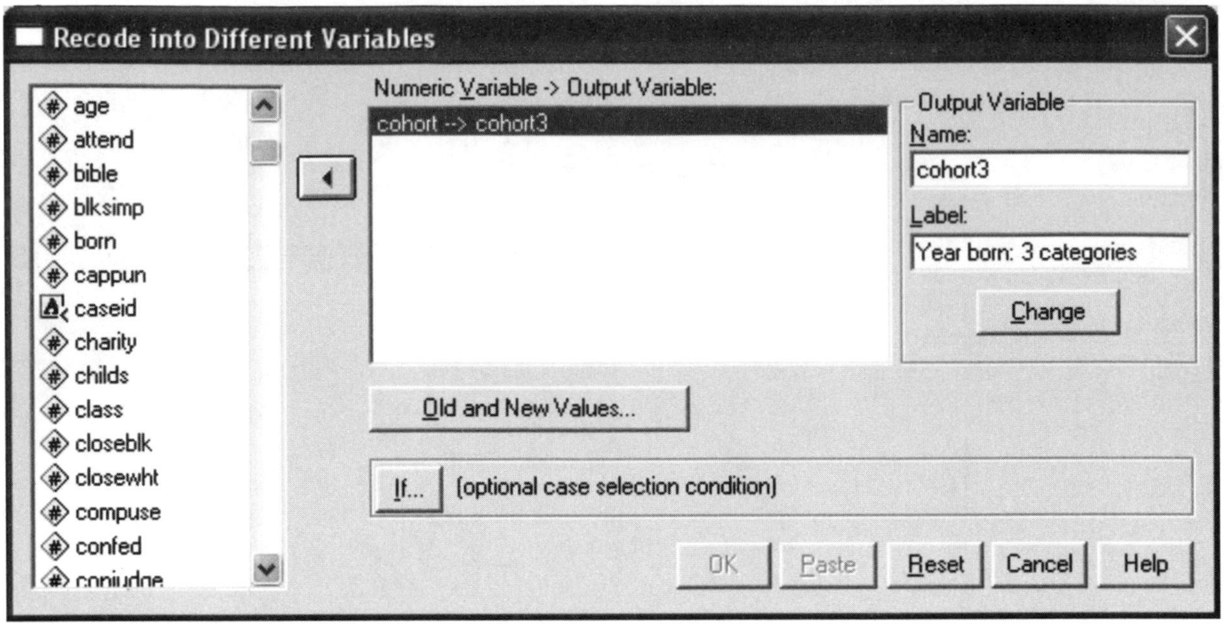

Figure 4–8 Collapsing an Interval-level Variable into Categories

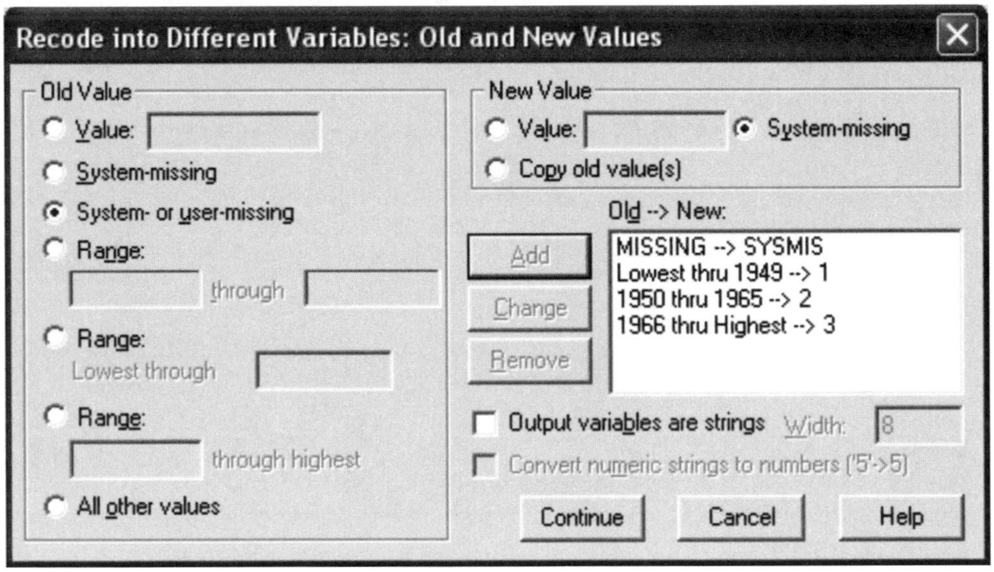

"2" in the Value box in the New Value panel and click Add. That's the middle "baby boomer" age group, now coded 2 on cohort3. In the Old Value panel, select the radio button next to "Range: through highest" and type "1966" in the box. Type "3" in the Value box in the New Value panel and click Add. That puts the youngest generation into code 3 on cohort3. Complete the recode by clicking the System- or user-missing button in the Old Value panel and the System-missing button in the New Value panel. Click Add. The Recode into Different Variables: Old and New Values window should now look like Figure 4-8. Click Continue. Click OK. Check your work by running Frequencies on cohort3 and examining the output (Figure 4-9).

The cumulative percent markers, 33.8 percent and 65.4 percent, are just where they are supposed to be. Cohort3 checks out. Before proceeding, scroll to the bottom of the Variable View in the Data Editor and make two changes to cohort3. First, change Decimals to 0. Second, click in the Values cell and label cohort3's values as follows:

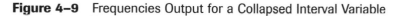

Value	Value label
1	Before 1950
2	1950–1965
3	After 1965

Figure 4–9   Frequencies Output for a Collapsed Interval Variable

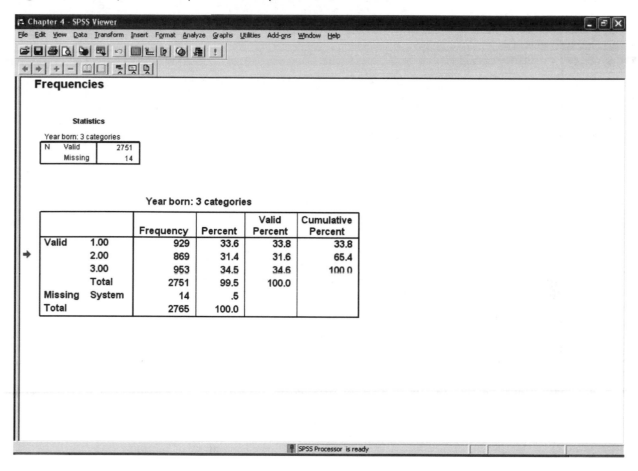

USING COMPUTE

As you have seen, SPSS Recode requires a certain amount of discernment and care. SPSS Compute, however, allows the creative juices to flow. Although SPSS permits the creation of new variables through a dizzying variety of complex transformations, the typical use of Compute is pretty straightforward. By and large, you will usually use Compute to create a simple *additive index* from similarly coded variables. Consider a simple illustration. Suppose you have three variables, each of which measures whether or not a respondent engaged in each of the following activities during an election campaign: tried to convince somebody how to vote, put a campaign bumper sticker on his or her car, or gave money to one of the candidates or parties. Each variable is coded identically: 0 if the respondent did not engage in the activity and 1 if he or she did. Now, each of these variables is interesting in its own right, but you might want to add them together, creating an overall measure of campaigning: People who did not engage in any of these activities would end up with a value of 0 on the new variable; those who engaged in one activity, a code of 1; two activities, a code of 2; and all three activities, a code of 3.

Here are some suggested guidelines to follow in using Compute to create a simple additive index. First, before running Compute, make sure that each of the variables is coded identically. In the preceding illustration, if the "bumper sticker" variable were coded 1 for no and 2 for yes, and the other variables were coded 0 and 1, the resulting additive index would be incorrect. Second, make sure that the variables are all coded in the

Figure 4–10 Compute Variable Window

same *direction*. If the "contribute money" variable were coded 0 for yes and 1 for no, and the other variables were coded 0 for no and 1 for yes, the additive index would again be incorrect.[1] Third, after running Compute, obtain a frequency distribution of the newly created variable. Upon examining the frequency distribution, you may decide to use Recode to collapse the new variable into more useful categories. Suppose, for example, that we add the three campaign acts together and get the following frequency distribution for the new variable:

Additive index: Number of campaign acts

Value label	Value	Percentage of sample
Engaged in none	0	60
Engaged in one	1	25
Engaged in two	2	13
Engaged in three	3	2
Total		100

Clearly, it looks like a Recode run may be in order—collapsing respondents coded 2 or 3 into the same category.

These points are best understood firsthand. GSS2002.sav contains two variables, each of which measures respondents' levels of intolerance toward a specific group: homosexuals (tolhomo) or racists (tolracis). Each of these variables is coded identically in the same direction: 0 for "tolerant," 1 for "middle," and 2 for "intolerant." We are going to add these variables together, using the expression "tolhomo + tolracis." Think about this expression for a moment. If a respondent were coded as "tolerant" on both variables, what would be his or her score on an additive index? It would be 0 + 0 = 0. What if the respondent were "intolerant" on both? In that case, 2 + 2 = 4. Thus we know from the get-go that the values of the new variable will range from 0 (at the tolerant end) to 4 (at the intolerant end).

Let's get SPSS to compute a new variable, which we will name intoler, by summing the codes of tolhomo and tolracis. Click Transform → Compute, invoking the SPSS Compute Variable window (Figure 4-10). A box labeled "Target Variable" is in the window's upper left-hand corner. This is where we name the new variable. Click in the Target Variable box and type "intoler," as shown in Figure 4-11. The large box on the right

Figure 4-11 Computing a New Variable

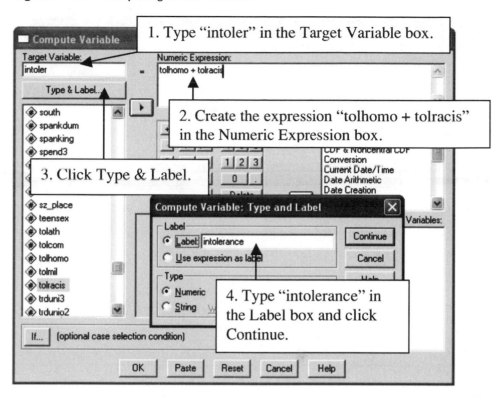

side of the window, labeled "Numeric Expression," is where we tell SPSS which variables we wish to use and how we wish to combine them. Scroll down the left-hand variable list until you find tolhomo. Click tolhomo into the Numeric Expression box. Using the keyboard (or the calculator pad beneath the Numeric Expression box), type or click a plus sign (+) to the right of tolhomo. Returning to the variable list, click tolracis into the Numeric Expression box. Before we create intoler, let's give it a descriptive label. Click the Type & Label button, which opens the Compute Variable: Type and Label window (see Figure 4-11). Type "intolerance" in the Label box and click Continue. You are ready to run the compute. Click OK. SPSS does its work and returns benignly to the Data Editor.

What does the new variable, intoler, look like? To find out, run Frequencies on intoler (Figure 4-12). This is an interesting variable. Respondents are heavily grouped in the 0 code, the most tolerant combination. Codes 1 and 2 together comprise a little over 40 percent of the sample, and the higher values, codes 3 and 4, are more thinly populated with cases. Before making intoler a permanent fixture in the dataset, let's use Recode to collapse it into three categories. We'll leave code 0 as its own category (cumulative percent, 44.3), but we'll combine codes 1 and 2 into one category (cumulative percent, 86.2), and codes 3 and 4 into one category (cumulative percent, 100.0).

This is a situation in which Recode → Into Same Variables is appropriate.[2] Click Recode → Into Same Variables. In the Recode into Same Variables window, click intoler into the Numeric Variables box, as shown in Figure 4-13. Click Old and New Values. Follow this recoding protocol:

Old value	New value
0	0
Range: 1 through 2	1
Range: 3 through 4	2
System- or user-missing	System-missing

The Recode into Same Variables: Old and New Values window should look like Figure 4-14. Click Continue. Click OK. Again run Frequencies on intoler to check the recode (Figure 4-15).

Figure 4–12 Frequency Output for a Computed Variable

		Frequency	Percent	Valid Percent	Cumulative Percent
Valid	.00	389	14.1	44.3	44.3
	1.00	158	5.7	18.0	62.3
	2.00	210	7.6	23.9	86.2
	3.00	45	1.6	5.1	91.3
	4.00	76	2.7	8.7	100.0
	Total	878	31.8	100.0	
Missing	System	1887	68.2		
Total		2765	100.0		

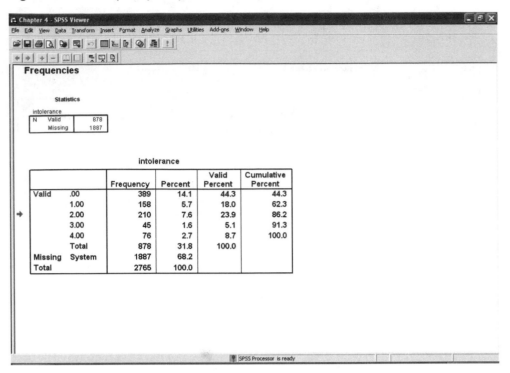

Figure 4–13 Recoding a New Variable

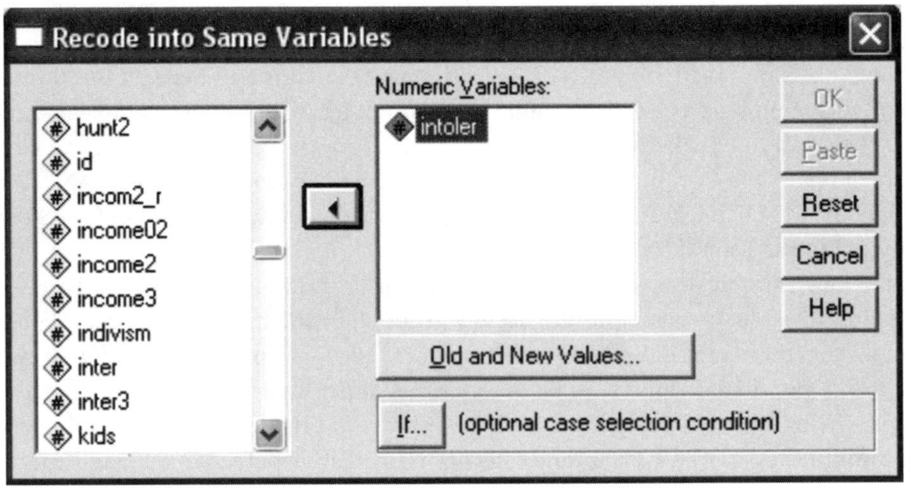

A flawless recode is a thing of beauty. Just as you did with married and cohort3, scroll to the bottom of the Variable View of the Data Editor and make the same two changes to intoler. First, change Decimals to 0. Second, click in the Values cell and assign these value labels:

Value	Value label
0	Tolerant
1	Middle
2	Intolerant

Before proceeding with the exercises, you will want to save the dataset.

Figure 4–14 Collapsing a New Variable into Categories

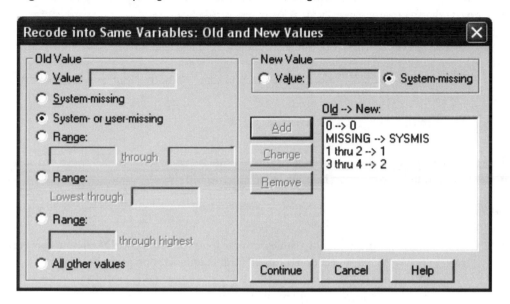

Figure 4–15 Frequency Output for a Computed and Collapsed Variable

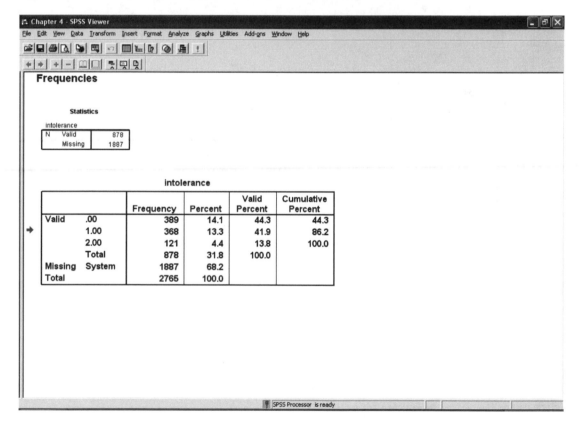

EXERCISES

1. GSS2002.sav has two variables that measure respondents' attitudes toward the role of government in "solving our country's problems" (helpnot) and in "improving the standard of living of poor Americans" (helppoor). Both variables are 5-point scales. Codes range from 1 (the respondent thinks that more government action is required) through 5 (the respondent thinks that the government is already doing too much or that people should help themselves). So each respondent is coded 1, 2, 3, 4, or 5 on helpnot and helppoor.

A. Imagine creating an additive index from these two variables. The additive index would have scores that range between what two values?

Between a score of _____ and a score of _____.

B. A respondent taking the strongest progovernment action stand on both variables would have what score on the index?

A score of _____.

C. Suppose that a respondent takes the strongest progovernment action stand on helppoor but stakes out the middle, fence-straddling position on helpnot. What score would this respondent have?

A score of _____.

D. Using SPSS Compute, compute an additive index from helpnot and helppoor. Name the new variable govhelp. Give govhelp this label: "Govt action required?" Run Frequencies on govhelp.

What percentage of respondents score 5 or less on govhelp?

_____ percent.

What percentage of respondents score 6 or less on govhelp?

_____ percent.

E. Use Recode → Into Same Variables to collapse govhelp into three categories according to the following recode protocol:

Old value	New value
2–5	1
6	2
7–10	3
Missing	Missing

Run Frequencies on govhelp.

What percentage of respondents score 1 on govhelp?

_____ percent.

What percentage of respondents score 2 or less on govhelp?

_____ percent.

F. In the Variable View of the Data Editor, change Decimals to 0 and supply these value labels:

Value	Value label
1	Govt action
2	Middle
3	No govt action

Run Frequencies on govhelp to make sure that everything worked out okay. Based on your results, fill in the table that follows.

Govt action required?

	Frequency	Valid percent	Cumulative percent
Govt action			
Middle			
No govt action			100.0
Total		100.0	

2. GSS2002.sav contains polviews, which measures political ideology—the extent to which individuals "think of themselves as liberal or conservative." Here is how polviews is coded:

Value	Value label
1	Extremely liberal
2	Liberal
3	Slightly liberal
4	Moderate
5	Slightly conservative
6	Conservative
7	Extremely conservative

A. Run Frequencies on polviews. Eyeball the "Valid Percent" column and make some rough-and-ready estimates.

The percentage of respondents who are either "extremely liberal," "liberal," or "slightly liberal" is (circle one)

about 15 percent.   about 25 percent.   about 35 percent.

The percentage of respondents who are either "slightly conservative," "conservative," or "extremely conservative" is (circle one)

about 15 percent.   about 25 percent.   about 35 percent.

B. Use Recode ➞ Into Different Variables to create a new variable named polview3. Give polview3 this label: "Ideology: 3 categories." Collapse the three liberal codes into one category (coded 1 on polview3), put the moderates into their own category (coded 2 on polview3), and collapse the three conservative codes into one category (coded 3 on polview3). (Don't forget to recode missing values on polviews into missing values on polview3.) Run Frequencies on polview3.

The percentage of respondents who are coded 1 on polview3 is (circle one)

about 15 percent.   about 25 percent.   about 35 percent.

The percentage of respondents who are coded 3 on polview3 is (circle one)

about 15 percent.   about 25 percent.   about 35 percent.

C. In the Variable View of the Data Editor, change Decimals to 0, and then click in the Values cell and supply the appropriate labels: "Liberal" for code 1, "Moderate" for code 2, and "Conservative" for code 3. Run Frequencies on polview3. Based on your findings, fill in the table that follows.

Ideology: 3 categories

	Frequency	Valid percent	Cumulative percent
Liberal			
Moderate			
Conservative			100.0
Total		100.0	

You have just added two very useful variables to GSS2002.sav. Before exiting SPSS, be sure to save the dataset.

NOTES

1. Survey datasets are notorious for reverse-coding. Survey designers do this so that respondents don't fall into the trap of response bias, or automatically giving the same response to a series of questions. Though you may need to be on the lookout for reverse-coding in your future research, none of the examples or exercises in this workbook will require that you "repair" the original coding of any variables.
2. Recode → Into Same Variables is an appropriate choice because the original variables, tolhomo and tolracis, are not being replaced or destroyed in the process. If the recode goes badly and intoler gets fouled up, you can always use the original variables to compute intoler again.

5

Making Controlled Comparisons

Political analysis often begins by making simple comparisons using cross-tabulation analysis or mean comparison analysis. Simple comparisons allow the researcher to examine the relationship between an independent variable, X, and a dependent variable, Y. However, there is always the possibility that alternative causes—rival explanations—are at work, affecting the observed relationship between X and Y. An alternative cause is symbolized by the letter Z. If the researcher does not control for Z, then he or she may misinterpret the relationship between X and Y.

What can happen to the relationship between an independent variable and a dependent variable, controlling for an alternative cause? One possibility is that the relationship between the independent variable and the dependent variable is spurious. In a spurious relationship, once the researcher controls for a rival causal factor, the original relationship becomes very weak, perhaps disappearing altogether. The control variable does all of the explanatory work. In another possibility, the researcher observes an additive relationship between the independent variable, the dependent variable, and the control variable. In an additive relationship, two sets of meaningful relationships exist. The independent variable maintains a relationship with the dependent variable and the control variable helps to explain the dependent variable. A third possibility, interaction, is somewhat more complex. If interaction is occurring, then the effect of the independent variable on the dependent variable depends on the value of the control variable. The strength or tendency of the relationship is different for one value of the control variable than for another value of the control variable.

These situations—a spurious relationship, an additive relationship, and interaction—are logical possibilities. Of course, SPSS cannot interpret a set of controlled comparisons for you. But it can produce tabular analysis and graphics that will give you the raw material you need to evaluate controlled comparisons.

In this chapter you will learn to use Crosstabs to analyze relationships when all three variables—the independent variable, the dependent variable, and the control variable—are nominal or ordinal. Because graphic displays are especially valuable tools for evaluating complex relationships, we will demonstrate how to use SPSS Graph to obtain bar charts and line charts. These graphics will help you to interpret cross-tabulations with control variables. In this chapter you will also learn to use Compare Means to analyze relationships in which the dependent variable is interval level and the independent and control variables are nominal or ordinal level. These skills are natural extensions of the procedures you learned in Chapter 3.

USING CROSSTABS WITH LAYERS

To demonstrate how to use SPSS Crosstabs to obtain control tables, we will work through an example with GSS2002.sav. This guided example uses one of the variables you created in Chapter 4, polview3.

Consider this hypothesis: In comparing individuals, liberals will be more likely to favor the legalization of marijuana than will conservatives. In this hypothesis, polview3, which categorizes respondents as liberal, moderate, or conservative, is the independent variable. GSS2002.sav contains the variable grass, which records respondents' opinions on the legalization of marijuana. (Code 1 is "legal," and code 2 is "not legal.")

Figure 5–1 Crosstabs Output without Control Variable

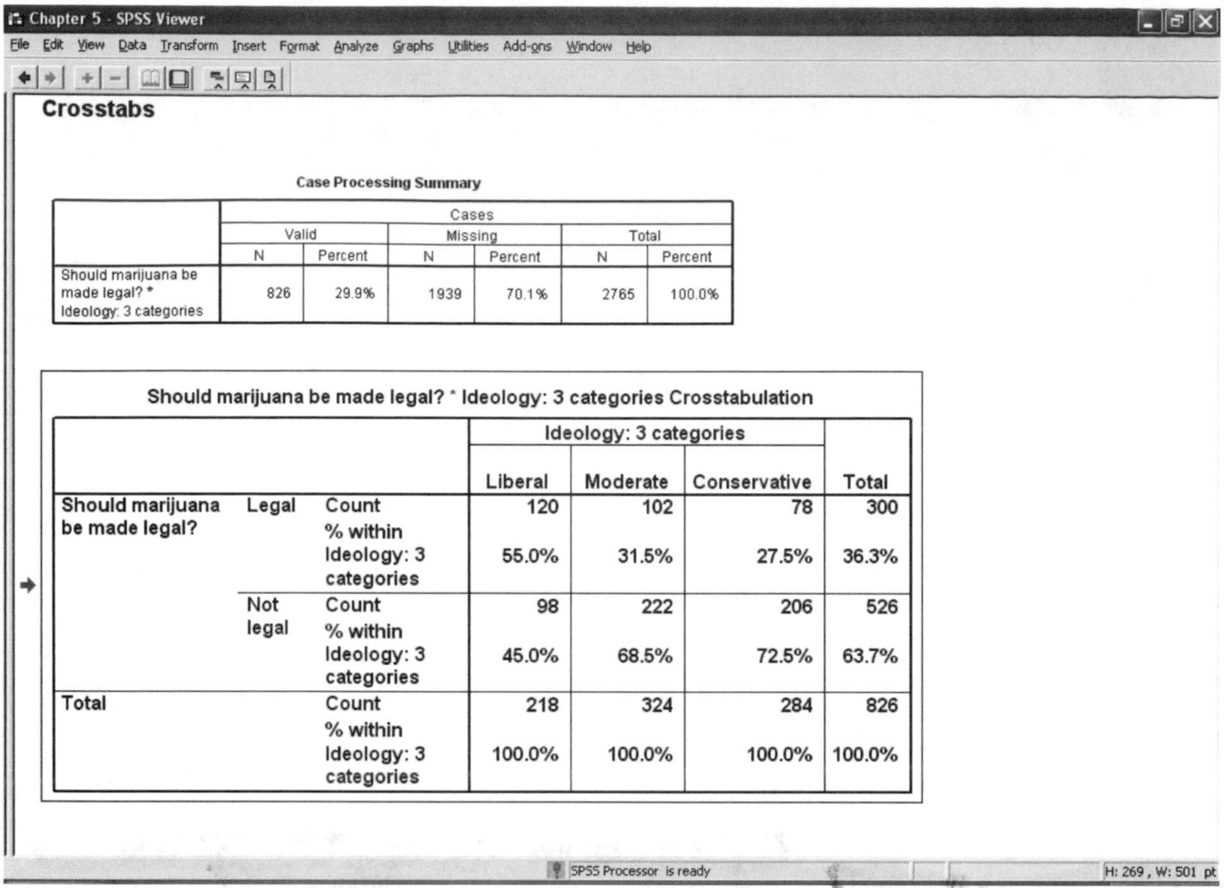

Case Processing Summary

	Cases					
	Valid		Missing		Total	
	N	Percent	N	Percent	N	Percent
Should marijuana be made legal? * Ideology: 3 categories	826	29.9%	1939	70.1%	2765	100.0%

Should marijuana be made legal? * Ideology: 3 categories Crosstabulation

			Ideology: 3 categories			
			Liberal	Moderate	Conservative	Total
Should marijuana be made legal?	Legal	Count	120	102	78	300
		% within Ideology: 3 categories	55.0%	31.5%	27.5%	36.3%
	Not legal	Count	98	222	206	526
		% within Ideology: 3 categories	45.0%	68.5%	72.5%	63.7%
Total		Count	218	324	284	826
		% within Ideology: 3 categories	100.0%	100.0%	100.0%	100.0%

To get reacquainted with cross-tabulation analysis, let's start by looking at the uncontrolled relationship between polview3 and grass. Then we will add a control variable.

Open GSS2002.sav. Go through the following steps, as covered in Chapter 3: In the SPSS Data Editor, click Analyze → Descriptive Statistics → Crosstabs. Find the dependent variable, grass, in the left-hand variable list and click it into the Row(s) panel. Find the independent variable, polview3, and click it into the Column(s) panel. Click the Cells button and select the box next to "Column" in the Percentages panel. Click Continue, and then click OK.

The SPSS Crosstabs output appears in the SPSS Viewer (Figure 5-1). Clearly the hypothesis has merit. Of the liberals, 55.0 percent favor legalization, compared with 31.5 percent of moderates and 27.5 percent of conservatives.

What other factors, besides ideology, might account for differing opinions on marijuana legalization? A plausible answer: whether the respondent has children. Regardless of ideology, people with children may be less inclined to endorse the legalization of an illegal drug than are people who do not have children. GSS2002.sav contains the variable kids, which classifies respondents into one of two categories: those with children (coded 1 and labeled "Yes" on kids) or those without (coded 0 and labeled "No" on kids). Let's run the analysis again, this time adding kids as a control variable.

Again click Analyze → Descriptive Statistics → Crosstabs, returning to the Crosstabs window. You will find the dependent variable, grass, and the independent variable, polview3, just where you left them. To obtain a controlled comparison—the relationship between grass and polview3, controlling for kids—scroll down the variable list until you find kids and click it into the box labeled "Layer 1 of 1," as shown in Figure 5-2. SPSS will run a separate cross-tabulation analysis for each value of the variable that appears in the Layer box. And that is precisely what we want: a cross-tabulation of grass and polview3 for respondents without children and a separate analysis for those with children. Click OK. SPSS's version of a control table appears in the SPSS Viewer (Figure 5-3).

Figure 5–2 Crosstabs with Layers

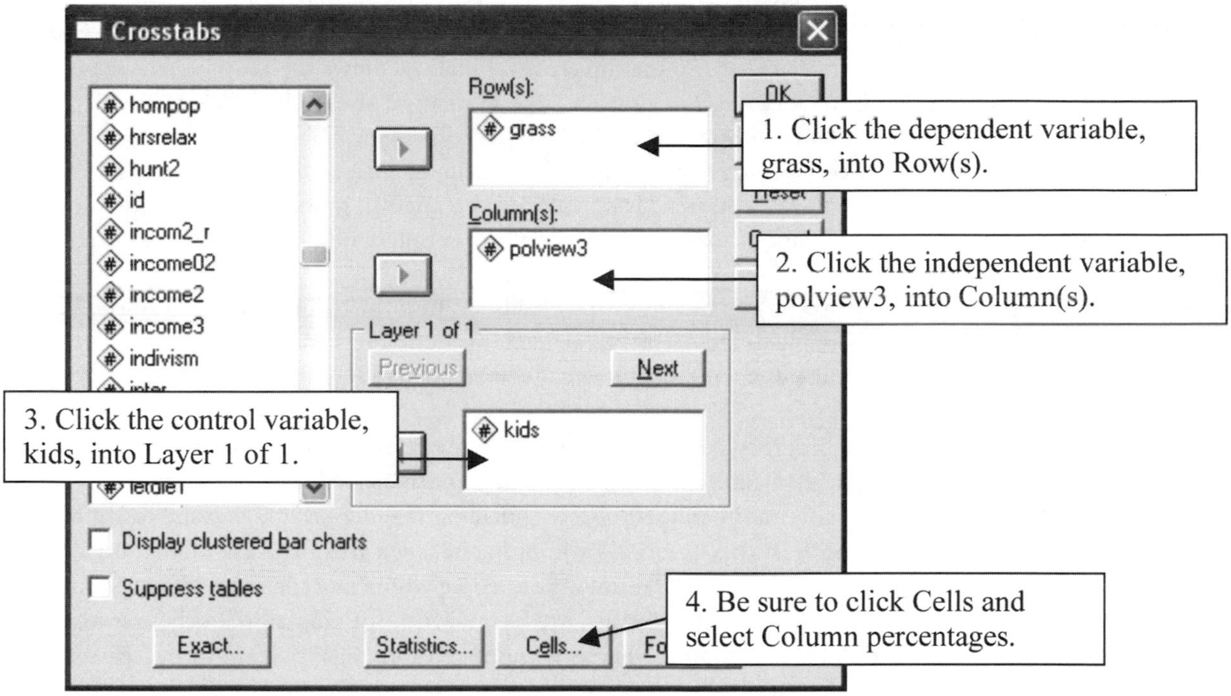

Figure 5–3 Crosstabs Output with Control Variable

Chapter 5 - SPSS Viewer

File Edit View Data Transform Insert Format Analyze Graphs Utilities Add-ons Window Help

Crosstabs

Should marijuana be made legal? * Ideology: 3 categories * Does R have children? Crosstabulation

Does R have children?				Ideology: 3 categories Liberal	Moderate	Conservative	Total
No	Should marijuana be made legal?	Legal	Count	61	39	24	124
			% within Ideology: 3 categories	72.6%	42.4%	38.1%	51.9%
		Not legal	Count	23	53	39	115
			% within Ideology: 3 categories	27.4%	57.6%	61.9%	48.1%
	Total		Count	84	92	63	239
			% within Ideology: 3 categories	100.0%	100.0%	100.0%	100.0%
Yes	Should marijuana be made legal?	Legal	Count	59	63	54	176
			% within Ideology: 3 categories	44.0%	27.2%	24.4%	30.0%
		Not legal	Count	75	169	167	411
			% within Ideology: 3 categories	56.0%	72.8%	75.6%	70.0%
	Total		Count	134	232	221	587
			% within Ideology: 3 categories	100.0%	100.0%	100.0%	100.0%

SPSS Processor is ready

SPSS output using Crosstabs with layers can be a bit confusing at first, so let's consider closely what SPSS has produced. There are two cross-tabulations in the SPSS Viewer, appearing as one table. To the left-hand side of the table you will see the label of the control variable, kids: "Does R have children?" The first value of kids, "No," appears beneath that label. So the top cross-tabulation shows the grass-polview3 relationship for people who do not have children. The bottom cross-tabulation shows the relationship for respondents with children, respondents with the value "Yes" on the control variable.

What is the relationship between ideology and support for marijuana legalization among respondents who do not have children? For those with children? Is polview3 still related to grass? You can see that ideology is related to marijuana opinions for both values of kids. Among people without children, 72.6 percent of the liberals favor legalization, compared with 42.4 percent of the moderates and 38.1 percent of the conservatives. The more conservative people are, the lower the likelihood that they will favor legalization. The same general pattern holds for people with children: 44.0 percent of the liberals favor legalization, compared with 27.2 percent of moderates and 24.4 percent of conservatives. So, controlling for kids, polview3 is related to grass in the hypothesized way.

One bonus of control tables is that they permit you to evaluate the relationship between the control variable and the dependent variable, controlling for the independent variable. What is the relationship between the control variable, kids, and marijuana attitudes, controlling for ideology? Using the control tables produced by SPSS, you can address this question by jumping between the top cross-tabulation and the bottom cross-tabulation, comparing marijuana opinions of people who share the same ideology but who differ on the control variable, kids. Consider liberals. Are liberals without kids more likely to favor legalization than are liberals with kids? Yes. Among liberals without children, 72.6 percent favor legalization versus only 44.0 percent for liberals with children. How about moderates? Yes, again. There is a noticeable difference between the percentage of moderates without children who favor legalization (42.4 percent) and that of moderates with children who favor legalization (27.2 percent). For conservatives, too, having children decreases the likelihood of a pro-legalization response.

How would you characterize this set of relationships? Does a spurious relationship exist between grass and polview3? Or are these additive relationships, with polview3 helping to explain legalization opinions and kids adding to the explanation? Or is interaction going on? Is the grass-polview3 relationship different for people without children than for people with children? If the grass-polview3 relationship were spurious, then the relationship would weaken or disappear after controlling for kids. Among respondents without children, liberals, moderates, and conservatives would all hold the same opinion about marijuana legalization. Ditto for people with children: Ideology would not play a role in explaining the dependent variable. Because the relationship persists after controlling for kids, we can rule out spuriousness. Now, it is sometimes difficult to distinguish between additive relationships and interaction relationships, so let's dwell on this question. In additive relationships, the effect of the independent variable on the dependent variable is the same or quite similar for each value of the control variable. In interaction relationships, by contrast, the effect of the independent variable on the dependent variable varies in size or tendency for different values of the control variable. Return to the cross-tabulation output. The grass-polview3 relationship has the same tendency for people with and without children: For both values of the control, liberals are more pro-legalization than are conservatives. But notice that this effect is much larger for people without children. As you compare percentages across the "Legal" row, the percentage drops nearly 35 percentage points, from 72.6 percent among liberals to 38.1 percent among conservatives. Now examine the bottom portion of the control table, the grass-polview3 relationship for people with children. Here we find a weaker effect of ideology on legalization opinions: from 44.0 percent among liberals to 24.4 percent among conservatives, a drop of about 20 percentage points. Because polview3 has a much larger effect on grass for one value of the control (respondents without children) than for the other value of the control (respondents with children), this is a set of interaction relationships.

OBTAINING CLUSTERED BAR CHARTS

In Chapter 3 you learned how to obtain a bar chart or line chart depicting the relationship between an independent variable and a dependent variable. SPSS also produces graphics for controlled comparisons. Here we demonstrate procedures for creating clustered bar charts. In the following guided example, we produce a bar chart that illustrates the relationship between grass and polview3, controlling for kids.

Figure 5–4   Define Clustered Bar Window

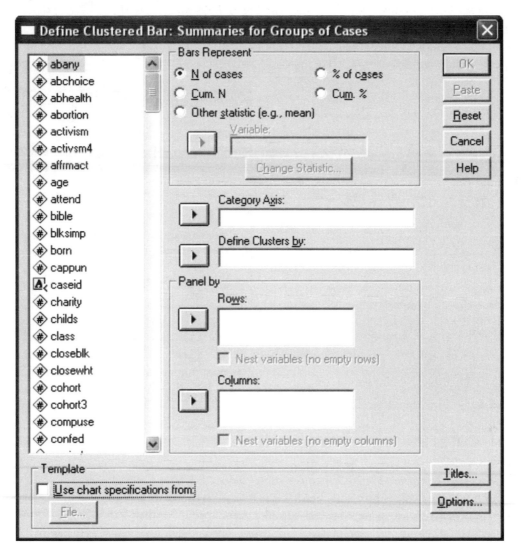

Click Graphs → Bar. When the Bar Charts window opens, click Clustered and make sure that the Summaries for Groups of Cases radio button is selected. Click Define. The Define Clustered Bar: Summaries for Groups of Cases window appears (Figure 5-4). What do we want the bar chart to depict? We want to see the percentage of respondents who favor legalization (coded 1 on grass) for each value of the independent variable (polview3). But we want to see the grass-polview3 relationship separately for each value of the control variable, kids. In an SPSS clustered bar chart, the values of the independent variable appear along the category axis. Because polview3 is the independent variable, click polview3 into the Category Axis box. For each value of polview3, we want to see the relationship separately for different values of the control variable, kids. In a clustered bar chart, the values of the control variable define the "clusters." The variable kids is the control variable, so click kids into the Define Clusters by box, as shown in Figure 5-5.

Now let's make sure that the bars will represent the percentages of respondents favoring legalization. In the Bars Represent panel, select the Other statistic radio button, which activates the Variable box. (In SPSS 12.0 or earlier, the radio button is labeled "Other summary function.") Find grass in the variable list and then click it into the Variable box. By default, of course, SPSS will display the mean value of grass, "MEAN(grass)," which does not suit our purpose (see Figure 5-5). Click Change Statistic. In the Statistic window, click the Percentage inside radio button. Type "1" in the Low box and "1" in the High box. As in Figure 5-5, these instructions tell SPSS to display the percentage of respondents in one category of the dependent variable, the percentage coded 1 on grass. Click Continue, returning to the Define Clustered Bar window. The Variable box should now read "PIN(1 1) (grass)," meaning "The bars will display the percentages of respondents inside the value of 1 on grass at the low end and the value of 1 on grass at the high end" (Figure 5-6). If you

Figure 5–5 Obtaining a Clustered Bar Chart

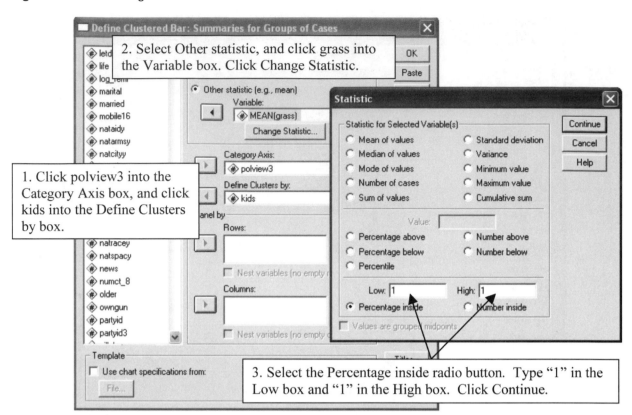

Note: In SPSS 12.0 or earlier, the Other statistic radio button is labeled "Other summary function," Change Statistic is labeled "Change Summary," and the Statistic window is the Summary Function window.

are running SPSS 11.5 or earlier, there is one more thing to do: Click Options and ensure that the Display groups defined by missing values box is unchecked. Click Continue, and then click OK.

The clustered bar chart, constructed to our specifications, appears in the SPSS Viewer (Figure 5-7). This graphic greatly facilitates interpretation of the relationship. The left-hand bars in the clusters (which appear dark gray in Figure 5-7) show the relationship between grass and polview3 for people without children, and the right-hand bars (light gray) depict the relationship for people with children. Notice that, for both sets of bars, the percentages favoring legalization decline as you move across the values of polview3. Note, too, that within each cluster the without-kids bar is taller than the with-kids bar, revealing the effect of the control variable, kids, on the dependent variable. Finally, as you move from liberal to moderate to conservative, observe the precipitous drop in the heights of the bars for respondents without children and the milder decline among respondents with children. This is a beautiful bar chart. But let's spruce it up using the SPSS Chart Editor.

We will make three changes to the chart: First, we will change the scale axis title. Second, we will label each bar, communicating the percentage of cases each bar represents. Finally, we will change the fill color or fill pattern on one set of bars, clearly distinguishing the category of the control variable, kids. (If you print graphics in black and white, as we do in this book, it is sometimes difficult to tell the difference between bars in the same cluster.) As in Chapter 3, first we will describe the Chart Editor in SPSS 12.0 or later, and then we will discuss SPSS 11.5 or earlier.

SPSS 12.0 or Later

Place the cursor anywhere on the chart and double-click. This invokes the Chart Editor. To change the scale axis title (Figure 5-8), first select it with a single-click. Single-click again to edit it. Replace the current title with this new title: "Percent favoring legalization of marijuana." (Clicking anywhere else on the chart returns the axis title to its proper position.) Next let's add data labels to the bars so that each bar displays the percentage of respondents favoring legalization. Click the Data Labels icon on the toolbar above the chart (Figure 5-9). Doing so has the desired consequence of labeling the bars. It also has the not necessarily

Figure 5–6 Define Clustered Bar Window (modified)

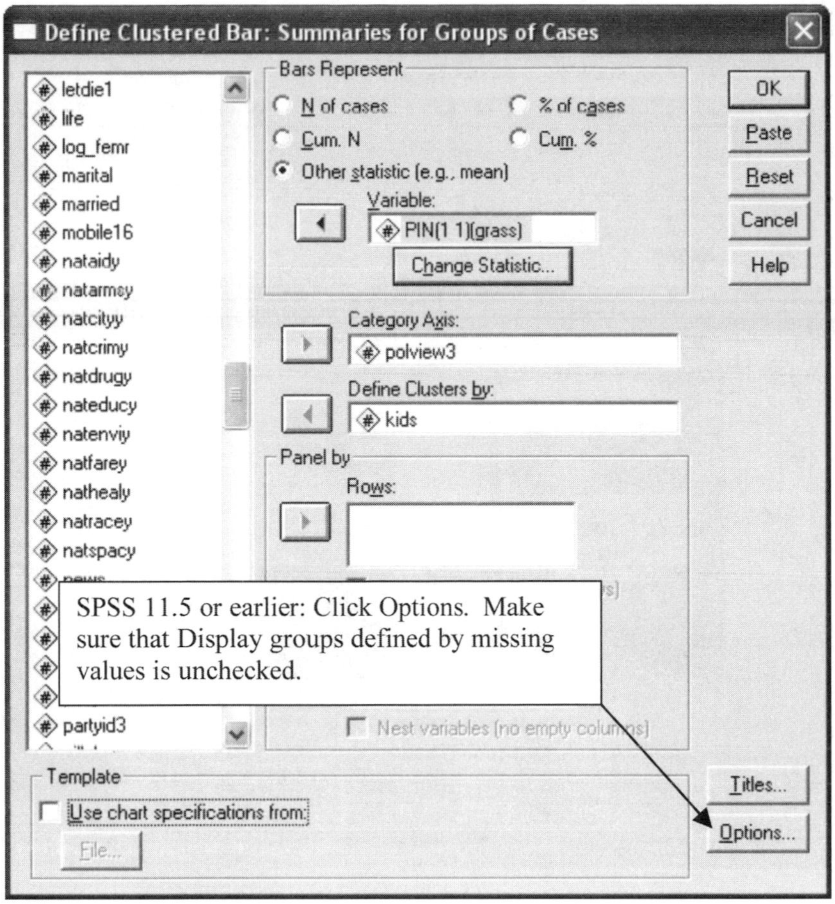

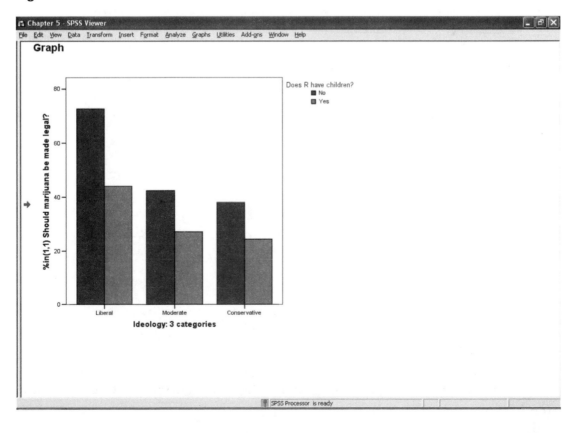

Figure 5–7 Clustered Bar Chart with Control Variable

Figure 5–8 Changing the Scale Axis Title (SPSS 12.0 or later)

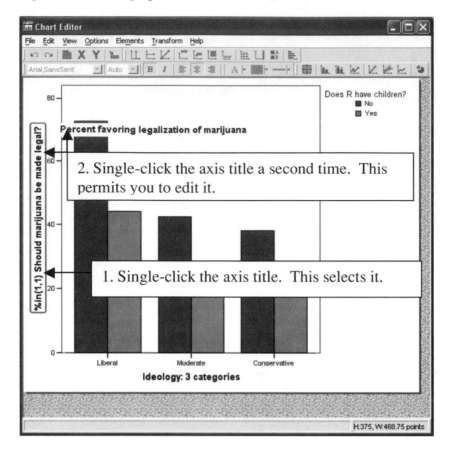

Figure 5–9 Adding Data Labels (SPSS 12.0 or later)

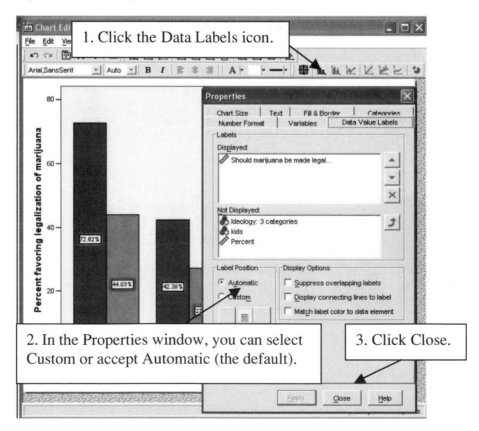

Figure 5–10 Changing the Fill Color on One Set of Bars (SPSS 12.0 or later)

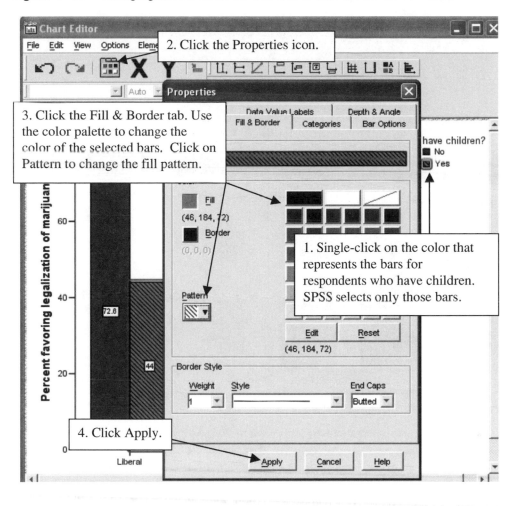

desired consequence of opening the Data Value Labels tab of the Properties window. Here you can accept the Automatic positioning of the data labels. Alternatively, you can select Custom and modify the positioning of the data labels. We will accept the default. Close the Properties window. Now we will modify the appearance of the shorter set of bars, the bars depicting marijuana opinions among respondents who have children. In the chart's legend area—the area that tells you which colors go with which values of the control variable—click on the color that represents the "Yes" value of kids (Figure 5-10). On the toolbar, click the Properties icon. In the Properties Window, click the Fill & Border tab. You may use the color palette to change the color of the bars, and you can edit the fill pattern by clicking on Pattern and selecting something different. We will leave the color alone but pick a lined fill pattern. After clicking Apply, closing the Properties Window, and exiting the Chart Editor, we will find our newly edited bar chart in the SPSS Viewer (Figure 5-11).

SPSS 11.5 or Earlier

Place the cursor anywhere on the chart and double-click, invoking the Chart Editor. To change the scale axis title, double-click on the current title, which opens the Scale Axis window (Figure 5-12). In the Scale Axis window, replace the current title with this new title: "Percent favoring legalization of marijuana." Select Center for Title Justification and click OK. The Chart Editor records the change. Now click the Bar Label Style icon on the toolbar (Figure 5-13). Click Standard, and then click Apply All. SPSS labels each bar with the percentage of respondents favoring legalization. Close the Bar Label Styles window. Now let's change the fill pattern on the shorter set of bars, those displaying marijuana opinions for respondents who have children. In the chart's legend area—the area that tells you which colors go with which values of the control variable—click on the color that represents the "Yes" value of kids (Figure 5-14). SPSS selects the bars for that

Figure 5–11   Edited Clustered Bar Chart with Control Variable (SPSS 12.0 or later)

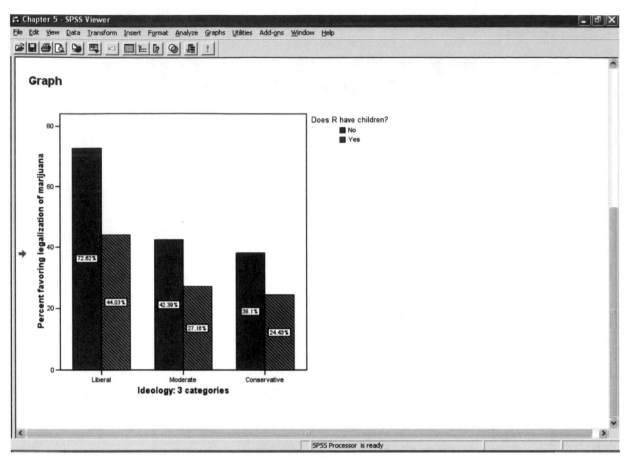

Figure 5–12   Changing the Scale Axis Title (SPSS 11.5 or earlier)

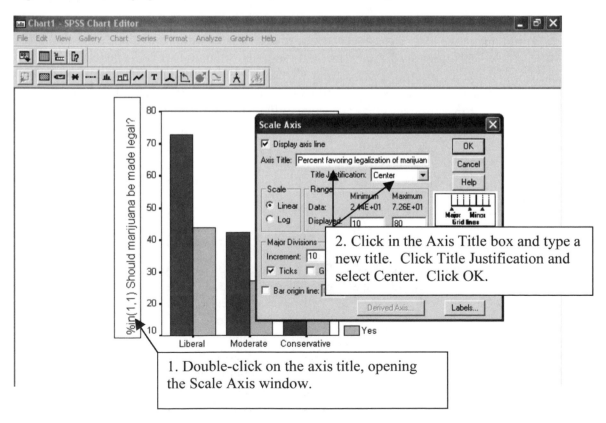

Figure 5–13 Adding Bar Labels (SPSS 11.5 or earlier)

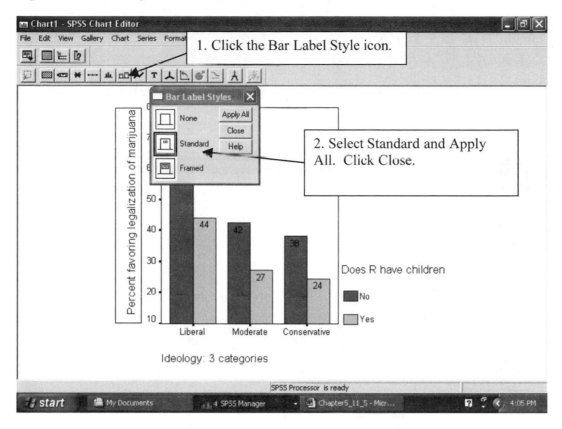

Figure 5–14 Changing the Fill Pattern on One Set of Bars (SPSS 11.5 or earlier)

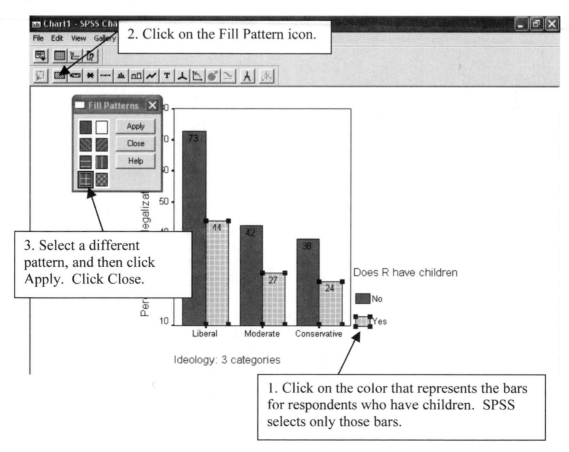

Figure 5-15 Edited Clustered Bar Chart with Control Variable (SPSS 11.5 or earlier)

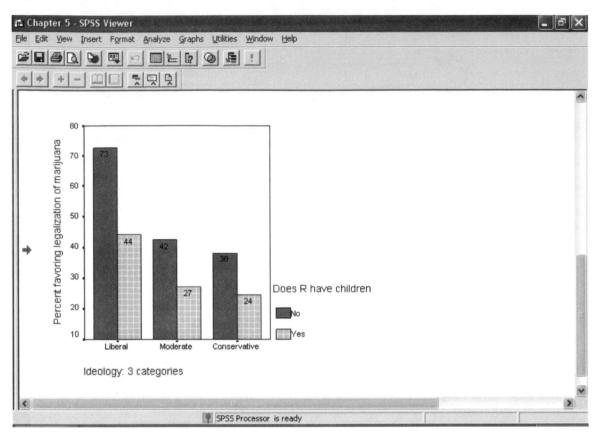

value of the control. Click the Fill Pattern icon on the toolbar. In the Fill Patterns window, select one of the patterns (such as the box-like pattern at the lower left), and then click Apply. The Chart Editor adds the pattern to the selected bars. Close the Fill Pattern window. Looks good. Close the Chart Editor and return to the SPSS Viewer. The newly edited clustered bar chart is now part of your output file (Figure 5-15).

OBTAINING MULTIPLE LINE CHARTS

Clustered bar charts provide useful graphic support for cross-tabulation relationships. You can also use another graphic style, line charts. Sometimes line charts are better, particularly if the control variable has a lot of categories. The choice between clustered bar charts and multiple line charts is largely a matter of personal preference. So that you can become familiar with both styles, we will demonstrate line charts using NES2000.sav. Before beginning the next example, close GSS2002.sav and open NES2000.sav.

Who favors laws that would permit homosexual couples to adopt children? Who opposes such laws? Consider this hypothesis: In comparing individuals, people with more education will be more likely to favor gay adoptions than will people with less education. NES2000.sav contains gayadopt, coded 1 for people who said yes when asked if they favored gay adoption laws and coded 2 for people who said no. This is the dependent variable. Another variable, educ3, measures education using three values—less than high school, high school, and more than high school. This is the independent variable. For a control variable, we will use gender. First, we will ask SPSS Crosstabs to produce a control table showing the relationship between gayadopt and educ3, controlling for gender. Then we will create a line chart of the relationship.

Go ahead and run the Crosstabs analysis. Put gayadopt in the Row(s), educ3 in the Column(s), and gender in the Layers box. Remember to click Cells and request column percentages. After you run the analysis, the SPSS Viewer should look like Figure 5-16. Apply your table-reading skills. You can see that, among males and females alike, education has the hypothesized effect on opinions: Individuals with more education are more likely to favor gay adoption laws than are individuals with less education. Yet the control variable, gender, is related to opinions as well. Controlling for education, females are more favorably disposed toward gay adoption laws than are males.

Figure 5–16 Crosstabs Output: Preparing to Produce a Line Chart

Chapter 5 - SPSS Viewer

File Edit View Data Transform Insert Format Analyze Graphs Utilities Add-ons Window Help

Crosstabs

Homosexual couples adopt chldn * Education: 3 categories * Gender Crosstabulation

Gender				Education: 3 categories 1. Less than HS	2. HS	3. More than HS	Total
1. Male	Homosexual couples adopt chldn	1. Yes	Count	19	61	209	289
			% within Education: 3 categories	24.4%	32.8%	44.7%	39.5%
		5. No	Count	59	125	259	443
			% within Education: 3 categories	75.6%	67.2%	55.3%	60.5%
	Total		Count	78	186	468	732
			% within Education: 3 categories	100.0%	100.0%	100.0%	100.0%
2. Female	Homosexual couples adopt chldn	1. Yes	Count	31	119	307	457
			% within Education: 3 categories	34.1%	40.6%	57.2%	49.6%
		5. No	Count	60	174	230	464
			% within Education: 3 categories	65.9%	59.4%	42.8%	50.4%
	Total		Count	91	293	537	921
			% within Education: 3 categories	100.0%	100.0%	100.0%	100.0%

SPSS Processor is ready

Let's get a line chart of these relationships. Then we will decide which scenario applies—a spurious relationship, an additive relationship, or interaction. Click Graphs → Line. In the Line Charts window, click Multiple. Click Define. The Define Multiple Line window opens (Figure 5-17). The procedures here are virtually identical to those for clustered bar charts, described earlier. We want the lines to represent the percentages of respondents favoring gay adoptions (coded 1 on gayadopt). To achieve that end, we click the Other statistic radio button, and then click gayadopt into the Variable box. Next, we click Change Statistic and request the percentage inside 1 (Low) and 1 (High). The category axis, as before, is defined by the independent variable—in this case, educ3. Click educ3 into the Category Axis box. Because we are after separate lines—one for men and one for women—the control variable, gender, goes in the Define Lines by box. (SPSS 11.5 or earlier: In Options, uncheck the Display groups defined by missing values box.) The Define Multiple Line window should look like Figure 5-18. Click OK. SPSS gives us a multiple line chart (Figure 5-19).

Again, we can appreciate the clarity of graphic depictions. Reading along each line, from left to right, we see the effect of education on opinions. For both males and females, an increase in education is associated with increased percentages in the "favor" category of the dependent variable. Looking at the distance between the lines, we see the effect of gender on opinions. At all values of education, higher percentages of females than of males favor gay adoption laws. The gayadopt-educ3 relationship is not spurious. Instead, this is a set of additive relationships. Why additive? Why not interaction? Because the strength and tendency of the gayadopt-educ3 relationship is much the same for women and men. Focus on the line for males. Tracing from less-educated to more-educated males, the percentage favoring gay adoptions rises from 24.4 percent to 44.7 percent. So for one value of the control variable, male, education has about a 20-percentage-point effect on the dependent variable. Now focus on the female line. Tracing from less-educated to more-educated females, the percentage favoring gay adoptions rises from 34.1 percent to 57.2 percent, also about a 20-percentage-point effect on the dependent variable. Notice, too, that the control variable, gender, has roughly the same impact at each level of education. Among the least educated, the percentage of women

Figure 5–17 Define Multiple Line Window

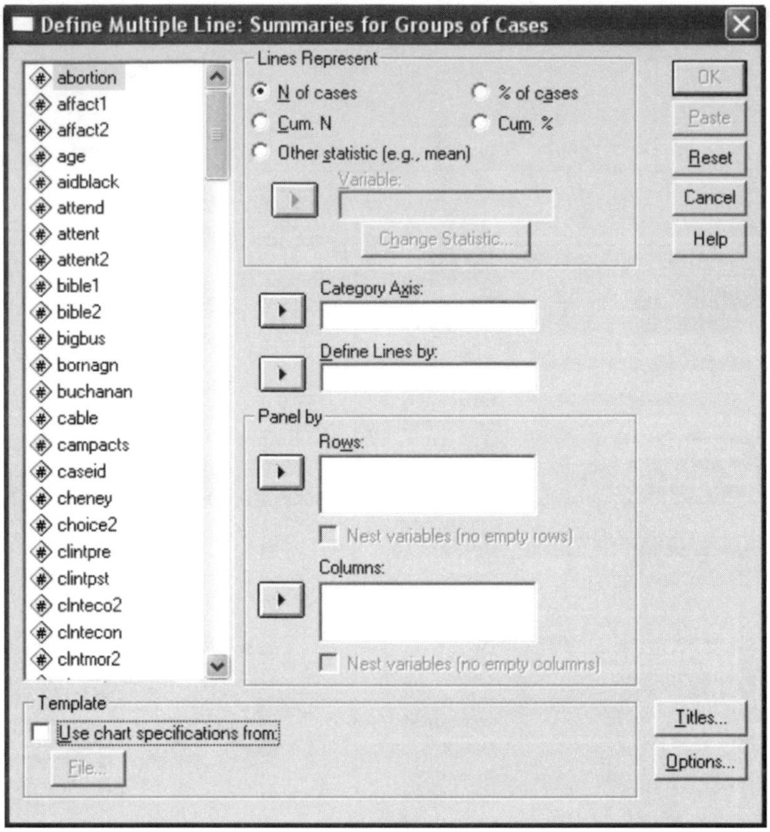

Figure 5–18 Define Multiple Line Window (modified)

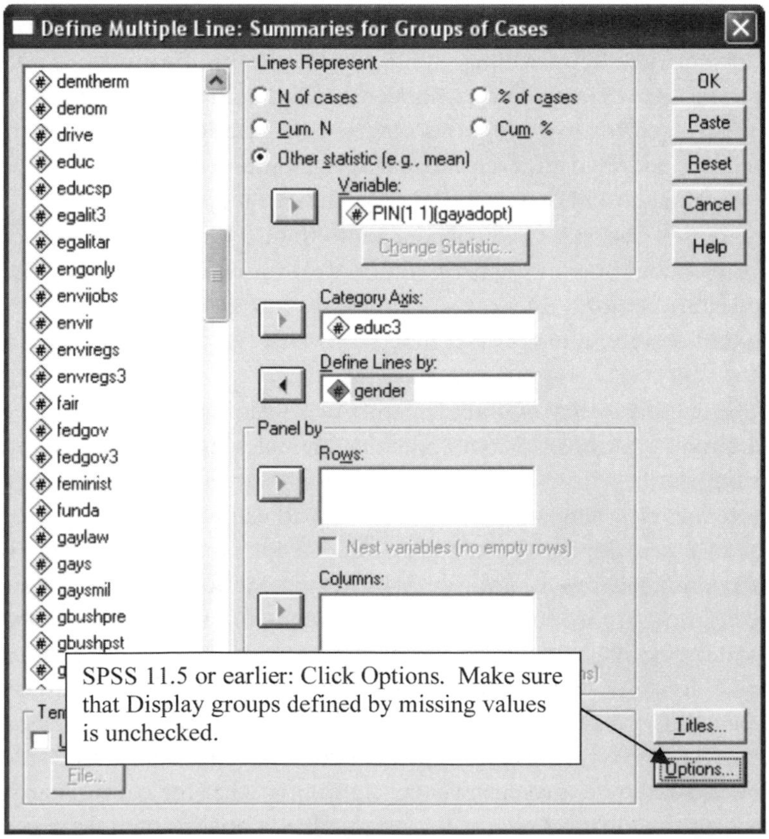

SPSS 11.5 or earlier: Click Options. Make sure that Display groups defined by missing values is unchecked.

Figure 5–19 Multiple Line Chart with Control Variable

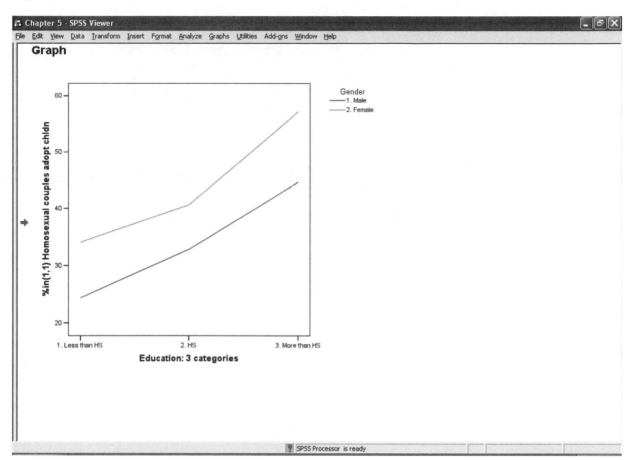

favoring gay adoptions is 10 points higher than the percentage of men who hold this opinion. Among the most educated, the gender difference is about 13 points.

A brief excursion into the SPSS Chart Editor will serve to enhance the line chart's appearance. We will make three changes. First (as usual), we will change the scale axis title. Second, we will change the line weights of both lines. (SPSS's default line weights don't print very clearly.) Third, we will change the style of one of the lines, clarifying the distinction between men and women.

SPSS 12.0 or Later

Double-click on the line chart to get into the Chart Editor. Go ahead and change the scale axis title to "Percent favoring gay adoptions." To change the line weights, first click on one of the lines (Figure 5-20). SPSS selects both lines. Next, click on the Properties icon on the toolbar. The Properties window appears, with the Lines tab in front. Click in the Weight box, select a heavier weight, and then click Apply. SPSS makes both lines heavier. All right. Now let's change the line style of the Female line to clearly distinguish it from the Male line. With the Properties window still open, click once on the Female line. SPSS selects the Female line and deselects the Male line. In the Style box of the Properties window, select a different line style, such as one of the dashed styles. Click Apply, and then click Close. Your newly edited multiple line chart appears in the SPSS Viewer (Figure 5-21).

SPSS 11.5 or Earlier

Double-click the chart to get into the Chart Editor. Go ahead and change the scale axis title to "Percent favoring gay adoptions." Now let's change the style and weight of the Female line, to clearly distinguish it from the Male line (Figure 5-22). Click on the Female line. SPSS selects the line. Click the Line Style icon on the toolbar. In the Line Styles window, select one of the broken or dashed line styles and pick a heavier line weight. Click Apply. The Chart Editor makes the change. With the Line Styles window still open, click the cursor pointer anywhere on the Male line. Leave the line style as is but choose a heavier weight. Click Apply.

Figure 5–20 Changing Line Weights and Line Styles (SPSS 12.0 or later)

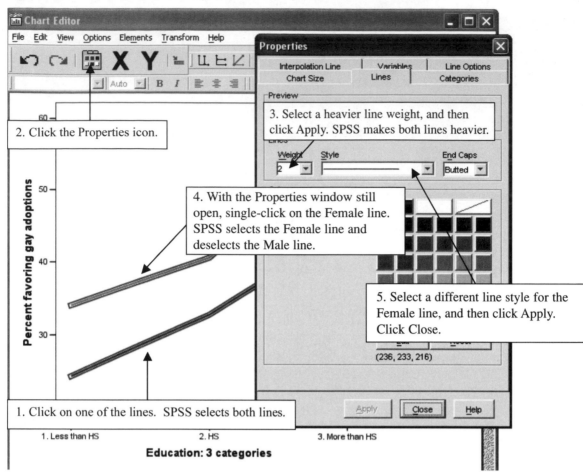

Figure 5–21 Edited Multiple Line Chart (SPSS 12.0 or later)

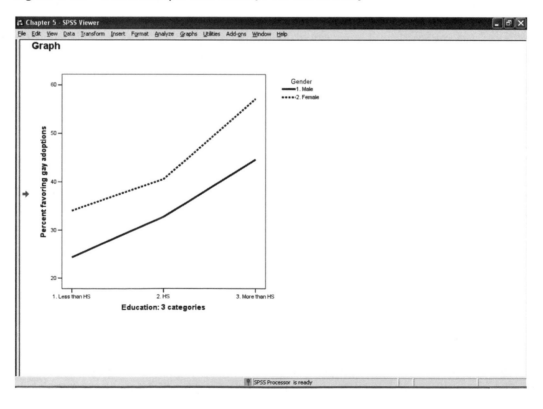

Figure 5–22   Changing Line Weights and Line Styles (SPSS 11.5 or earlier)

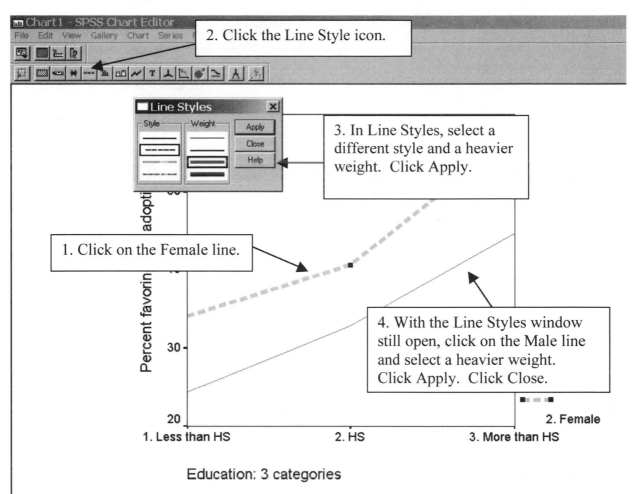

The Chart Editor makes the line heavier. Close the Line Styles window. You may want to experiment and make other changes. For example, you can edit and center the category axis title (currently "Education: 3 categories") by double-clicking it and typing a new title, such as "Level of education." In any event, the line chart looks fine. Close the Chart Editor and return to the SPSS Viewer (Figure 5-23).

USING COMPARE MEANS WITH LAYERS

Now we turn to the situation in which the dependent variable is interval level and the independent variable and the control variable are nominal or ordinal level. In most ways the procedure for using Compare Means with layers to obtain controlled comparisons is similar to that for using Crosstabs. However, the two procedures differ in one important way. We will work through a guided example using NES2000.sav.

One of the most durable fixtures in U.S. politics is the relationship between income and partisanship. For many years, people who made less money were more strongly attracted to the Democratic Party than were more affluent individuals. Yet newer partisan divisions, such as that based on gender, may be altering the relationship between partisanship and income. How can this be? Think about this question for a moment. Suppose that, among men, traditional partisan differences persist, with lower-income males more pro-Democratic than higher-income males. But suppose that, among women, income-based partisan differences are much weaker, with lower-income females and higher-income females holding similar pro-Democratic views. This idea suggests that the relationship between income and partisanship is weaker for females than for males. If this idea is correct, then we should find a set of interaction relationships between income, partisanship, and gender. Let's investigate.

NES2000.sav contains a number of feeling thermometer variables, which record respondents' ratings of different political groups and personalities on a scale from 0 (negative, or "cold") to 100 (positive, or

Figure 5–23 Edited Multiple Line Chart (SPSS 11.5 or earlier)

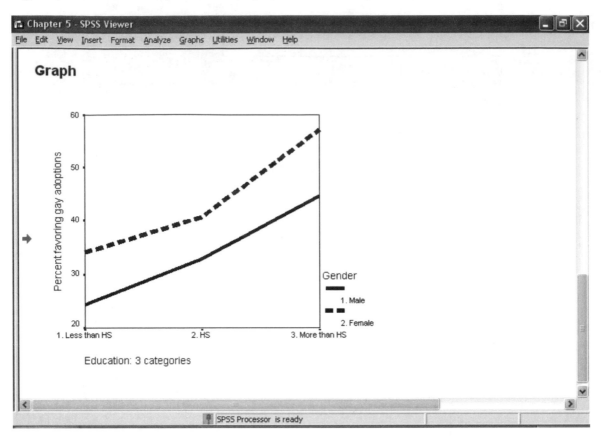

"warm."). One of these variables, demtherm, which gauges feelings toward the Democratic Party, will be the dependent variable in this example. The independent variable is an ordinal measure of income, income3, which classifies respondents into three income levels: less than $15,000, $15,000 to $34,999, and $35,000 or higher. The control variable is gender, coded 1 for males and coded 2 for females. We will use Analyze → Compare Means → Means to produce mean values of demtherm for each value of income3, controlling for gender.

Click Analyze → Compare Means → Means. Find demtherm in the variable list and click it into the Dependent List box. Now we want SPSS to proceed as follows. First, we want it to separate respondents into two groups, men and women, on the basis of the control variable, gender. Second, we want SPSS to calculate mean values of demtherm for each category of the independent variable, income3. In the way that SPSS handles mean comparisons, it first separates cases on the variable named in the first Layer box. It then calculates means of the dependent variable for variables named in subsequent Layer boxes. For this reason, it is best to put the control variable in the first layer and to put the independent variable in the second layer. Because gender is the control, locate gender in the variable list and click it into the Layer 1 of 1 box (Figure 5-24). Click Next. The next Layer box, labeled "Layer 2 of 2," opens. The independent variable, income3, goes in this box. Click income3 into the Layer 2 of 2 box (Figure 5-25). One last thing: Click Options. In Cell Statistics, click Standard Deviation back into the left-hand Statistics box, and then click Continue. Ready to go. Click OK.

An SPSS control table appears in the SPSS Viewer (Figure 5-26). This is a highly readable table. The values of the control variable, gender, appear along the left-hand side of the table. The topmost set of mean comparisons shows the mean Democratic Party thermometer ratings of males, the next set is for females, and the bottom set (labeled "Total") shows the uncontrolled relationship between demtherm and income3—for males and females combined. Let's interpret this table. What is the relationship for male respondents? As income increases, mean ratings of the Democratic Party decline. Males in the lowest income category averaged 65.45, compared with 56.46 for the males in the middle income category and 52.55 for those in the highest value of income3. For males, then, the mean drops about 13 degrees between the lowest income group and the highest income group. Do we find the same pattern for females? Well, as

Figure 5–24   Means Window with Dependent Variable and Control Variable

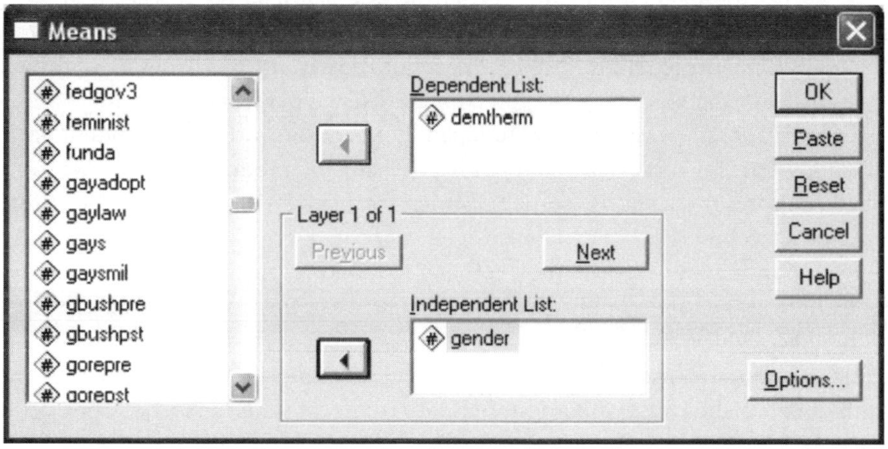

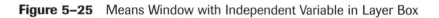

Figure 5–25   Means Window with Independent Variable in Layer Box

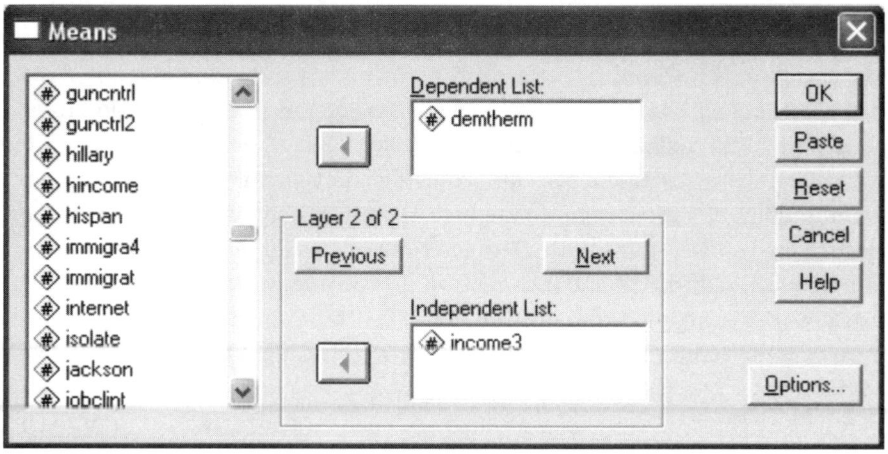

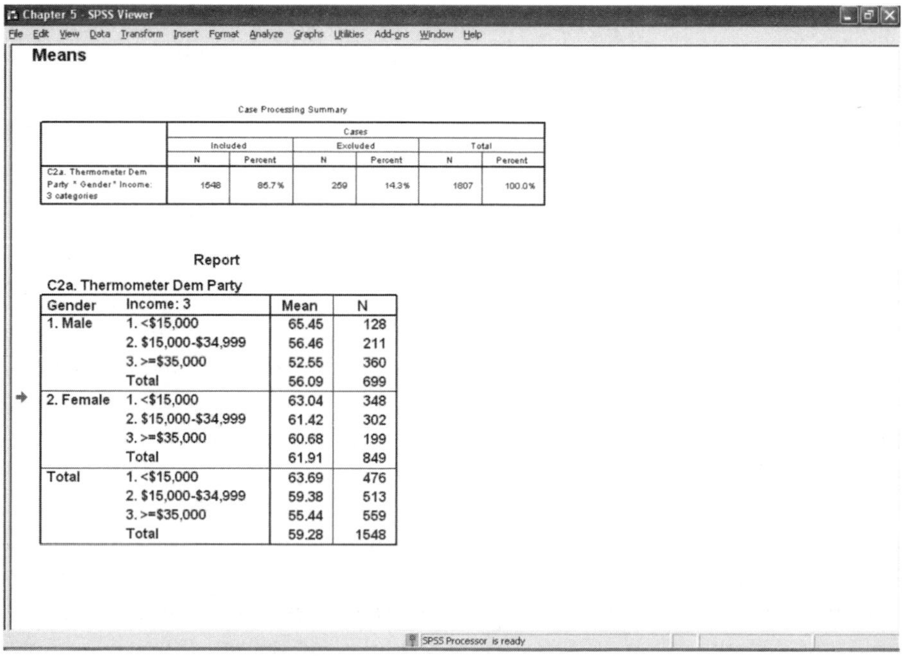

Figure 5–26   Mean Comparison Table with Control Variable

income goes up, mean ratings decline: from 63.04 for females in the lowest value of income3, to 61.42 for those in the middle group, to 60.68 among the most affluent females. So the direction of the relationship is the same for females and males. But would you say that the demtherm-income3 relationship is as strong for women as it is for men? No, you would not. With an overall drop in mean ratings of slightly more than 2 degrees—from about 63 among women in the lowest income category to about 61 for women in the highest income category—the relationship between the independent variable and the dependent variable is noticeably weaker for women than for men. This is a clear example of interaction. Why can we say this? Because the relationship between demtherm and income3 is much stronger for one value of the control variable (Male) than for the other value of the control (Female).

By examining this control table more closely, we can make some further observations about how the gender gap may be altering the long-standing relationship between income and partisanship. Consider the bottom panel of the table, which shows the overall relationship between demtherm and income3 for the entire sample. Consider, too, the distribution of cases (N) across the values of income3 for the whole sample. The overall relationship shows the time-honored pattern: decreasing mean values of demtherm between low-income people (63.69, or about 64 degrees) and those in the highest income category (55.44, or about 55 degrees). This is a mean difference of about 9 degrees. Which gender, male or female, makes a greater contribution to the low-income mean of 64? Well, there are 476 low-income people in the sample. From the Male panel of the table, we can see that only 128 of them are men, whereas the Female panel shows that 348 are women. Because the low-income category is populated more heavily with women than with men, women make a larger contribution to the low-income mean of demtherm. What about the highest value of income3? Here the situation is reversed. There are 559 high-income individuals: 360 males and only 199 females. So males make a bigger contribution to the high-income mean, tugging it down to about 55.

Now let's speculate a bit. Imagine what the data would look like if, over time, more and more women were to enter the higher-income category, perhaps achieving equity with men. Under this scenario, women would make a larger and larger contribution to the high-income mean. Assuming, of course, that these women were as favorably disposed toward the Democratic Party as are the women in our control table, the *overall* relationship between demtherm and income3 would become weaker and weaker. Speculation aside, this example illustrates why controlled comparisons are of central importance to the methodology of political research. Controlling for gender reveals the true gender-specific relationship between the independent and dependent variables.

Now let's obtain a line chart of these relationships and make some further substantive observations about the gender gap. Click Graphs → Line. In the Line Charts window, click Multiple, and then click Define. (The variables from our previous example are still occupying all the boxes. Click the Reset button.) In the Lines Represent panel of the Define Multiple Line window, select the Other statistic radio button. Click demtherm into the Variable box. SPSS moves demtherm into the Variable box with its default designation, "MEAN(demtherm)." This default suits our purpose. In this case, we want to graph mean values of the dependent variable, demtherm, for different values of income3. We want two lines to appear within the graph: one line showing the demtherm-income3 relationship for men and a separate line showing the relationship for women. Because income3 is the independent variable, click income3 into the Category Axis box. Click gender into the Define Lines by box. (A reminder to 11.5 users: Be sure to click Options and uncheck the Display groups defined by missing values box.) Click OK. We now have a tailor-made line chart of the relationship (Figure 5-27).

You can see why line charts lend clarity and simplicity to complex relationships. By tracing along each line, from lower income to higher income, you can see the effect of income on thermometer ratings. Among males, the line drops sharply. The drop among females, by contrast, indicates a much weaker effect. Notice, too, the relationship between gender and the dependent variable at different levels of income. For the lowest-income group, something of a reverse gender gap occurs, with males giving ratings to the Democratic Party that are slightly higher than those given by females. As income increases, however, the gender gap widens. This pattern suggests some general questions that you may wish to investigate in your own research. Do male-female differences on other political and social issues become more pronounced as income increases? Do some issues produce a larger gender gap than others?

If you planned to include the demtherm-income3-gender line chart in a report or research paper, you would of course want to edit its appearance. If you would like, go ahead and practice using the SPSS Chart Editor. You might end up with a line chart that looks something like Figure 5-28.

Figure 5–27   Multiple Line Chart Showing Mean Values

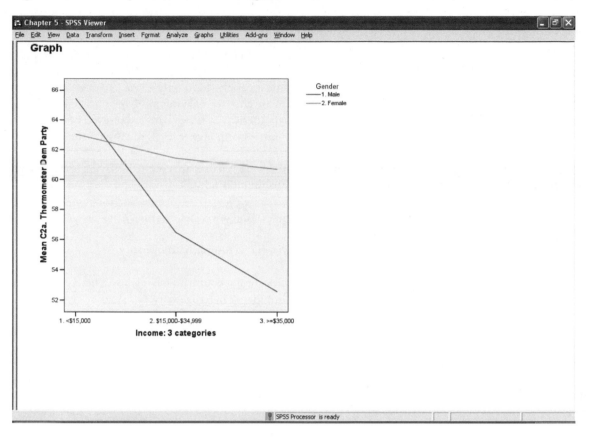

Figure 5–28   Edited Multiple Line Chart Showing Mean Values

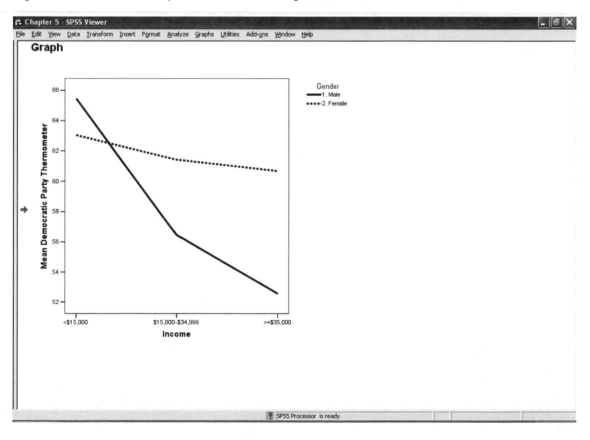

EXERCISES

For Exercises 1 and 2 you will analyze World.sav. For Exercises 3 and 4 you will analyze NES2000.sav.

1. Some countries have democratic regimes, and other countries do not. What factors help to explain this difference? One idea is that the type of government is shaped by the ethnic and religious diversity in a country's population. Countries that are relatively homogeneous, with most people sharing the same language and religious beliefs, are more likely to develop democratic systems than are countries having more linguistic conflicts and religious differences. Consider the ethnic heterogeneity hypothesis: Countries with lower levels of ethnic heterogeneity will be more likely to be democracies than will countries with higher levels of ethnic heterogeneity.

   A. According to the ethnic heterogeneity hypothesis, if you were to compare countries having lower heterogeneity with countries having higher heterogeneity, you should find (check one)

      ❏ a lower percentage of democracies among countries having lower heterogeneity.

      ❏ a higher percentage of democracies among countries having lower heterogeneity.

      ❏ no difference between the percentage of democracies among countries having lower heterogeneity and the percentage of democracies among countries with higher heterogeneity.

   B. World.sav contains the variable regime, which classifies each country as a democracy (coded 0 on regime) or a dictatorship (coded 1 on regime). This is the dependent variable. World.sav also contains eth_het3, which classifies countries according to their level of ethnic, linguistic, and religious heterogeneity: low (coded 1), moderate (coded 2), or high (coded 3). This is the independent variable. Run Crosstabs, testing the ethnic heterogeneity hypothesis. Fill in the percentages of democracies:

	Ethno-linguistic heterogeneity		
	Low	Moderate	High
Percentage of democracies	_____	_____	_____

   C. Based on these results, you could say that (check one)

      ❏ as ethnic heterogeneity increases, the percentage of democracies increases.

      ❏ as ethnic heterogeneity increases, the percentage of democracies decreases.

      ❏ as ethnic heterogeneity increases, there is little change in the percentage of democracies.

   D. A country's level of economic development also might be linked to its type of government. According to this perspective, countries with higher levels of economic development will be more likely to be democracies than will countries with lower levels. World.sav contains the variable gdpcap2. This variable, based on gross domestic product per capita, is an indicator of economic development. Countries are classified as low (coded 1 on gdpcap2) or high (coded 2 on gdpcap2). Obtain a cross-tabulation analysis of the regime-eth_het3 relationship, controlling for gdpcap2. Fill in the percentages of democracies:

	Ethno-linguistic heterogeneity		
	Low	Moderate	High
Low GDP per capita Percentage of democracies			
High GDP per capita Percentage of democracies			

C. NES2000.sav contains three variables: gorepre, which provides a feeling thermometer of Al Gore; jobclnt2, which measures whether respondents either approved or disapproved of Clinton's job performance; and partyid3, which classifies respondents as Democrats, independents, or Republicans. Run Compare Means → Means, using gorepre as the dependent variable, jobclnt2 as the independent variable, and partyid3 as the control variable. (Remember to put the control variable, partyid3, in the first Layer box and the independent variable, jobclnt2, in the second Layer box.) Based on your analysis, fill in the following table, recording mean thermometer ratings of Al Gore and the number of cases (N) for each value of partyid3 and jobclnt2.

Party ID: 3 categories	Clinton approval	Mean thermometer rating of Al Gore	Number of cases (N)
Democrat	Approve	_____	_____
	Disapprove	_____	_____
	Total	_____	_____
Independent	Approve	_____	_____
	Disapprove	_____	_____
	Total	_____	_____
Republican	Approve	_____	_____
	Disapprove	_____	_____
	Total	_____	_____
Total	Approve	_____	_____
	Disapprove	_____	_____
	Total		

D. The bottom three rows of this table, which show mean thermometer ratings of Al Gore for the total sample, permit you to test political analyst 1's idea. Based on the total sample, you could conclude that (check one)

❑ people who approved of Clinton's job performance gave Al Gore a higher mean rating than did people who disapproved of Clinton's job performance.

❑ people who approved of Clinton's job performance gave Al Gore a lower mean rating than did people who disapproved of Clinton's job performance.

E. Now examine the table and make some further observations. Let's compare the group of Democrats with the group of Republicans. Examine the "Number of cases" column. By dividing the number of Democrats who approved of Clinton by the total number of Democrats, you can determine the percentage of Democrats who approved of Clinton's job performance. By dividing the number of Republicans who approved of Clinton by the total number of Republicans, you can determine the percentage of Republicans who approved of Clinton.

The percentage of Democrats who approved of Clinton is about (circle one)

      10 percent.   35 percent.   50 percent.   65 percent.   90 percent.

The percentage of Republicans who approved of Clinton is about (circle one)

      10 percent.   35 percent.   50 percent.   65 percent.   90 percent.

Based on these rough estimates, you could conclude that (check one)

❑ Democrats were more likely than Republicans to approve of Clinton's job performance.

❑ Democrats were less likely than Republicans to approve of Clinton's job performance.

F. Now let's gauge the effect of Clinton approval on Gore thermometer ratings for each value of party identification. For Democrats, for example, you would start with the mean rating of Democrats who approved of Clinton and subtract the mean Gore rating of Democrats who disapproved of Clinton. This would show you the effect of Clinton approval on Gore ratings among Democrats. You would do the same thing for independents and Republicans. For each group, subtract the mean rating of those who disapproved of Clinton (critics) from the mean rating of those who approved of him (supporters). Record the mean differences in the table that follows.

Party identification	Mean difference: Mean rating of Clinton Supporters minus mean rating of Clinton critics
Democrat	_____
Independent	_____
Republican	_____

G. Based on the results in letter F, you could conclude that (check one)

❑ the effect of Clinton approval on Gore thermometer ratings is about the same for Democrats, independents, and Republicans.

❑ the effect of Clinton approval on Gore thermometer ratings is weaker for Democrats than for independents or Republicans.

❑ the effect of Clinton approval on Gore thermometer ratings is stronger for Democrats than for independents or Republicans.

❑ the relationship between Clinton approval and ratings of Gore is spurious.

That concludes the exercises for this chapter. Before exiting SPSS, be sure to save your output file.

6

Making Inferences about Sample Means

Political research has much to do with observing patterns, creating explanations, framing hypotheses, and analyzing relationships. In interpreting their findings, however, researchers often operate in an environment of uncertainty. This uncertainty arises, in large measure, from the complexity of the political world. As we have seen, when we infer a causal connection between an independent variable and a dependent variable, it is hard to know for sure whether the independent variable is causing the dependent variable. Other, uncontrolled variables might be affecting the relationship, too. Yet uncertainty arises, as well, from the simple fact that research findings are often based on random samples. In an ideal world, we could observe and measure the characteristics of every element in the population of interest—every voting-age adult, every student enrolled at a university, every bill introduced in every state legislature, and so on. In such an ideal situation, we would enjoy a high degree of certainty that the variables we have described and the relationships we have analyzed mirror what is really going on in the population. But of course we often do not have access to every member of a population. Instead we rely on a sample, a subset drawn at random from the population. By taking a random sample, we introduce random sampling error. In using a sample to draw inferences about a population, therefore, we never use the word *certainty*. Rather, we talk about *confidence* or *probability*. We know that the measurements we make on the sample will reflect the characteristics of the population, within the boundaries of random sampling error.

What are those boundaries? If we calculate the mean income of a random sample of adults, for example, how confident can we be that the mean income we observe in our sample is the same as the mean income in the population? The answer depends on the standard error of the sample mean, the extent to which the mean income of the sample departs by chance from the mean income of the population. If we use a sample to calculate a mean income for women and a mean income for men, how confident can we be that the difference between these two sample means reflects the true income difference between women and men in the population? Again, the answer depends on the standard error—in this case, the standard error of the *difference* between the sample means, the extent to which the difference in the sample departs from the difference in the population.

In this chapter you will use three SPSS procedures to explore and apply inferential statistics. First, you will learn to use SPSS Descriptives to obtain basic information about interval-level variables. Second, using the One-Sample T Test procedure, you will obtain confidence intervals for a sample mean. The 95 percent confidence interval will tell you the boundaries within which there is a .95 probability that the true population mean falls. You will also find the 90 percent confidence interval, which is applied in testing hypotheses at the .05 level of significance. Third, using the Independent-Samples T Test procedure, you will test for statistically significant differences between two sample means.

USING SPSS DESCRIPTIVES AND ONE-SAMPLE T TEST

To gain insight into the properties and application of inferential statistics, we will work through an example using NES2000.sav. We begin by looking at the Descriptives procedure, which yields basic information about

Figure 6–1 Descriptives Window

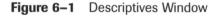

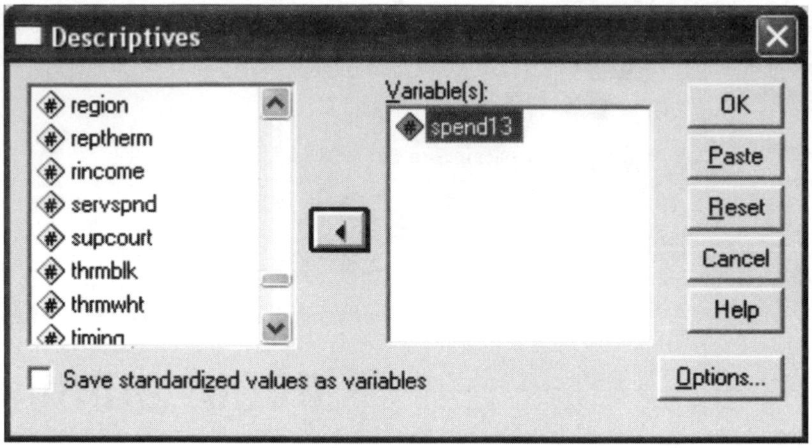

interval-level variables. We then demonstrate the fundamentals of inference using the SPSS One-Sample T Test procedure.

NES2000.sav contains spend13, a measure of individuals' opinions about federal spending. Respondents were asked whether spending should be increased, kept the same, or decreased for each of thirteen federal programs. Spend13 was created by adding up the number of times the respondent said "increased."[1] We can use Descriptives to obtain summary information about spend13. Open NES2000.sav. In the Data Editor, click Analyze → Descriptive Statistics → Descriptives. In the main Descriptives window, scroll down the left-hand variable list until you find spend13. Click spend13 into the Variable(s) list (Figure 6-1). Click the Options button in the lower right-hand corner of the Descriptives window. Now you can specify which descriptive statistics you would like SPSS to produce. These defaults should already be checked: mean, standard deviation, minimum, and maximum. That's fine. Also check the box beside "S.E. mean," which stands for "standard error of the mean" (Figure 6-2). Click Continue, and then click OK. SPSS reports the requested statistics for spend13 in the SPSS Viewer: number of cases analyzed (N), minimum and maximum observed values for spend13, mean value of spend13, standard error of the mean, and standard devia-

Figure 6–2 Descriptives: Options Window (modified)

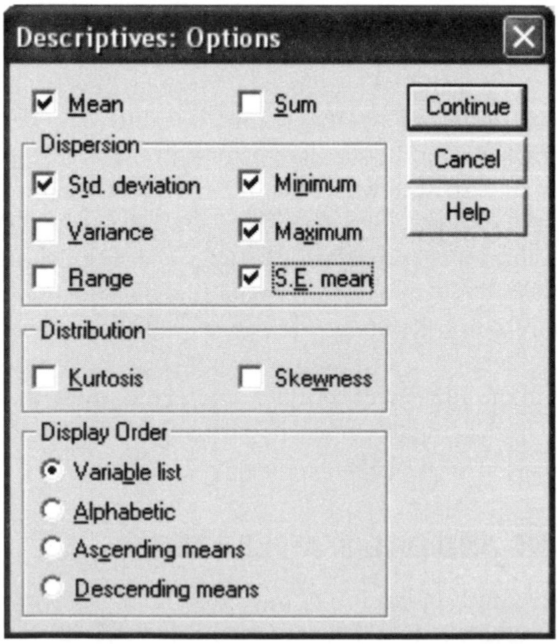

Figure 6–3 Descriptives Output

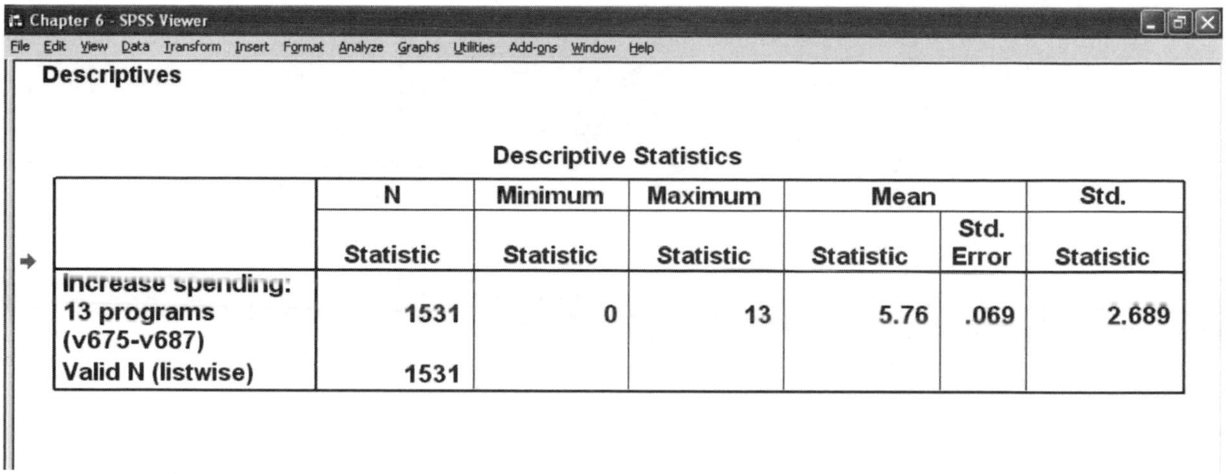

Descriptive Statistics

	N	Minimum	Maximum	Mean		Std.
	Statistic	Statistic	Statistic	Statistic	Std. Error	Statistic
Increase spending: 13 programs (v675-v687)	1531	0	13	5.76	.069	2.689
Valid N (listwise)	1531					

tion, which bears the minimalist label "Std." (Figure 6-3). Among the 1,531 respondents, scores on spend13 range from 0 (increase spending in none of the programs) to 13 (increase spending in all of the programs). The mean value of spend13 is 5.76, with a standard deviation of 2.689. How closely does the mean of 5.76 reflect the true mean in the population from which this sample was drawn?

The answer depends on the standard error of the sample mean. The standard error of a sample mean is based on the standard deviation and the size of the sample. SPSS determines the standard error just as you would—by dividing the standard deviation by the square root of the sample size. For spend13, the standard error is the standard deviation, 2.689, divided by the square root of 1,531, 39.13, which is equal to .069. (If you are running SPSS 11.5 or earlier, SPSS may have expressed this value using scientific notation: 6.87E-02, meaning "move the decimal point two places to the left." Doing so would yield .0687, which rounds to .069.) This number, .069, tells us the extent to which the sample mean of 5.76 departs by chance from the population mean. The standard error is the essential ingredient for making inferences about the population mean. Next, we will use the One-Sample T Test procedure to perform three inferential tasks. We will find the 95 percent confidence interval of the mean, calculate the 90 percent confidence interval of the mean, and then test a hypothetical claim about the population mean using the .05 level of significance.

First, let's use One-Sample T Test to obtain the 95 percent confidence interval of spend13. Click Analyze → Compare Means → One-Sample T Test, causing the One-Sample T Test window to open (Figure 6-4). The user supplies SPSS with information in two places: the Test Variable(s) panel and the Test Value box, which currently contains the default value of 0. Now, One-Sample T Test is not naturally designed to report the 95 percent confidence interval for a mean. Rather, it is set up to compare the mean of a variable

Figure 6–4 One-Sample T Test Window

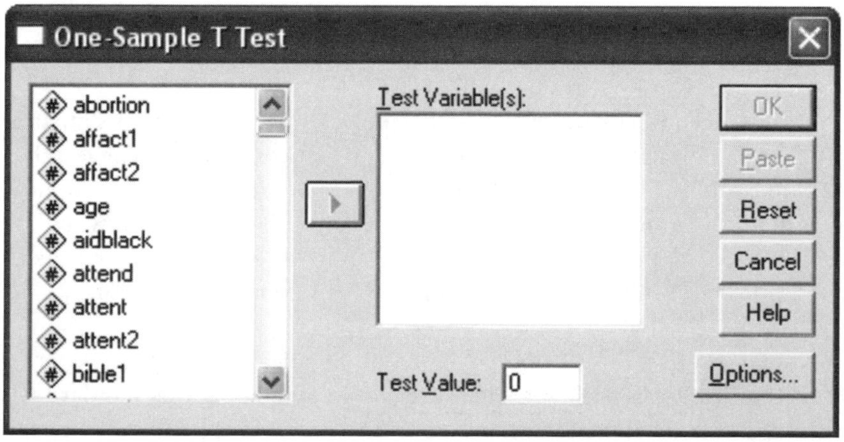

Figure 6–5 Setting Up the Confidence Interval

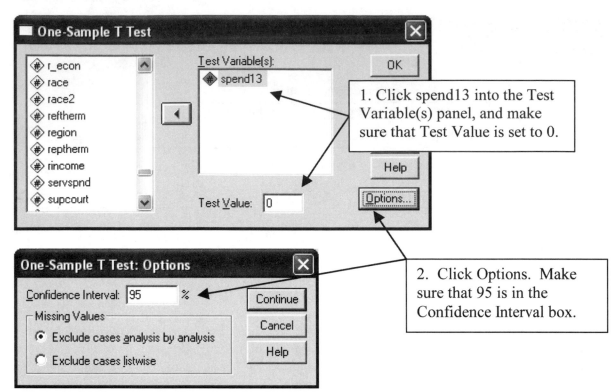

in the Test Variable(s) panel with a hypothetical mean (provided by the user in the Test Value box) and to see if random error could account for the difference. (We will discuss this calculation below.) However, if you run One-Sample T Test on its defaults, it will provide the 95 percent confidence interval. To obtain the 95 percent confidence interval for the mean of a variable, do three things. First, click the variable into the Test Variable(s) panel. Second, make sure that the Test Value box contains the default value of 0. Third, click Options and ensure that the confidence interval is set at 95 percent (Figure 6-5). To follow these steps for spend13, we would click it into the Test Variable(s) panel and leave the Test Value box as it is. After clicking Options to make sure that the confidence interval is set at 95 percent, we would run the analysis.

SPSS output for One-Sample T Test includes two tables (Figure 6-6). In the One-Sample Statistics table, SPSS reports summary information about spend13. This information is similar to the Descriptives output discussed earlier. Again, we can see that spend13 has a mean of 5.76, a standard deviation of 2.689, and a standard error of .069. We are interested mainly in the second table, the One-Sample Test table. In fact, when using One-Sample T Test to obtain confidence intervals, you may safely ignore all of the information in the One-Sample Test table except for the rightmost cells. The values appearing under the label "95% Confidence Interval of the Difference," 5.62 and 5.89, define the lower and upper boundaries of the 95 percent confidence interval. There is a high probability, a 95 percent probability, that the true population mean lies in the region between 5.62 at the low end and 5.89 at the high end. There is a 5 percent probability that the population mean lies outside these boundaries—a 2.5 percent chance that the population mean is less than 5.62 and a 2.5 percent chance that it is greater than 5.89.

The 95 percent confidence interval provides a stringent .025 one-tailed test of statistical significance for hypothetical claims about a population mean. For example, if someone were to suggest that the true population mean is 5.92, you could confidently reject this idea. Why? Because the proposed mean of 5.92 lies beyond the upper confidence boundary. If the population mean really is 5.92, you would obtain a sample mean of 5.76 less than 2.5 percent of the time. Similarly, if someone else claimed that the population mean falls below 5.62, you could reject this claim, too, because such an event would occur by chance fewer than 2.5 times out of 100.

A somewhat less stringent test, the .05 one-tailed test of statistical significance, is perhaps the most common standard used in testing hypotheses. There are two ways to apply this standard—the confidence interval approach and the P-value approach. In the confidence interval approach, the researcher finds the

Figure 6–6 Finding the 95 Percent Confidence Interval

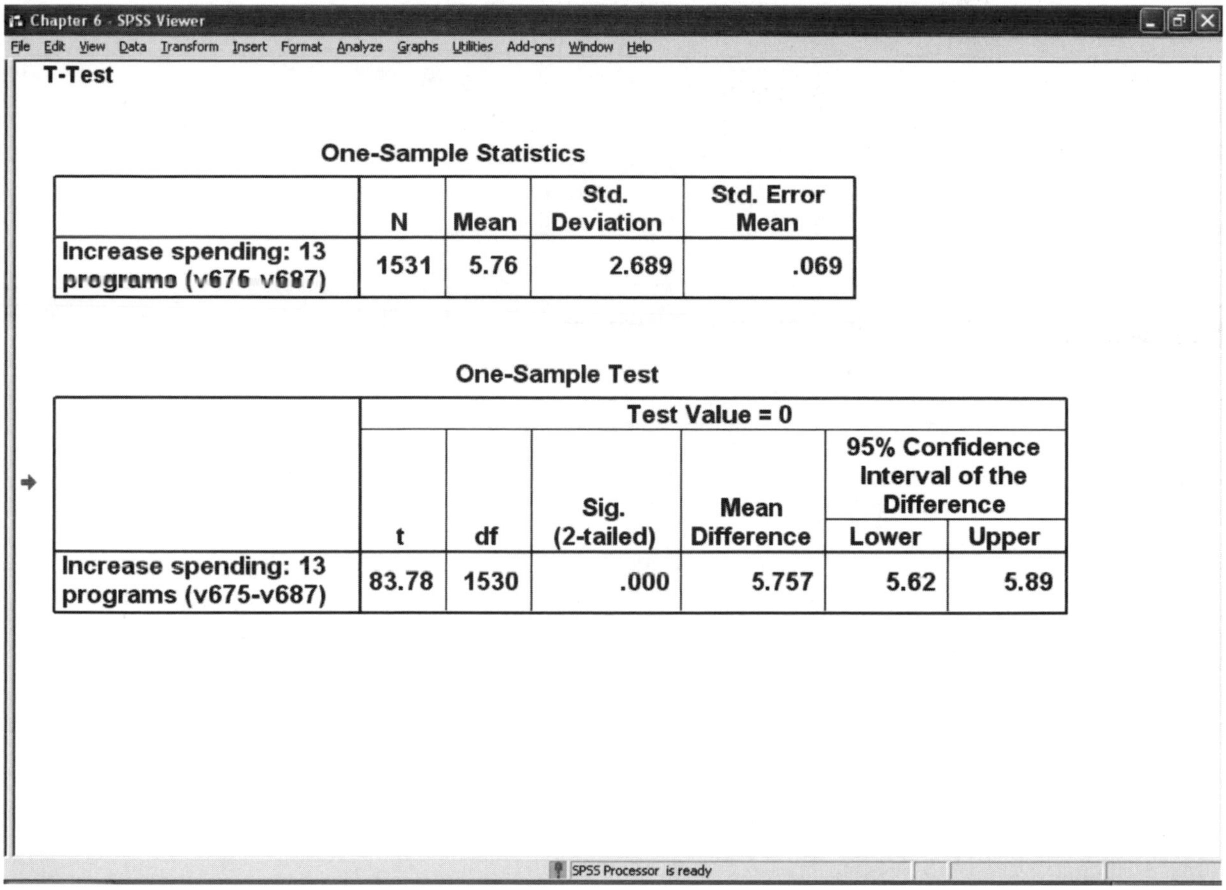

T-Test

One-Sample Statistics

	N	Mean	Std. Deviation	Std. Error Mean
Increase spending: 13 programs (v676 v687)	1531	5.76	2.689	.069

One-Sample Test

	Test Value = 0					
					95% Confidence Interval of the Difference	
	t	df	Sig. (2-tailed)	Mean Difference	Lower	Upper
Increase spending: 13 programs (v675-v687)	83.78	1530	.000	5.757	5.62	5.89

90 percent confidence interval of the mean. Why the 90 percent confidence interval? There is a 90 percent probability that the population mean falls between the lower value and the higher value of this interval. There is a 10 percent chance that the population mean falls outside these limits—5 percent *below* the lower boundary and 5 percent *above* the upper boundary. The values of the 90 percent confidence interval, therefore, set the limits of random sampling error in applying the .05 standard. In the P-value approach the researcher determines the exact probability associated with a hypothetical claim about the population mean. First, let's find the 90 percent confidence interval for spend13. Then we will use the P-value approach to evaluate a hypothetical claim about the mean of spend13.

Click Analyze → Compare Means → One-Sample T Test. Make sure that spend13 is still in the Test Variable(s) panel and that the default value of 0 appears in the Test Value box. Click Options. This time, type "90" in the confidence interval box. Click Continue, and then click OK. The One-Sample Test table in the SPSS Viewer provides the 90 percent confidence interval (Figure 6-7). You can be confident, 90 percent confident anyway, that the population mean of spend13 lies between 5.64 at the low end and 5.87 at the high end. There is a probability of .10 that the population mean lies beyond these limits—a .05 probability that it is less than 5.64 and a .05 probability that it is greater than 5.87.

We can apply this knowledge to the task of testing a hypothetical claim. Suppose you hypothesized that political science majors will be more likely to favor government spending than will most people. To test this idea, you ask a group of political science majors a series of 13 questions about federal programs—the same set of questions that appears in the 2000 National Election Study (NES). Whereas the 2000 NES reports a mean value of 5.76 on spend13, you find a higher mean value, 5.86, among the subjects in your study. Thus it would appear that your subjects are, on average, more supportive of government spending than are the individuals in the NES's random sample of U.S. adults. But is this difference, 5.76 versus 5.86, *statistically* significant at the .05 level? No, it is not. Why can we say this? Because the political science majors' mean, 5.86, does not exceed the NES sample's upper confidence boundary, 5.87.

Think about it this way. Imagine a population of U.S. adults in which spend13's true mean is equal to 5.76. Now suppose you were to draw a random sample from this population and calculate the mean of

Figure 6–7 Finding the 90 Percent Confidence Interval

```
┌─ Chapter 6 - SPSS Viewer ──────────────────────────────────────── _ ⮺ ✕ ┐
 File Edit View Data Transform Insert Format Analyze Graphs Utilities Add-ons Window Help
```

T-Test

One-Sample Statistics

	N	Mean	Std. Deviation	Std. Error Mean
Increase spending: 13 programs (v675-v687)	1531	5.76	2.689	.069

One-Sample Test

	Test Value = 0					
					90% Confidence Interval of the Difference	
	t	df	Sig. (2-tailed)	Mean Difference	Lower	Upper
Increase spending: 13 programs (v675-v687)	83.78	1530	.000	5.757	5.64	5.87

```
                              SPSS Processor is ready
```

spend13. The upper confidence boundary tells you that such a sample would yield a mean of greater than 5.87 *less frequently* than 5 times out of 100. The upper confidence boundary also says that such a sample would produce a mean of less than 5.87 *more frequently* than 5 times out of 100. Because 5.86 is less than 5.87, you must conclude that the political science majors' mean is not significantly higher than the NES mean. Put another way, there is a probability of greater than .05 that your sample of political science majors and the NES's sample of adults were both drawn from the same population—a population in which spend13 has a mean equal to 5.76.

Confidence interval approaches to statistical significance work fine. Find the 90 percent confidence interval and compare the hypothetical mean to the appropriate interval boundary. If the hypothetical mean falls above the upper boundary (or below the lower boundary), then conclude that the two numbers are significantly different at the .05 level. If the hypothetical mean falls below the upper boundary (or above the lower boundary), then conclude that the two numbers are not significantly different at the .05 level. Thus the confidence interval approach tells you that a random sample of U.S. adults would produce a sample mean of 5.86 more frequently than 5 percent of the time. However, the P-value approach to statistical significance is more precise. The P-value will tell you *exactly* how frequently a sample mean of 5.86 would occur.

Let's run One-Sample T Test on spend13 one more time and obtain the information we need to determine the P-value associated with the political science majors' mean of 5.86. Click Analyze → Compare Means → One-Sample T Test. Spend13 should still be in the Test Variable(s) panel. Now click in the Test Value box and type "5.86" (Figure 6-8). SPSS will calculate the difference between the mean of the test variable, spend13, and the test value, 5.86. SPSS will then report the probability that the test value, 5.86, came from the same population as did the mean of the test variable, spend13. Click OK. Again, we have One-Sample T Test output (Figure 6-9).

Consider the One-Sample Test table. What do these numbers mean? SPSS follows this protocol in comparing the mean of a test variable with a test value. First, it finds the difference between them: test variable

Figure 6–8   Testing a Hypothetical Claim about a Sample Mean

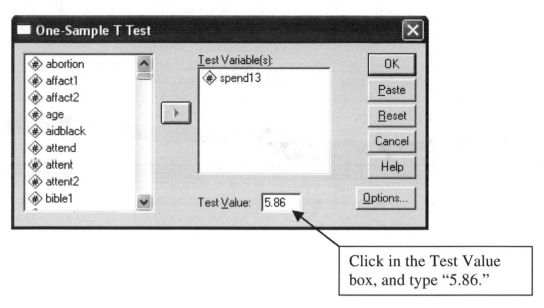

Click in the Test Value
box, and type "5.86."

Figure 6–9   Testing for Statistical Significance

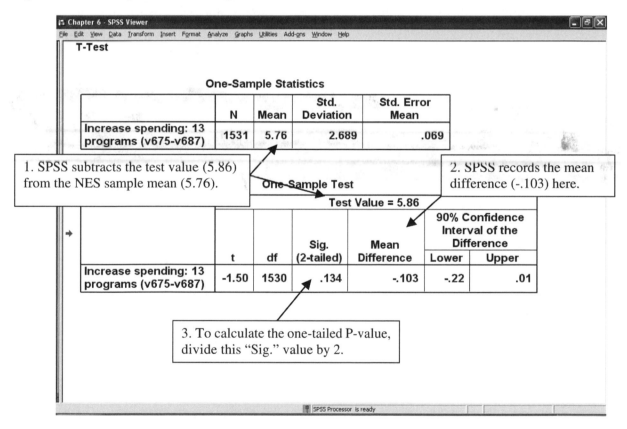

1. SPSS subtracts the test value (5.86)
from the NES sample mean (5.76).

2. SPSS records the mean
difference (-.103) here.

3. To calculate the one-tailed P-value,
divide this "Sig." value by 2.

mean minus test value. So SPSS calculates 5.76 – 5.86 and reports the result, –.103, in the "Mean Difference" column of the One-Sample Test table.

SPSS then asks itself this question: If in the population there is really no difference between the test variable mean and the test value, how often would one obtain a difference of at least .103 in *either direction*? That is, how often would one observe a difference of less than –.103 *or* more than +.103? To answer this inferential question, SPSS calculates a Student's t-test statistic, or t-ratio, the mean difference divided by spend13's standard error.[2] This value of t, –1.50, appears in the leftmost cell of the One-Sample Test table.

Thus spend13's mean falls 1.50 standard errors below the political science majors' mean. Turn your attention to the cell labeled "Sig. (2-tailed)," which contains the number .134. This two-tailed value tells you the proportion of the curve that lies below t = −1.50 *and* above t = +1.50.

Now, we are not testing the hypothesis that the political science majors' mean is *different from* the mean of the adult population. We are not asking SPSS to tell us if the majors' mean is less than or greater than the population mean. Rather, we are testing the hypothesis that the majors' mean is *greater than* the population mean. In testing this hypothesis, we do not want to know the proportion of the curve that lies above t = +1.50. We only want to know the P-value associated with t = −1.50, the test statistic for spend13's mean of 5.76 minus the political science majors' mean of 5.86. Because the Student's t-distribution is perfectly symmetrical, one-half of .134, or .067, falls below t = −1.50. From the confidence interval approach we already know that there is a probability of greater than .05 that the political science majors' mean and the NES sample mean came from the same population. We can now put a finer point on this probability. We can say that, if the majors' mean and the NES mean came from the same population, then the observed difference between them (−.103) would occur, by chance, .067 of the time. Because .067 exceeds the .05 threshold, we would conclude again that the test subjects' mean is not significantly higher than the population mean.

Before proceeding, let's pause to review the steps for obtaining a P-value from the One-Sample T Test procedure. This is also the appropriate place to introduce a useful template for writing an interpretation of your results. First, click the variable of interest into the Test Variable(s) panel. Second, type the hypothetical value in the Test Value box and click OK. Third, obtain a P-value by dividing the number in the "Sig. (2-tailed)" cell by 2. Use the P-value to fill in the blank in the following template:

> If in the population there is no difference between the mean of [the test variable] and [the test value], then the observed difference of [the mean difference] would occur _____ of the time by chance.

For the spend13 example, we would complete the sentence this way: "If in the population there is no difference between the mean of spend13 and 5.86, then the observed difference of −.103 would occur .067 of the time by chance." The .05 benchmark is the standard for testing your hypothesis. If the P-value is less than or equal to .05, then you can infer that the test value is significantly greater than (or less than) the mean of the test variable. If the P-value is greater than .05, then you can infer that the test value is not significantly greater than (or less than) the mean of the test variable.

USING INDEPENDENT-SAMPLES T TEST

We now turn to a common hypothesis-testing situation: comparing the sample means of a dependent variable for two groups that differ on an independent variable. Someone investigating the gender gap, for example, might test a series of hypotheses about the political differences between men and women. In the next guided example, we test two gender gap hypotheses using two feeling thermometer scales as the dependent variables:

Hypothesis 1: In comparing individuals, men will give the military higher feeling thermometer ratings than will women.
Hypothesis 2: In comparing individuals, men will give the women's movement lower feeling thermometer ratings than will women.

The first hypothesis suggests that when we divide the sample on the basis of the independent variable, gender, and compare mean values of the military feeling thermometer, the male mean will be higher than the female mean. The second hypothesis suggests that a similar male-female comparison on the women's movement feeling thermometer will show the male mean to be lower than the female mean.

The researcher always tests his or her hypotheses against a skeptical foil, the null hypothesis. The null hypothesis claims that, regardless of any group differences that a researcher observes in a random sample, no group differences exist in the population from which the sample was drawn. How does the null hypothesis explain systematic patterns that might turn up in a sample, such as a mean difference between women and men on the military feeling thermometer? Random sampling error. In essence the null hypothesis says,

Figure 6–10 Independent-Samples T Test Window

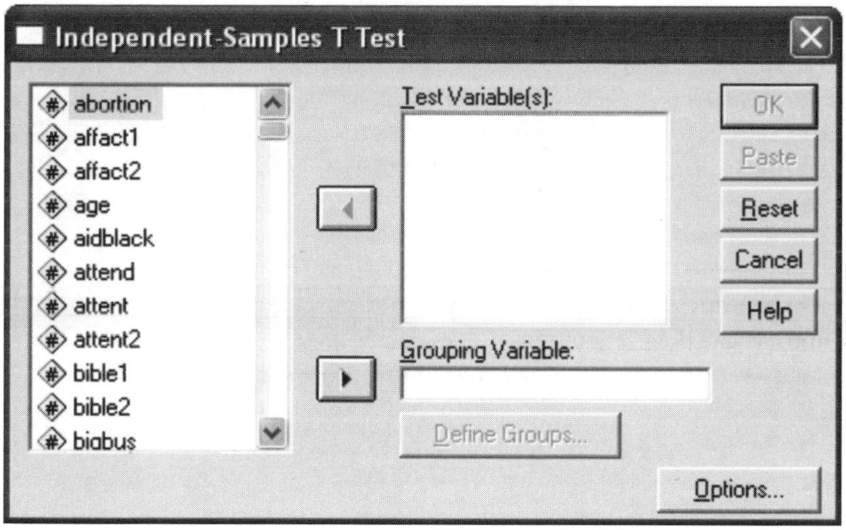

"You observed such and such a difference between two groups in your random sample. But, in reality, no difference exists in the population. When you took the sample, you introduced random sampling error. Thus random sampling error accounts for the difference you observed." For both hypotheses 1 and 2 above, the null hypothesis says that there are no real differences between men and women in the population, that men do not give the military higher ratings or the women's movement lower ratings. The null hypothesis further asserts that any observed differences in the sample can be accounted for by random sampling error.

The null hypothesis is so central to the methodology of statistical inference that we always begin by assuming it to be correct. We then set a fairly tough standard for rejecting it. The researcher's hypotheses—such as the military hypothesis and the women's movement hypothesis—are considered alternative hypotheses. The Independent-Samples T Test procedure permits us to test each alternative hypothesis against the null hypothesis and to decide whether the observed differences between males and females are too large to have occurred by random chance when the sample was drawn. For each mean comparison, the Independent-Samples T Test procedure will give us a P-value: the probability of obtaining the sample difference under the working assumption that the null hypothesis is true.

Click Analyze → Compare Means → Independent-Samples T Test. The Independent-Samples T Test window appears (Figure 6-10). SPSS wants to know two things: the name or names of the test variable(s) and the name of the grouping variable. SPSS will calculate the mean values of the variables named in the Test Variable(s) panel for each category of the variable named in the Grouping Variable box. It will then test to see if the differences between the means are significantly different from 0, as claimed by the null hypothesis.

We want to compare the means for men and women on two feeling thermometers, one for the military (military) and one for the women's movement (wommov). Find military and wommov in the variable list and click both of them into the Test Variable(s) panel. Because we want the means of these variables to be calculated separately for each sex, gender is the grouping variable. When you click gender into the Grouping Variable box, SPSS moves it into the box with the designation "gender(? ?)." The Define Groups button is activated (Figure 6-11). SPSS needs more information. It needs to know the codes of the two groups we wish to compare. Men are coded 1 on gender and women are coded 2. (Recall that by right-clicking on a variable you can reacquaint yourself with that variable's codes.) Click Define Groups (Figure 6-12). There are two ways to define the groups we want to compare: Use specified values (the default) and Cut point. The choice, of course, depends on the situation. If you opt for Use specified values, then SPSS will divide the cases into two groups based on the codes you supply for Group 1 and Group 2. If the grouping variable has more than two categories, then you may wish to use Cut point. SPSS will divide the cases into two groups based on the code entered in the Cut point box—one group for all cases having codes equal to or greater than the Cut point code and one group having codes less than the Cut point code. (You will use Cut point in one of the exercises at the end of this chapter.) Because gender has two codes—1 for males and 2 for females—we will go with the Use specified values option in this example.

Figure 6–11   Specifying Test Variables and a Grouping Variable

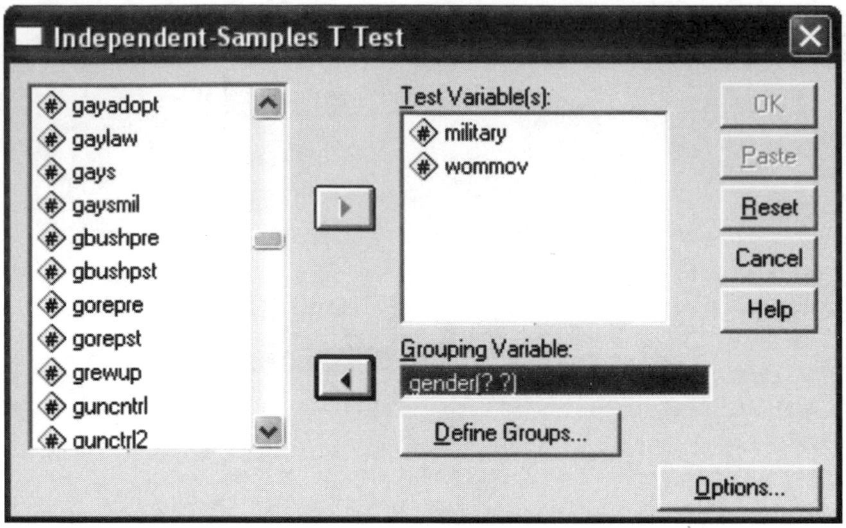

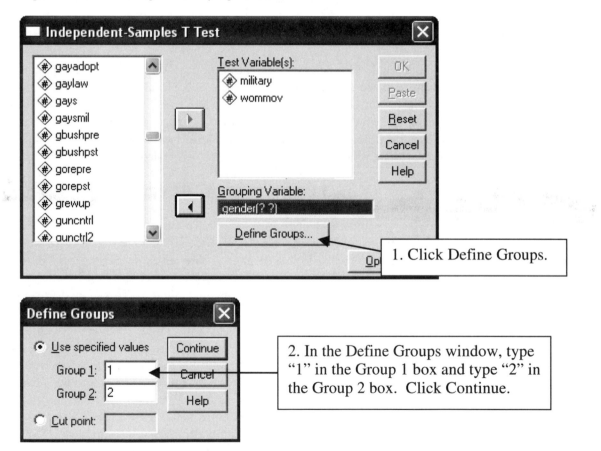

Figure 6–12   Defining the Grouping Variable

Click in the Group 1 box and type "1," and then click in the Group 2 box and type "2." Click Continue. The Independent-Samples T Test window should now look like Figure 6-13. Notice that SPSS has replaced the question marks next to gender with the codes for males and females. One more thing: Because we will be applying the .05 standard in testing the null hypothesis, click Options and change the confidence interval to 90 percent. Click Continue, and then click OK.

SPSS runs both mean comparisons and reports the results in the SPSS Viewer (Figure 6-14). The top table, labeled "Group Statistics," shows descriptive information about the means of military and wommov.

Figure 6–13 Independent-Samples T Test Window (with defined grouping variable)

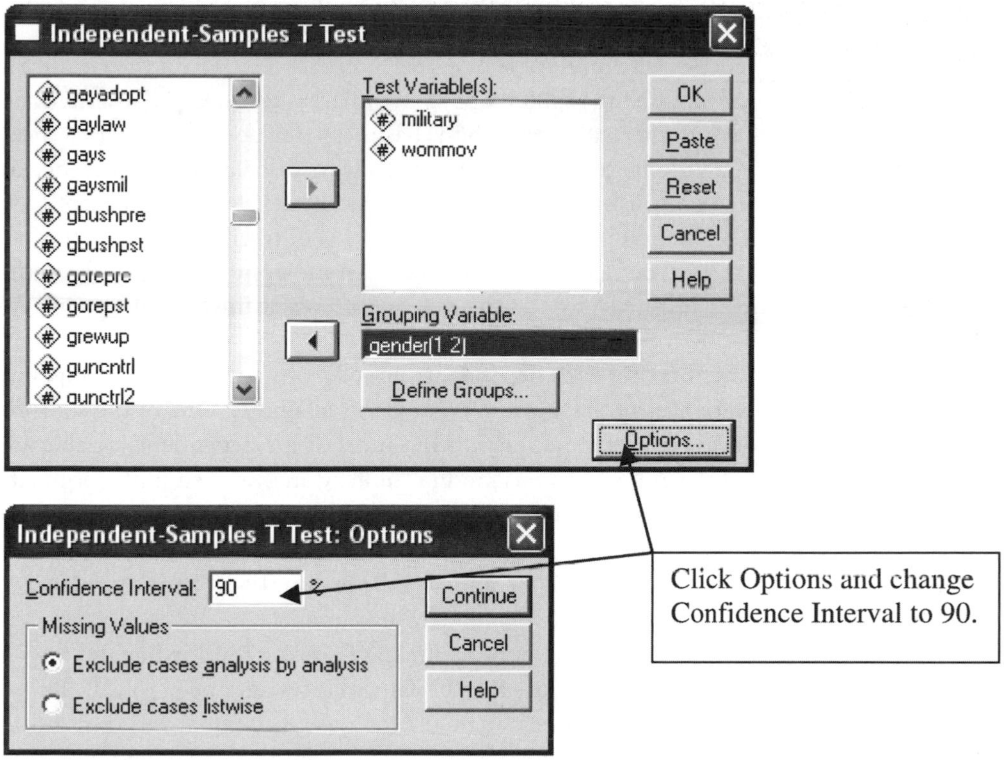

Figure 6–14 Results of Independent-Samples T Test

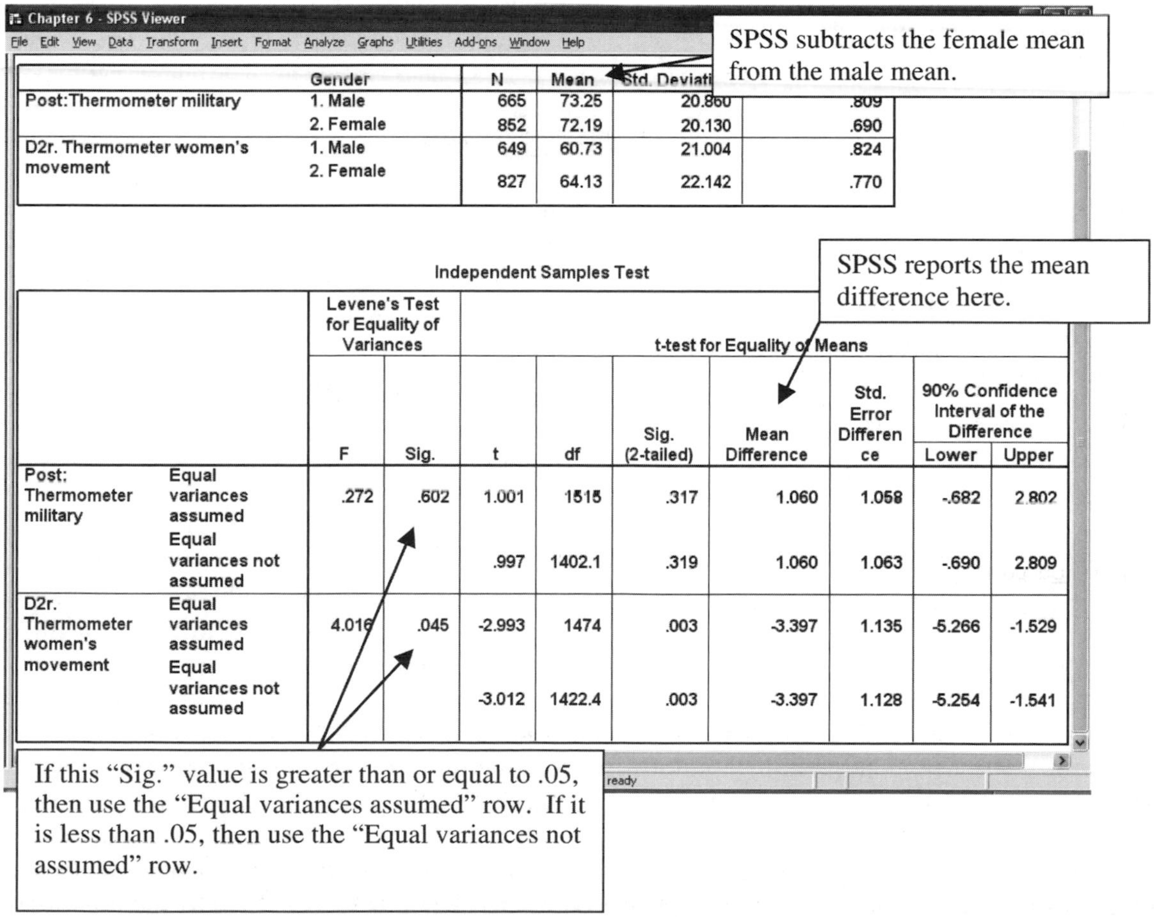

	Gender	N	Mean	Std. Deviati...
Post:Thermometer military	1. Male	665	73.25	20.860	.809
	2. Female	852	72.19	20.130	.690
D2r. Thermometer women's movement	1. Male	649	60.73	21.004	.824
	2. Female	827	64.13	22.142	.770

SPSS subtracts the female mean from the male mean.

Independent Samples Test

SPSS reports the mean difference here.

		Levene's Test for Equality of Variances		t-test for Equality of Means					90% Confidence Interval of the Difference	
		F	Sig.	t	df	Sig. (2-tailed)	Mean Difference	Std. Error Differen ce	Lower	Upper
Post: Thermometer military	Equal variances assumed	.272	.602	1.001	1515	.317	1.060	1.058	-.682	2.802
	Equal variances not assumed			.997	1402.1	.319	1.060	1.063	-.690	2.809
D2r. Thermometer women's movement	Equal variances assumed	4.016	.045	-2.993	1474	.003	-3.397	1.135	-5.266	-1.529
	Equal variances not assumed			-3.012	1422.4	.003	-3.397	1.128	-5.254	-1.541

If this "Sig." value is greater than or equal to .05, then use the "Equal variances assumed" row. If it is less than .05, then use the "Equal variances not assumed" row.

The bottom table, "Independent Samples Test," tests for statistically significant differences between men and women on each dependent variable. There is a lot of information to digest here, so let's take it one step at a time.

We will evaluate the gender difference on the military feeling thermometer first. From the Group Statistics table we can see that males, on average, rated the military at 73.25, whereas females had a somewhat lower mean, 72.19. It would appear that our alternative hypothesis has merit. Or does it? The difference between these two sample means is 73.25 minus 72.19, or 1.060 (SPSS always calculates the difference by subtracting the Group 2 mean from the Group 1 mean. This value appears in the "Mean Difference" column of the Independent-Samples Test table.) The null hypothesis claims that this difference is the result of random sampling error and, therefore, that the true male-female difference in the population is 0. Using the information in the Independent-Samples Test table, we test the null hypothesis against the alternative hypothesis that the male mean is higher than the female mean.

Notice that there are two rows of numbers for each dependent variable. One row is labeled "Equal variances assumed" and the other "Equal variances not assumed." What is this all about? One of the statistical assumptions for comparing sample means is that the population variances of the dependent variable are the same for both groups—in this case, that the amount of variation in military among men in the population is equal to the amount of variation in military among women in the population. If this assumption holds up, then you would use the first row of numbers to test the hypothesis. If this assumption is incorrect, however, then you would use the second row of numbers. SPSS evaluates the assumption of equal variances using Levene's test, which tests the hypothesis that the two variances are equal.

Here is how to proceed. Look at the "Sig." value that appears under "Levene's Test for Equality of Variances." If this value is greater than or equal to .05, then use the "Equal variances assumed" row. If the "Sig." Value under "Levene's Test for Equality of Variances" is less than .05, then use the "Equal variances not assumed" row. Because this "Sig." value for military is greater than .05, we would go ahead and use the first row of numbers to evaluate the mean difference between men and women.

Let's use the 90 percent confidence interval to apply the .05 standard. There are, of course, two boundaries—a lower boundary, −.682, and an upper boundary, 2.802. Which one should we use? Here is a fool-proof method for testing a hypothesis using the correct confidence boundary. First, make sure that the direction of the mean difference is consistent with the alternative hypothesis. If the mean difference runs in the direction opposite from the one you hypothesized, then the game is already up: The alternative hypothesis is incorrect. If the direction of the mean difference checks out okay, then begin at the mean difference and start moving toward 0, which lies at the heart of the null's territory. If you cross a confidence boundary before you hit 0, then the mean difference is statistically significant at the .05 level. The difference would occur by chance fewer than 5 times out of 100. If, however, you hit 0 first—before you cross a boundary— then the mean difference is not statistically significant at the .05 level. It would occur by chance more often than 5 times out of 100.

In the current example, the difference between men and women on military runs in the hypothesized direction: Males have a higher mean rating than do females. So the alternative hypothesis is still alive. Now start at the mean difference, 1.060, and move toward 0. To beat the null hypothesis, we have to cross a confidence interval boundary before we hit 0. Do we cross a boundary first? No, we hit 0 first. The confidence boundary is below 0, at −.682. Conclusion: If the null hypothesis is correct, then the probability of observing a mean difference of 1.060 is greater than .05. Do not reject the null hypothesis.

Just as with the One-Sample T Test, we can arrive at an exact probability, or P-value, by dividing the "Sig. (2-tailed)" value by 2. The value in the "Sig. (2-tailed)" cell is .317. Dividing by 2, we have .159. More precise conclusion: If the null hypothesis is correct, then random sampling error would produce a mean difference of 1.060 about 16 percent of the time. If we were to say that, in the population, men score higher than do women on military, we could too easily be making an inferential mistake. Do not reject the null hypothesis.

The military gender gap hypothesis did not fare too well against the null hypothesis. How about the women's movement hypothesis? Again, the information on wommov in the Group Statistics table would appear consistent with the hypothesis. Men, with a mean of 60.73, score lower than do women, who averaged 64.13. SPSS reports the mean difference, − 3.397, in the Independent-Samples Test table. Does this difference pass muster with the null hypothesis? Let's look at the Independent-Samples Test table and decide which row of numbers to use. In this case the "Sig." value under "Levene's Test for Equality of Variances" is

NOTES

1. Respondents were asked whether spending should be increased, kept the same, or decreased in these 13 federal programs: building and repairing highways, welfare programs, AIDS research, foreign aid, food stamps, aid to poor people, Social Security, environmental protection, public schools, dealing with crime, child care, tightening border security to prevent illegal immigration, and aid to blacks.
2. SPSS performs this calculation at 32-decimal precision. So if you were to check SPSS's math, using the mean difference and standard error that appear in the SPSS Viewer, you would arrive at a slightly different t-ratio than the value of t reported in the One-Sample Test table.

.48

.914

.457

2

917

7

Chi-square and
Measures of Association

In the preceding chapter you learned how to test for mean differences on an interval-level dependent variable. But what if you are not dealing with interval-level variables? What if you are doing cross-tabulation analysis and are trying to figure out whether an observed relationship between two nominal or ordinal variables mirrors the true relationship in the population? Just as with mean differences, the answer depends on the boundaries of random sampling error, the extent to which your observed results "happened by chance" when you took the sample. The SPSS Crosstabs procedure can provide the information needed to test the statistical significance of nominal or ordinal relationships, and it will yield appropriate measures of association.

You are familiar with the SPSS Crosstabs procedure. For analyzing datasets that contain a preponderance of categorical variables—variables measured by nominal or ordinal categories—cross-tabulation is by far the most common mode of analysis in political research. In this section we will revisit Crosstabs and use the Statistics subroutine to obtain the oldest and most widely applied test of statistical significance in cross-tabulation analysis, the chi-square test. With some exceptions, chi-square can always be used to determine whether an observed cross-tab relationship departs significantly from the expectations of the null hypothesis.

In this chapter you will also learn how to obtain measures of association for the relationships you are analyzing. SPSS is programmed to produce, at the user's discretion, a large array of such measures. In doing your own analysis, you will have to tell SPSS which measure or measures you are after. Before starting the first guided example, therefore, let's review the measures of association that you should use for different situations. Here we review the application and interpretation of four measures: Kendall's tau-b, Kendall's tau-c, lambda, and Cramer's V.

One of the Kendall's statistics will be appropriate when both variables in the cross-tabulation are ordinal-level variables. If the table is *square*—if both variables have the same number of categories—ask SPSS to produce tau-b. If the table is *nonsquare*—the variables have a different number of categories—use tau-c. Both tau-b and tau-c are directional measures. A plus (+) sign says that increasing values of the independent variable are associated with increasing values of the dependent variable. A minus (–) sign says that increasing values of the independent variable are related to decreasing values of the dependent variable.

Both Kendall's statistics provide a proportional reduction in error (PRE) measure of the strength of a relationship. A PRE measure tells you the extent to which the values of the independent variable predict the values of the dependent variable. A value close to 0 says that the independent variable provides little predictive leverage; the relationship is weak. Values close to the poles—to –1 for negative associations or to +1 for positive relationships—tell you that the independent variable provides a lot of help in predicting the dependent variable; the relationship is strong.

Lambda, too, is a PRE measure that you can request when one or both variables in the cross-tabulation are nominal level. Lambda's PRE status stands it in good stead with political researchers because PRE measures are generally preferred over measures that do not permit a PRE interpretation. Even so, lambda tends to underestimate the strength of a relationship, especially when one of the variables has low variation.

Figure 7–1 Crosstabs Output (ordinal-level relationship)

Chapter 7 - SPSS Viewer

File Edit View Data Transform Insert Format Analyze Graphs Utilities Add-ons Window Help

Crosstabs

Case Processing Summary

	Cases					
	Valid		Missing		Total	
	N	Percent	N	Percent	N	Percent
Environmental regulations:3 cats * Education: 3 categories	1349	74.7%	458	25.3%	1807	100.0%

Environmental regulations:3 cats * Education: 3 categories Crosstabulation

			Education: 3 categories			
			1. Less than HS	2. HS	3. More than HS	Total
Environmental regulations:3 cats	Tougher regs	Count	44	169	445	658
		% within Education: 3 categories	46.8%	48.4%	49.1%	48.8%
	Depends	Count	34	116	325	475
		% within Education: 3 categories	36.2%	33.2%	35.9%	35.2%
	Regs a burden	Count	16	64	136	216
		% within Education: 3 categories	17.0%	18.3%	15.0%	16.0%
Total		Count	94	349	906	1349
		% within Education: 3 categories	100.0%	100.0%	100.0%	100%

SPSS Processor is ready

Therefore, when you are analyzing a relationship in which one or both of the variables are nominal, it is a good practice to request Cramer's V as well as lambda. Cramer's V, one of a variety of chi-square-based measures, does not measure strength by the PRE criterion. However, it is bounded by 0 (no relationship) and 1 (a perfect relationship).

ANALYZING AN ORDINAL-LEVEL RELATIONSHIP

Let's begin by using NES2000.sav to analyze an ordinal-level relationship. Consider this hypothesis: In comparing individuals, people with higher levels of education will be more likely to favor environmental regulations than will people with lower levels of education. NES2000.sav contains envregs3, an ordinal variable that measures opinions about government regulation of business designed to protect the environment. Respondents who favor "tougher regulations" are coded 1, those who say "it depends" are coded 2, and those responding that regulations are "too much of a burden" on business are coded 3. Envregs3 is the dependent variable. A familiar three-category measure of education, educ3, is the independent variable. This variable, you will recall, gives each respondent a code of 1 (less than high school), 2 (high school), or 3 (more than high school).

Let's first test this hypothesis the old-fashioned way—by running the Crosstabs analysis and comparing column percentages. Click Analyze → Descriptive Statistics → Crosstabs. Remember to put the dependent variable, envregs3, on the rows and the independent variable, educ3, on the columns. Request column percentages. Run the analysis and consider the output (Figure 7-1).

How would you evaluate the envregs3-educ3 hypothesis in light of this analysis? Focus on the column percentages in the "Tougher regs" row. According to the hypothesis, as we move along this row, from less education to more education, the percentages of respondents favoring regulation should increase. Is this what happens? Sort of. The percentages increase from 46.8 percent among people with less than high school to 48.4 percent for high school graduates to 49.1 percent for those with more than high school. So the difference between the least-educated and the most-educated respondents is something on the order of 2 percentage points—not a terribly robust relationship between the independent and dependent variables. Using your own interpretive skills, you would probably say that the findings are too weak to support the envregs3-educ3 hypothesis.

Now let's reconsider the envregs3-educ3 cross-tabulation from the standpoint of inferential statistics, the way the chi-square test of statistical significance would approach it. Chi-square begins by looking at the "Total" column, which contains the distribution of the entire sample across the values of the dependent variable, envregs3. Thus 48.8 percent of the sample favor tougher regulations, 35.2 percent take a middle position, and 16.0 percent think regulations are too much of a burden on business. Chi-square then frames the null hypothesis, which claims that, in the population, envregs3 and educ3 are not related to each other, that individuals' levels of education are unrelated to their opinions about environmental regulations. If the null hypothesis is correct, then a random sample of people who have less than high school would produce the same distribution of environmental opinions as the total distribution. By the same token, a random sample of high school graduates would yield a distribution that looks just like the total distribution, as would a random sample of individuals with more than high school. If the null hypothesis is correct, then the distribution of cases down each column of the table will be the same as in the "Total" column. Of course, the null hypothesis asserts that any departures from this monotonous pattern resulted from random sampling error.

Now reexamine the table and make a considered judgment. Would you say that the observed distribution of cases within each category of educ3 conforms to the expectations of the null hypothesis? Well, for the category of least education, the distribution is pretty close to the total distribution, with only slight departures—for example, a somewhat lower percentage in the "Tougher regs" category than the null would expect and a slightly higher percentage in the "Regs a burden" category. In fact, for each value of educ3, there is fairly close conformity to what we would expect to find if the null hypothesis were true. The small departures from these expectations, furthermore, might easily be explained by random sampling error.

Let's rerun the analysis and find out if our considered judgment is borne out by the chi-square test. We will also obtain a measure of association for the relationship. Return to the Crosstabs window. Click Statistics. The Crosstabs: Statistics window pops up (Figure 7-2). There are many choices here, but we know what we want: We would like SPSS to perform a chi-square on the table. Check the Chi-square box. We also know which measure of association to request. Because both envregs3 and educ3 are ordinal-level variables—and because both have the same number of categories—we will need Kendall's tau-b. Check the box next to "Kendall's tau-b." Click Continue, and then click OK.

SPSS runs the cross-tabulation analysis again, and this time it has produced two additional tables of statistics: "Chi-Square Tests" and "Symmetric Measures" (Figure 7-3). Given the parsimony of our requests, SPSS has been rather generous in its statistical output. In the Chi-Square Tests table, focus exclusively on the row labeled "Pearson Chi-Square." The first column, labeled "Value," provides the chi-square test statistic. If the observed data perfectly fit the expectations of the null hypothesis, then this test statistic would be 0. As the observed data depart from the null's expectations, this value grows in size. For the envregs3-educ3 cross-tabulation, SPSS calculated a chi-square test statistic equal to 2.434. Is this number, 2.434, statistically different from 0, the value we would expect to obtain if the null hypothesis were true? Put another way: If the null hypothesis is correct, how often will we obtain a test statistic of 2.434 by chance? The answer is contained in the rightmost column of the Chi-Square Tests table, under the odd label "Asymp. Sig. (2-sided)." For the chi-square test of significance, this value *is* the P-value. In our example SPSS reports a P-value of .656. If the null hypothesis is correct in its assertion that no relationship exists between the independent and dependent variables, then we will obtain a test statistic of 2.434, by chance, about 66 percent of the time. The null hypothesis is on solid inferential ground. From our initial comparison of percentages, we suspected that the relationship might not trump the null hypothesis. The chi-square test has confirmed that suspicion. Do not reject the null hypothesis.

Turn your attention to our requested measure of association, Kendall's tau-b, which SPSS calculated to be −.020. Ignore (for the moment) the puny magnitude, .020, and consider the minus sign. The hypothesis suggested a positive relationship: As education increases, the percentage favoring tougher regulations should also increase. And our comparison of percentages did show a positive—if very weak—pattern. As education increases, the percentage of respondents favoring tougher regulations also increases. So shouldn't the sign

Figure 7–2 Requesting the Chi-square Test (ordinal-level relationship)

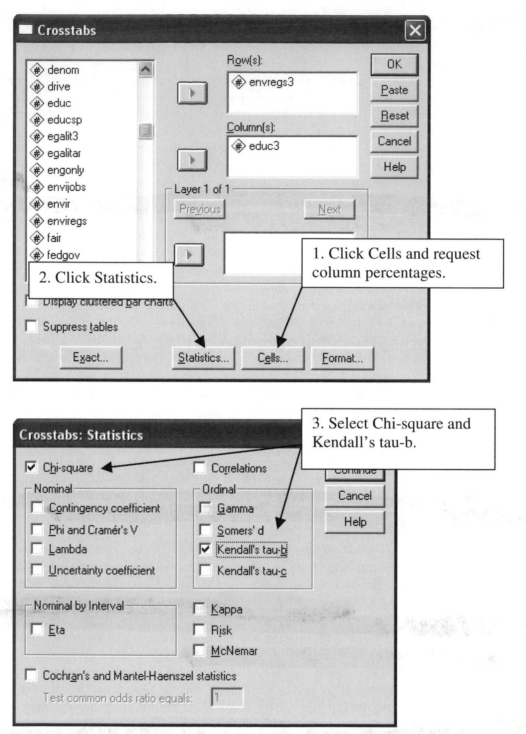

on Kendall's tau-b be positive? Indeed, confusion about what the sign means is common in computer analysis. So we need to be clear about what SPSS has done.

SPSS doesn't know how you framed your hypothesis, and it doesn't care. It only cares about how the variables are coded. If increasing codes on the independent variable are associated with increasing codes on the dependent variable, then SPSS calls it a positive relationship and puts a plus sign on the Kendall's statistic. If increasing codes on the independent variable are related to decreasing codes on the dependent variable, then SPSS calls it a negative relationship and places a minus sign on the Kendall's statistic. Because in our example people with higher codes on educ3 are (slightly) more likely to fall into lower codes of envregs3 ("Tougher regs"), SPSS has reported a negative relationship. Always use your substantive knowl-

Figure 7–3   Results of the Chi-square Test (ordinal-level relationship)

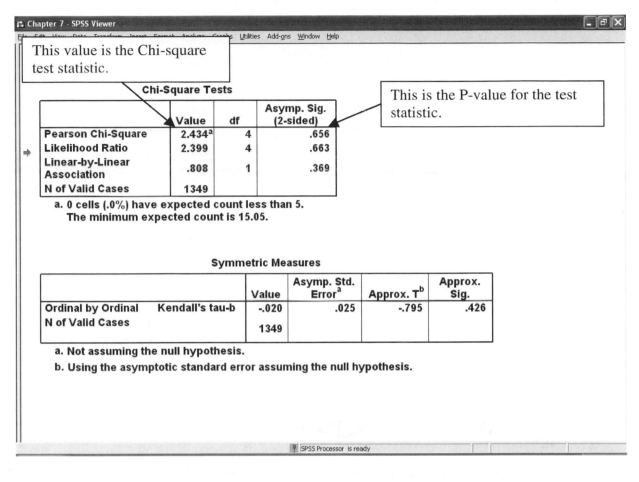

edge of the relationship in reporting your results. In this example we would say that there is a very weak but positive relationship between level of education and support for tougher environmental regulations.

Very weak, to be sure. What does the magnitude of Kendall's tau-b, .020, tell us about our ability to predict values of the dependent variable based on knowledge of the independent variable? It tells us this: Compared with how well we can predict individuals' environmental opinions without knowledge of their levels of education, knowledge of their levels of education improves our prediction by 2 percent. Not much going on there. Let's frame another hypothesis, using different variables, and see if our luck changes.

ANALYZING A NOMINAL-LEVEL RELATIONSHIP

For this guided example we will return to the gender gap, a good source for interesting relationships. We will test this hypothesis: In comparing individuals, women will be more likely to favor gun control than will men. To make things more interesting, we will control for another variable that might also affect attitudes toward gun laws, political trust. It stands to reason that people who are more trusting toward the government would be more willing to expand the government's authority to restrict gun ownership than would people who have a less trusting attitude. Would the gender gap on gun opinions be the same for less trusting and more trusting individuals? Or might the gender gap be weaker among men and women who have a higher level of trust? Let's investigate.

NES2000.sav contains gunctrl2, which classifies respondents' gun opinions by two categories: whether they think gun laws should make it "harder" to own a gun or whether they think such laws should be "kept the same or make it easier" to own a gun. Gunctrl2 is the dependent variable, and gender is the independent variable. For the control variable we will use poltrst2, which divides respondents into two categories: low trust and high trust.[1] Click Analyze → Descriptive Statistics → Crosstabs. Click Reset to clear the panels. Now set up our new analysis: gunctrl2 on the rows, gender on the columns, and poltrst2 in the Layer panel (Figure 7-4). Click Cells and request column percentages. Click Statistics. Again we want chi-square, so

Figure 7–4 Requesting the Chi-square Test (nominal-level relationship)

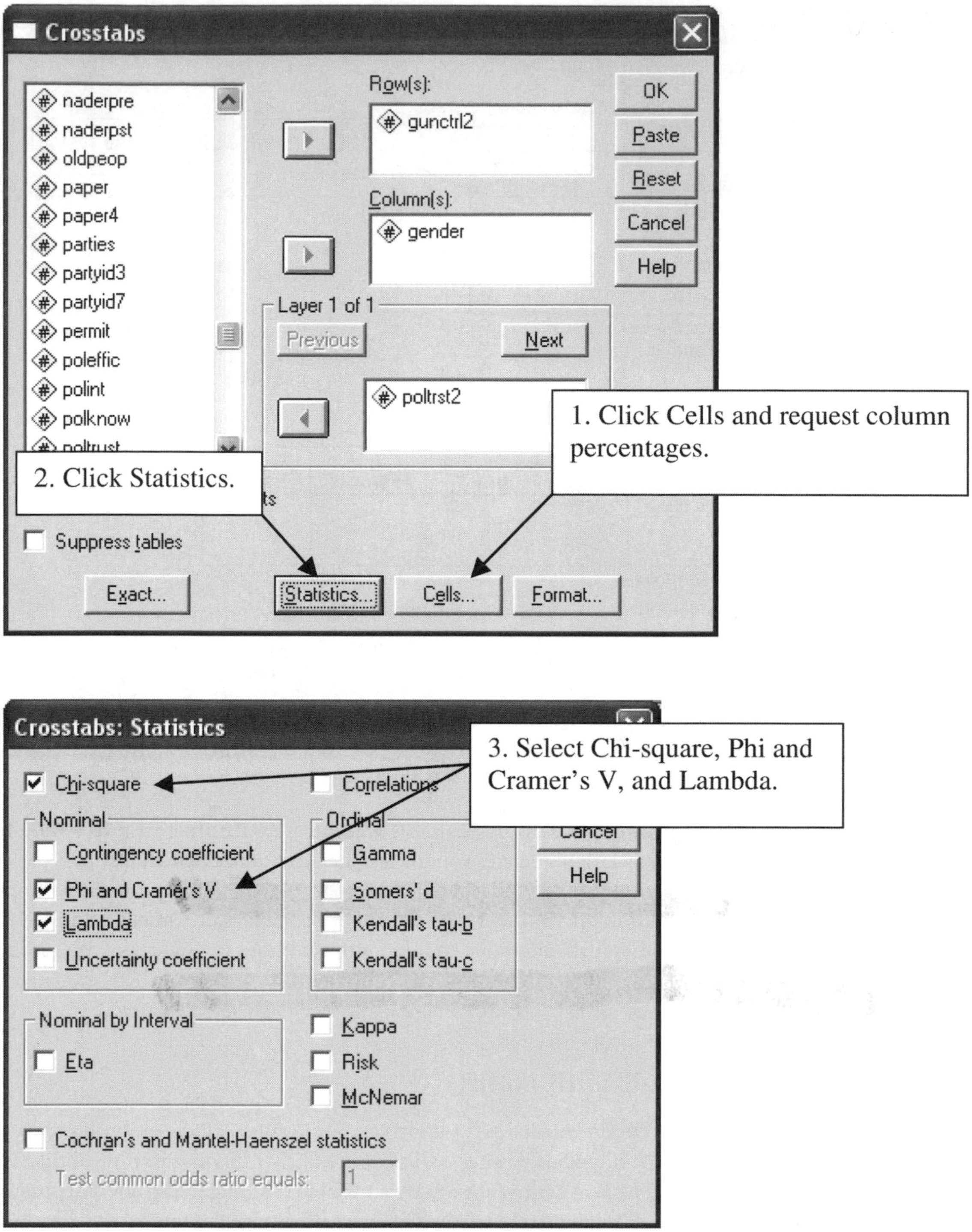

make sure that the Chi-square box is checked. Because gender is a nominal-level variable, we can't use any of the ordinal statistics. But we can use lambda and Cramer's V. In the Nominal panel, check the box next to "Phi and Cramer's V" and check the box next to "Lambda." Click Continue, and then click OK.

SPSS output for controlled comparisons is a familiar sight (Figure 7-5). Before examining the statistics, consider the substantive relationships depicted in the cross-tabulations. Among people with low trust, 39.7 percent of the males said that guns should be "harder to own," compared with 65.4 percent of the females—more than a 25-percentage-point gap. What happens when we switch to the high-trust category of the control? Among more trusting individuals, the percentage of males who favor stricter laws jumps to 54.6 percent, whereas there is a more modest increase in the percentage of women in this category, to 71.6 percent. Thus, among individuals with higher trust, there is a 17-percentage-point gender difference. Clearly interac-

Figure 7–5 Crosstabs Output (nominal-level relationship)

Gun ownership laws should make it...? * Gender * Political trust: 2 cats Crosstabulation

Political trust: 2 cats				Gender		
				1. Male	2. Female	Total
Low	Gun ownership laws should make it...?	Harder to own	Count	138	291	429
			% within Gender	39.7%	65.4%	54.1%
		Same/Easier to own	Count	210	154	364
			% within Gender	60.3%	34.6%	45.9%
	Total		Count	348	445	793
			% within Gender	100.0%	100.0%	100%
High	Gun ownership laws should make it...?	Harder to own	Count	159	260	419
			% within Gender	54.6%	71.6%	64.1%
		Same/Easier to own	Count	132	103	235
			% within Gender	45.4%	28.4%	35.9%
	Total		Count	291	363	654
			% within Gender	100.0%	100.0%	100%

Chi-Square Tests

Political trust: 2 cats		Value	df	Asymp. Sig. (2-sided)	Exact Sig. (2-sided)	Exact Sig. (1-sided)

SPSS Processor is ready

tion is going on here. Although a noticeable gender gap occurs among the more trusting, the gun opinions–gender relationship is stronger among males and females who have a lower level of political trust.

Now let's see what the statistics have to say. According to the Chi-Square Tests table (Figure 7-6), both relationships are statistically significant. The chi-square test statistic for the gunctrl2-gender relationship for individuals with low trust is 52.096, which, according to the P-value, would occur .000 of the time if the null hypothesis were correct. So we can reject the null hypothesis for this value of the control. The chi-square test statistic for the high-trust relationship, 20.244, also defeats the null hypothesis. Thus the likelihood of either relationship occurring by chance is highly remote.

Scroll down to the next table of numbers, "Directional Measures" (Figure 7-7). SPSS has reported three lambda statistics: "Symmetric," "Gun ownership laws should make it. . . ? Dependent," and "Gender Dependent." Again, SPSS doesn't know exactly what we want, so it has given us a choice. Always use the lambda statistic that names the dependent variable in your hypothesis. Because our dependent variable is labeled "Gun ownership laws should make it. . . ?" we would use that statistic. For the low-trust relationship, lambda is equal to .198. So for people with low trust, gender gives us a fair amount of predictive power. Compared with how accurately we could predict gun opinions by not knowing the independent variable, using gender as a predictive tool improves our prediction by about 20 percent—not stunning, but not bad.

Now consider the magnitude of lambda for people with high trust. Here lambda is equal to .000. Our inspection of the cross-tabulation showed a weaker relationship for the high-trust category, but .000 seems rather *too* weak. After all, we observed *some* relationship between gun opinions and gender. And the large chi-square test statistic for this relationship invited us to reject the null hypothesis. Even so, because of the way lambda is computed, it failed to detect a relationship. Lambda looks at the modal value of the dependent variable for each category of the independent variable. Lambda can detect a relationship only if the mode is different between categories. Scroll up to the Crosstabs output for this analysis (see Figure 7-5). In the low-trust cross-tab, men and women have different modes. The modal value for men is "Same/Easier to own," which contains 60.3 percent of the males, and the mode for women is "Harder to own," which has

Figure 7–6 Results of the Chi-square Test (nominal-level relationship)

Chapter 7 - SPSS Viewer

File Edit View Data Transform Insert Format Analyze Graphs Utilities Add-ons Window Help

Chi-Square Tests

Political trust: 2 cats		Value	df	Asymp. Sig. (2-sided)	Exact Sig. (2-sided)	Exact Sig. (1-sided)
Low	Pearson Chi-Square	52.096[b]	1	.000		
	Continuity Correction[a]	51.065	1	.000		
	Likelihood Ratio	52.541	1	.000		
	Fisher's Exact Test				.000	.000
	Linear-by-Linear Association	52.031	1	.000		
	N of Valid Cases	793				
High	Pearson Chi-Square	20.244[c]	1	.000		
	Continuity Correction[a]	19.512	1	.000		
	Likelihood Ratio	20.233	1	.000		
	Fisher's Exact Test				.000	.000
	Linear-by-Linear Association	20.213	1	.000		
	N of Valid Cases	654				

a. Computed only for a 2x2 table

b. 0 cells (.0%) have expected count less than 5. The minimum expected count is 159.74.

c. 0 cells (.0%) have expected count less than 5. The minimum expected count is 104.56.

Directional Measures

Political trust: 2 cats				Value	Asymp. Std. Error[a]	Approx. T[b]	Approx. Sig.
Low	Nominal by Nominal	Lambda	Symmetric	.180	.044	3.840	.000
			Gun ownership laws should make	.198	.046	3.896	.000

SPSS Processor is ready

Figure 7–7 Directional Measures

Chapter 7 - SPSS Viewer

File Edit View Data Transform Insert Format Analyze Graphs Utilities Add-ons Window Help

Directional Measures

Political trust: 2 cats				Value	Asymp. Std. Error[a]	Approx. T[b]	Approx. Sig.
Low	Nominal by Nominal	Lambda	Symmetric	.180	.044	3.840	.000
			Gun ownership laws should make it...? Dependent	.198	.046	3.896	.000
			Gender Dependent	.161	.050	2.951	.003
		man Kruskal	Gun ownership laws should make it...? Dependent	.066	.018		.000[c]
			Gender Dependent	.066	.018		.000[c]
High	Nominal by Nominal	Lambda	Symmetric	.055	.028	1.897	.058
			Gun ownership laws should make it...? Dependent	.000	.000	.[d]	.[d]
			Gender Dependent	.100	.050	1.897	.058
		Goodman and Kruskal tau	Gun ownership laws should make it...? Dependent	.031	.014		.000[c]
			Gender Dependent	.031	.014		.000[c]

Use the dependent variable in your hypothesis to pick the appropriate lambda.

a. Not assuming the null hypothesis.

b. Using the asymptotic standard error assuming the null hypothesis.

c. Based on chi-square approximation

d. Cannot be computed because the asymptotic standard error equals zero.

SPSS Processor is ready

❏ In comparing individuals, women will be more likely than men to think that abortion should "always" be allowed.

❏ In comparing individuals, women will be less likely than men to think that women should play a role in work and politics.

❏ In comparing individuals, women will be no more likely than men to think that women should play a role in work and politics.

❏ In comparing individuals, women will be more likely than men to think that women should play a role in work and politics.

B. Test pedantic pontificator's hypotheses using SPSS Crosstabs. GSS2002.sav contains two variables that will serve as dependent variables. The variable abchoice, a measure of abortion opinions, ranges from 0 ("never allow") to 3 ("always allow"). The variable femrole3, which measures attitudes toward the role of women in work and politics, ranges from 1 ("women domestic") to 3 ("women in work, politics"). The independent variable is sex. Obtain Chi-square. Because sex is a nominal variable, be sure to request lambda and Cramer's V. In the abchoice-sex cross-tabulation, focus on the percentage saying "always allow." In the femrole3-sex cross-tabulation, focus on the "women in work, politics" category. Record your results in the table that follows.

Dependent variable	Sex		Chi-square		Measures of association	
	Male	Female	Test statistic	P-value	Lambda	Cramer's V
Percent "always allow" (abchoice)						
Percent "women in work politics" (femrole3)						

C. Based on these results, you may conclude that (check all that apply)

❏ a statistically significant gender gap exists on abortion opinions.

❏ pedantic pontificator's hypothesis about the femrole3-sex relationship appears to be incorrect.

❏ the abchoice-sex relationship you obtained could have occurred by chance more frequently than 5 times out of 100.

❏ pedantic pontificator's hypothesis about the abchoice-sex relationship appears to be correct.

❏ a higher percentage of females than males think that women belong in work and politics.

D. (Fill in the blanks.) The value of lambda for the femrole3-sex relationship is equal to _____. This means that, compared with how well you can predict _____ by not knowing _____, by knowing _____ you can improve your predictive accuracy by about _____ percent.

3. While having lunch together, three researchers are discussing what the terms *liberal*, *moderate*, and *conservative* mean to most people. Each researcher is touting a favorite independent variable that may explain the way survey respondents describe themselves ideologically.

Researcher 1: "When people are asked a question about their ideological views, they think about their attitudes toward government spending. If people think the government should spend more on important programs, they will respond that they are 'liberal.' If they don't want too much spending, they will say that they are 'conservative.' "

Researcher 2: "Well, that's fine. But let's not forget about social policies, such as abortion and pornography. These issues must influence how people describe themselves ideologically. People with more permissive views on these sorts of issues will call themselves 'liberal.' People who favor government restrictions will label themselves as 'conservative.' "

Researcher 3: "Okay, you both make good points. But you're ignoring the importance of racial issues in American politics. When asked whether they are liberal or conservative, people probably think about their opinions on racial policies, such as affirmative action. Stronger proponents of racial equality will say they are 'liberal,' and weaker proponents will say they are 'conservative.'"

In an earlier chapter of this book, you created an ordinal measure of ideology, polview3, which is coded 1 for "liberal," 2 for "moderate," and 3 for "conservative." This is the dependent variable. GSS2002.sav also contains researcher 1's favorite independent variable, spend3, a three-category ordinal measure of attitudes toward government spending. Higher codes denote more favorable opinions toward spending. Researcher 2's favorite independent variable is social, a three-category ordinal measure of attitudes on social issues. Higher codes denote less permissive views. Researcher 3's favorite independent variable is racial, also a three-category ordinal variable. Higher codes denote more strongly egalitarian opinions on racial issues.

A. Think about how SPSS calculates Kendall's statistics. Assuming that each researcher is correct, SPSS should report (check all that apply)

❏ a negative relationship between polview3 and spend3.

❏ a positive relationship between polview3 and social.

❏ a negative relationship between polview3 and racial.

B. Run a Crosstabs analysis of each of the relationships, using polview3 as the dependent variable and spend3, social, and racial as independent variables. Obtain Chi-square. Because each relationship will produce a square cross-tabulation, request Kendall's tau-b. Examine the cross-tabulations and chi-square statistics. Based on these results, you may conclude that (check all that apply)

❏ as values of spend3 increase, the percentage of respondents describing themselves as liberal increases.

❏ as values of spend3 increase, the percentage of respondents describing themselves as liberal decreases.

❏ the polview3-social relationship is not statistically significant.

❏ if the null hypothesis is correct, you will obtain the polview3-racial relationship more frequently than 5 times out of 100.

❏ if the null hypothesis is correct, you will obtain the polview3-racial relationship less frequently than 5 times out of 100.

C. Kendall's tau-b for the polview3-social relationship is equal to _____. Thus compared with how well we can predict polview3 by not knowing social, using social as a predictive tool increases our predictive accuracy by about _____ percent.

D. The three researchers make a friendly wager. The researcher whose favorite independent variable does the worst job predicting values of the dependent variable has to buy lunch for the other two. Who pays for lunch (circle one)?

Researcher 1   Researcher 2   Researcher 3

4. Certainly you would expect partisanship and attitudes toward trade unions to be related. Unions have been mainstays of Democratic support since the New Deal of the 1930s, so you could hypothesize that people holding pro-union opinions are more likely to be Democrats than are people who are less favorably disposed toward unions. Yet it also seems reasonable to hypothesize that the relationship between union opinions (independent variable) and party identification (dependent variable) will not be the same for all age groups. It may be that, among older cohorts—those socialized into politics during or shortly after the New Deal—

8

Correlation and Linear Regression

Correlation and regression are powerful and flexible techniques used to analyze interval-level relationships. Pearson's correlation coefficient (Pearson's r) measures the strength and direction of the relationship between two interval-level variables. Pearson's r is not a proportional reduction in error (PRE) measure, but it does gauge strength by an easily understood scale—from –1, a perfectly negative association between the variables, to +1, a perfectly positive relationship. A correlation of 0 indicates no relationship. Researchers often use correlation techniques in the beginning stages of analysis to get an overall picture of the relationships between interesting variables.

Regression analysis produces a statistic, the regression coefficient, that estimates the effect of an independent variable on a dependent variable. Regression also produces a PRE measure of association, R-square, which indicates how completely the independent variable (or variables) explains the dependent variable. In regression analysis the dependent variable is measured at the interval level, but the independent variable can be of any variety—nominal, ordinal, or interval. Regression is more specialized than correlation. Researchers use regression analysis to model causal relationships between one or more independent variables and a dependent variable.

In the first part of this chapter, you will learn to perform correlation analysis using the SPSS Correlate procedure. You will learn to use Interactive Scatterplot, which yields a visual depiction of the relationship between two interval-level variables. Interactive Scatterplot also calculates basic regression statistics and fits a regression line to the data. In the second part of the chapter, you will run regression analysis using SPSS Regression → Linear. You will learn to perform bivariate regression and multiple regression. Bivariate regression uses one independent variable to predict a dependent variable, whereas multiple regression uses two or more independent variables to predict a dependent variable.

USING CORRELATE AND INTERACTIVE SCATTERPLOT

Suppose that a student of state politics is interested in the gender composition of state legislatures. Using SPSS Descriptives to analyze States.sav, this student finds that state legislatures range from 6 percent female to 40 percent female. (This student could be you, since you now know how to use Descriptives.) Why is there such variation in the female composition of state legislatures? The student researcher begins to formulate an explanation. Perhaps states with lower percentages of college graduates have lower percentages of women legislators than do states with more college-educated residents. And maybe a cultural variable, the percentage of Christian adherents, plays a role. Perhaps states with higher percentages of Christian residents have lower percentages of female lawmakers. Correlation analysis would give this researcher an overview of the relationships among these variables. Let's use SPSS Correlate and Interactive Scatterplot to investigate.

Open States.sav. In the SPSS menu bar, click Analyze → Correlate → Bivariate. The SPSS Bivariate Correlations window is a no-frills interface (Figure 8-1). The researcher simply clicks any variables of interest into the Variables panel. We are interested in three variables: the percentage of Christian adherents

Figure 8–1 Bivariate Correlations Window

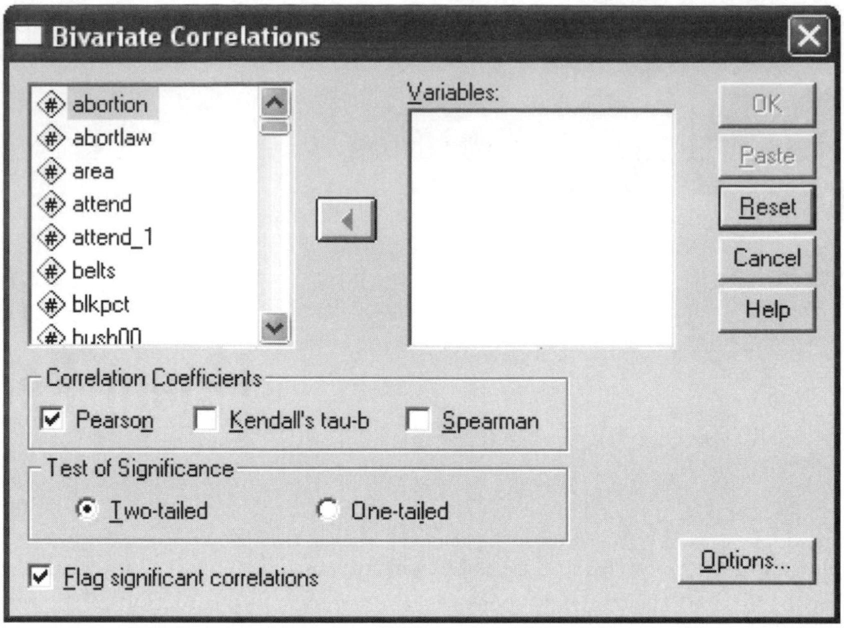

(christad), the percentage of college graduates (college), and the percentage of female state legislators (womleg). Click each of these variables into the Variables panel. By default, SPSS will return Pearson's correlation coefficients. So the Pearson box, which is already checked, suits our purpose. Click OK. SPSS reports the results in the SPSS Viewer (Figure 8-2).

The Correlations table, called a correlation matrix, shows the correlation of each variable with each of the other variables—it even shows the correlation between each variable and itself! Each of the correlations in which we are interested appears twice in the table: once above the upper-left-to-lower-right diagonal of 1s, and again below the diagonal. The correlation between christad and womleg is −.570, which tells us that increasing values of one of the variables is associated with decreasing values of the other variable. So as the percentage of Christian adherents goes up, the percentage of female legislators goes down. How strong is the relationship? We know that Pearson's r is bracketed by −1 and +1, so we could say that this relationship is a fairly strong negative association. The correlation between college and womleg, .410, indicates a positive relationship: As states' percentages of college graduates increase, so do their percentages of women legislators. This association is weaker, however, than the christad-womleg relationship. Finally, christad and college, with a Pearson's r of −.139, are weakly related. This value for Pearson's correlation coefficient suggests, of course, that the relationship has no clear, systematic pattern.

Producing and Editing a Scatterplot

Correlation analysis is a good place to start when analyzing interval-level relationships. One of SPSS's graphics routines, Interactive Scatterplot, can help to paint a richer portrait of a relationship. Interactive Scatterplot produces a graphic that plots all the cases in a two-dimensional space according to their values on two variables. The horizontal axis is defined by an independent variable (such as christad), and the vertical axis is defined by a dependent variable (such as womleg). Another SPSS graphics routine, Scatter, also produces a scatterplot. Interactive Scatterplot and Scatter are both good. But Interactive Scatterplot is better suited for our purposes in this chapter because it can be tailored to report regression estimates. Therefore, in this chapter we illustrate the use of Interactive Scatterplot.

Click Graphs → Interactive → Scatterplot. The Create Scatterplot window is different from any window we have discussed thus far in this book (Figure 8-3). It has five tabs: Assign Variables (the opening, main-tab window), Fit, Spikes, Titles, and Options. In the Assign Variables tab window we tell SPSS which variables to assign to the horizontal and vertical axes of the scatterplot. Notice the strange black arrow that runs vertically, interrupted by an elongated box near the top of the Assign Variables tab window. This means "put the vertical axis variable in this box." Similarly, the horizontal arrow, which is interrupted by another elongated

Figure 8–2 Correlation Matrix

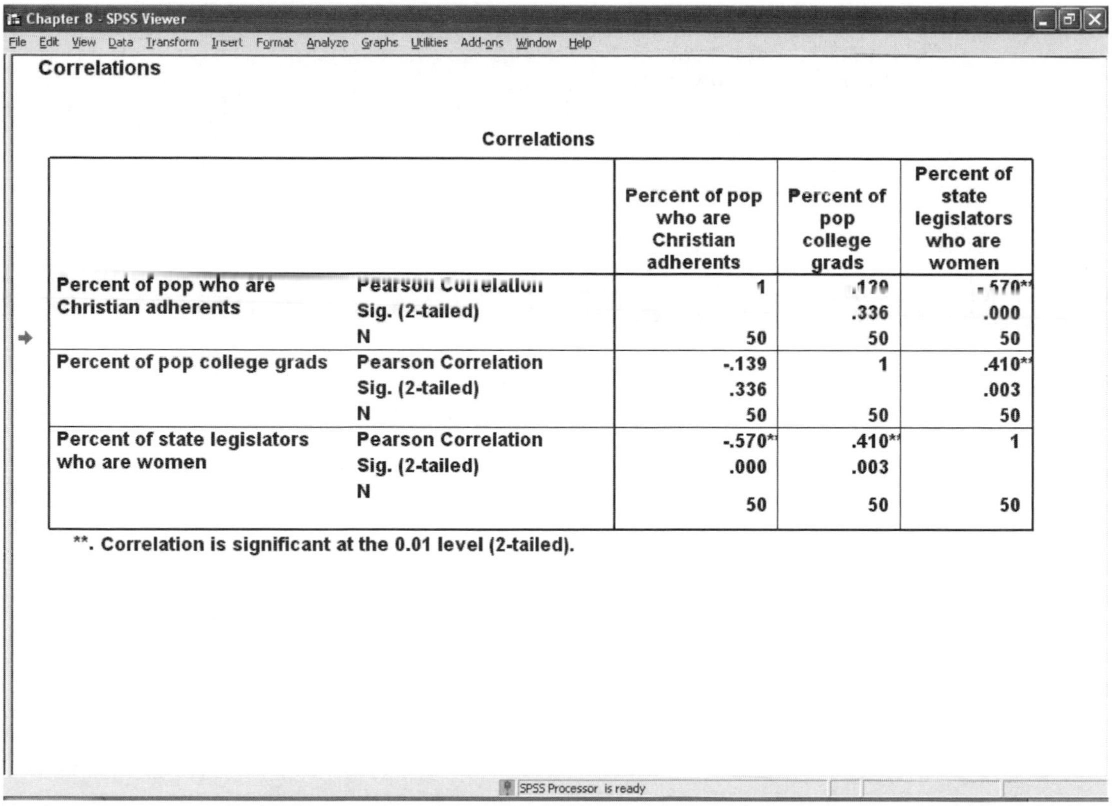

Correlations

Correlations

		Percent of pop who are Christian adherents	Percent of pop college grads	Percent of state legislators who are women
Percent of pop who are Christian adherents	Pearson Correlation	1	.139	-.570**
	Sig. (2-tailed)		.336	.000
	N	50	50	50
Percent of pop college grads	Pearson Correlation	-.139	1	.410**
	Sig. (2-tailed)	.336		.003
	N	50	50	50
Percent of state legislators who are women	Pearson Correlation	-.570**	.410**	1
	Sig. (2-tailed)	.000	.003	
	N	50	50	50

**. Correlation is significant at the 0.01 level (2-tailed).

Figure 8–3 Create Scatterplot Window: Assign Variables Tab

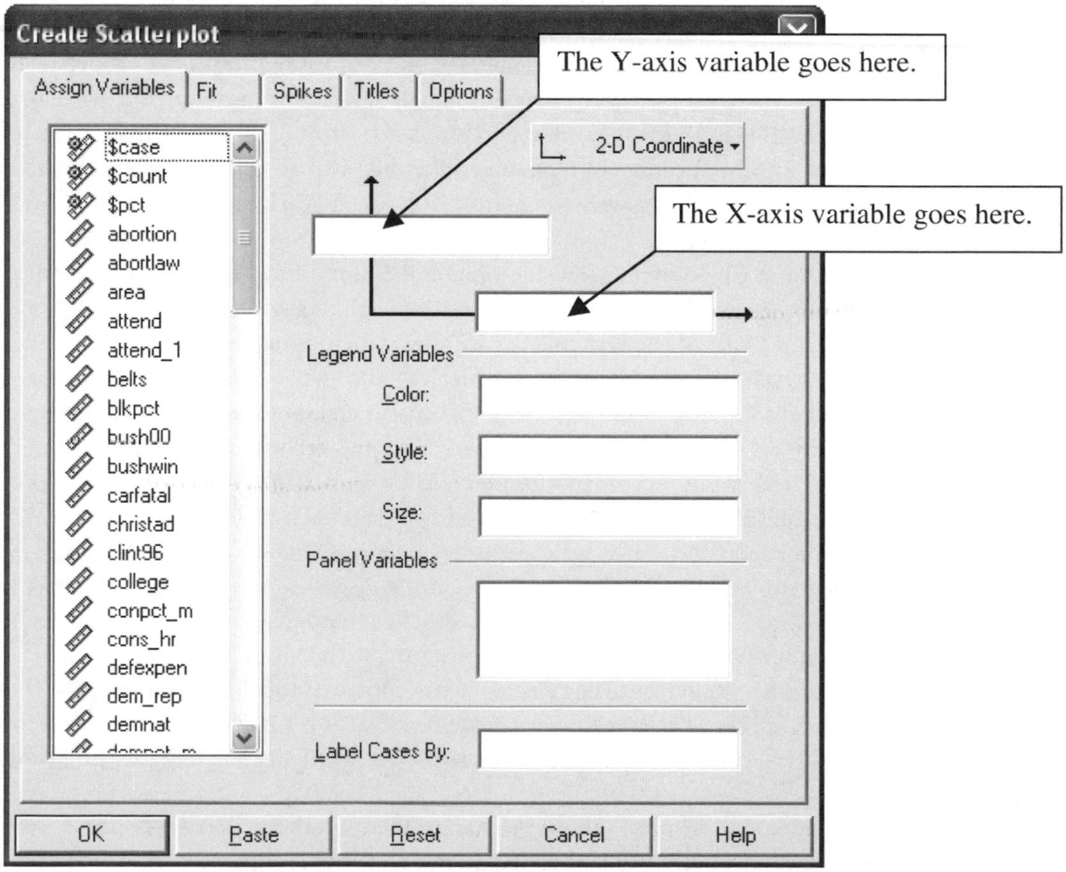

Figure 8–4   Create Scatterplot Window: Assign Variables Tab (modified)

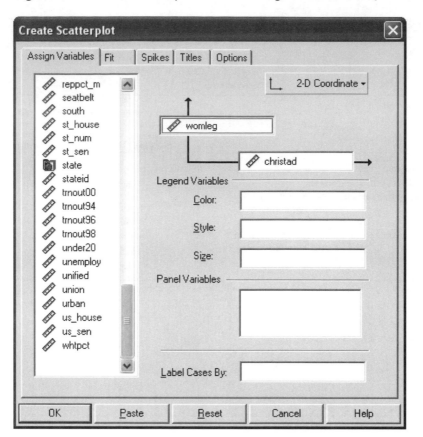

box, means "put the horizontal axis variable in this box." In other SPSS procedures we have discussed, the user selects variables in the variable list and clicks them into an analysis panel. In Interactive Scatterplot you select a variable for analysis by dragging it from the variable list and dropping it in the appropriate box—something different for a change. We want the percentage of female legislators to define the vertical axis, so locate womleg in the variable list, "grip" it by keeping the left mouse button depressed, drag it over, and drop it in the vertical axis box.[1] The percentage of Christian adherents will go on the horizontal axis. Find christad, and then drag and drop it in the horizontal axis box. The Assign Variables tab window should now look like Figure 8-4.

There is one more thing to do: Click the Options tab (Figure 8-5). In typical fashion SPSS permits the user to customize output in many ways. For our purposes, all of the defaults will work fine—with one exception. Notice the lower right-hand panel of the Options tab window, which is labeled "Axes." By default SPSS will construct a scatterplot that has a 3-inch Y-axis and a 3-inch X-axis. In a two-variable scatterplot, such as the one we are creating, SPSS calls the horizontal axis "X1." (SPSS also creates three-variable scatterplots. In these it labels the additional axis "X2." Ignore the X2 box.) Let's leave the vertical axis at 3 inches but change the horizontal axis to 4 inches, making the scatterplot more readable.[2] Click in the X1 box, delete "3.00," and type "4" in its place. (Just type "4." SPSS will automatically add two decimal points, "4.00.") Click OK. SPSS runs Interactive Scatterplot and constructs a graphic to our specifications (Figure 8-6).

We know from our earlier run that Pearson's r for this relationship is –.570. The scatterplot gives us a clearer idea of what the correlation "looks like." As you can see, states that have lower percentages of Christian adherents tend to have higher percentages of women legislators, with values on the Y-axis that range between roughly 20 percent and 35–40 percent. The percentages of women legislators for states at the higher end of the X-axis, furthermore, fall between less than 10 percent and around 20 percent. So as you move from left to right along the X-axis, values on the Y-axis generally decline, just as the negative correlation coefficient suggested.

Let's do some basic editing of this graphic. Double-click anywhere on the scatterplot. This activates the interactive editing toolbars, which appear around the sides of the scatterplot (Figure 8-7). There are, of

Figure 8–5 Create Scatterplot Window: Options Tab

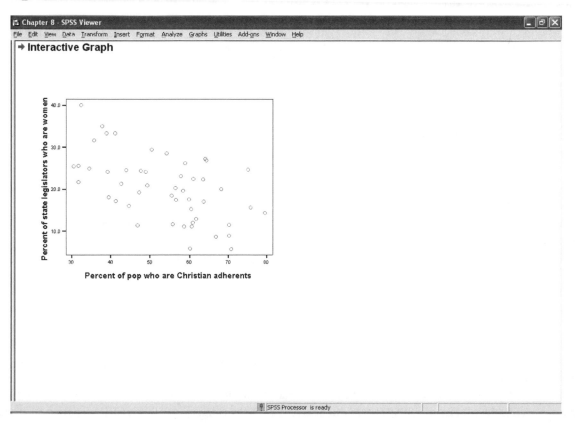

Figure 8–6 Interactive Scatterplot

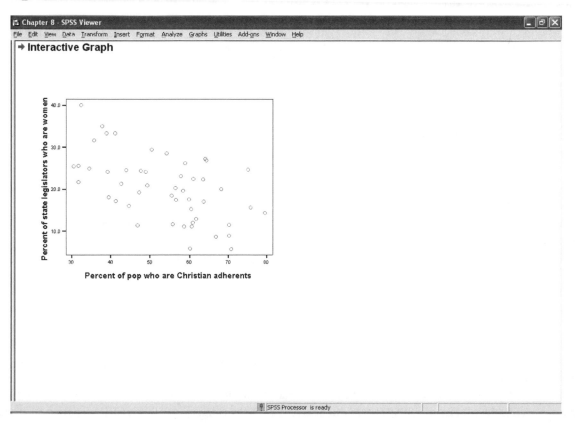

Figure 8–7   Interactive Scatterplot, Ready for Editing

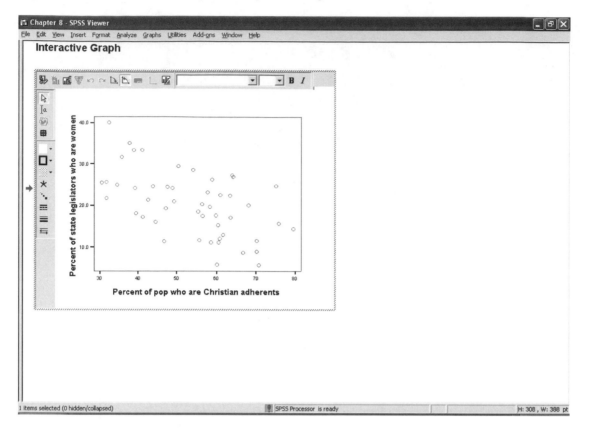

course, many changes that you can make to the appearance of the graph. You may want to experiment. (Don't worry. If the scatterplot gets messed up, you can always rerun the analysis.) We will do three things: make the dots solid and a little larger (the current empty dots do not print well), change the Y-axis title, and change the X-axis title. Put the cursor on any dot and double-click. This opens the Cloud window, as shown in Figure 8-8. (SPSS collectively refers to the symbols inside a scatterplot as a "cloud.") Click Style and select one of the solid symbols, such as the solid dot. Click Size and select a larger size, such as 7 point or 8 point. Click Apply, and then click OK. We've now got larger, solid dots. Let's make the wordy Y-axis title more concise. Double-click anywhere on the current title: "Percent of state legislators who are women." SPSS relocates the title to a convenient editing spot, across the top of the graphic. Change the title to read "State legislators: % women." (As soon as you click anywhere else on the scatterplot, SPSS will replace the old title with the new one.) Now double-click on the X-axis title. Change it to read "State population: % Christian adherents." Looks better. Click anywhere outside the editing toolbars. The newly edited scatterplot is now part of the output file (Figure 8-9).

Obtaining Regression Estimates

So that you can become comfortable using Interactive Scatterplot, and to demonstrate its application to regression analysis, let's run the routine again—with a couple of modifications. This time we will obtain a scatterplot of the womleg-college relationship. We will also ask SPSS to fit a regression line to the data points.

Click Graphs → Interactive → Scatterplot. All of our choices from the last run should still be in place. For this run we want college to define the horizontal axis. Remove christad from the horizontal axis box by dragging it out of the box and dropping it back into the variable list. (Drop it anywhere in the variable list. SPSS will return it to its proper position in the list.) Find college, and then drag and drop it into the horizontal axis box. Now click the Fit tab. Click the drop-down menu in the Method panel. Select Regression, as shown in Figure 8-10. All set. Click OK. SPSS creates a scatterplot, just as before, only this time it fits a regression line to the data (Figure 8-11).

Later we can tidy up this somewhat cluttered display. But first let's consider the substantive meaning of the regression line. How did SPSS figure out where the line should go? SPSS ran ordinary least squares,

Figure 8–8 Editing Cloud Points and Axis Titles

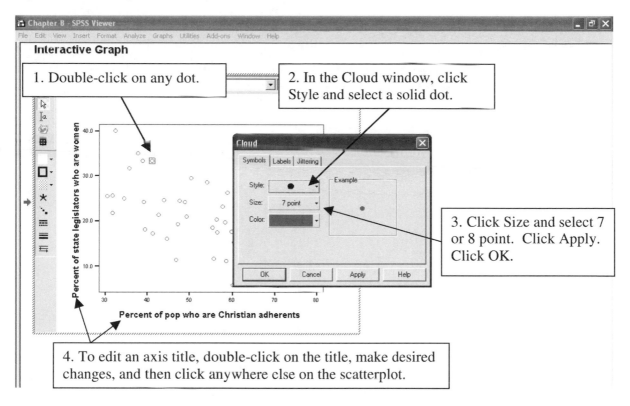

Figure 8–9 Edited Interactive Scatterplot

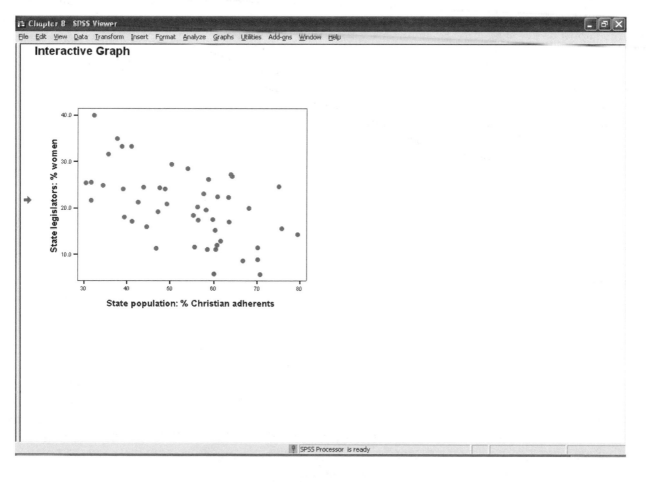

Figure 8–10   Create Scatterplot Window: Fit Tab

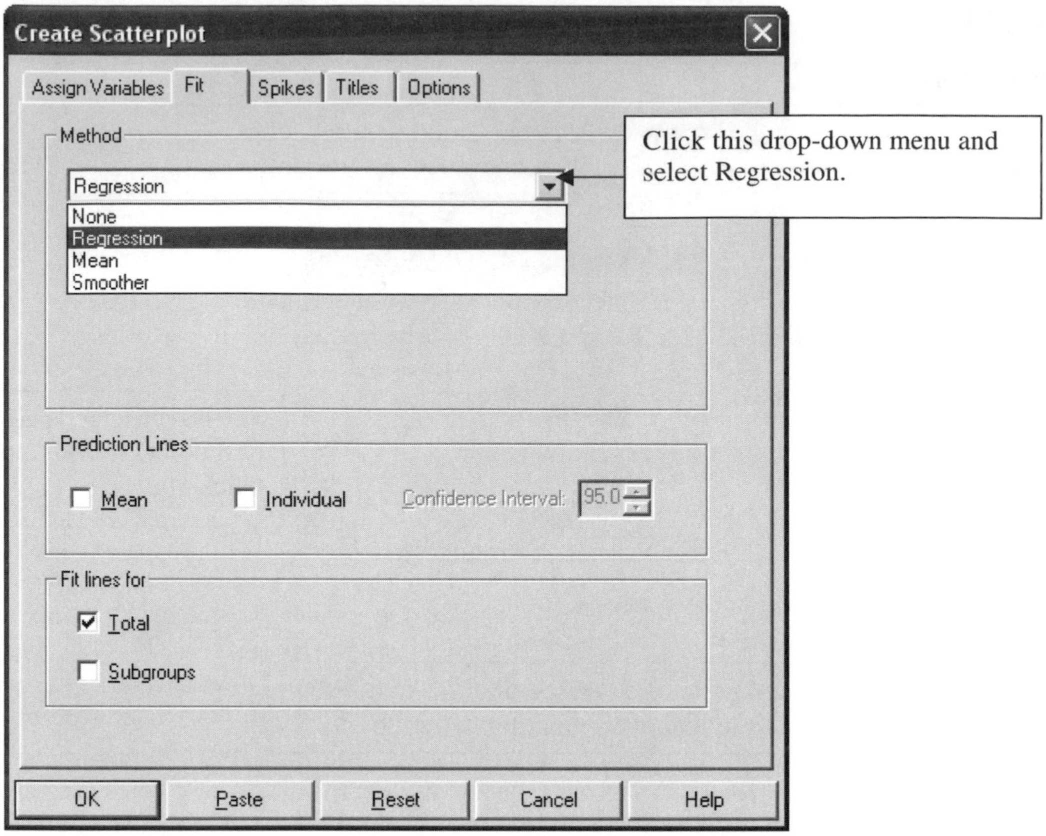

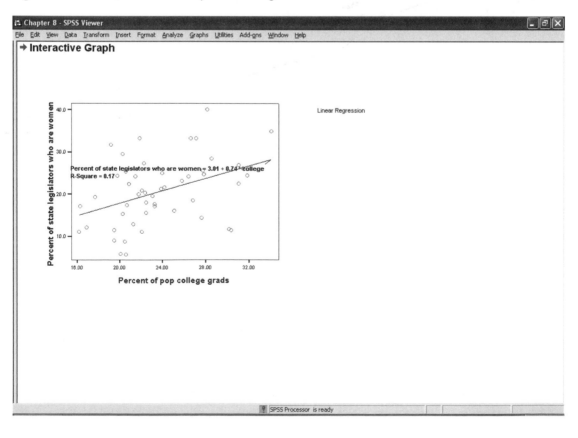

Figure 8–11   Interactive Scatterplot with Regression Fit

or OLS, regression, using the percentage of legislators who are women (womleg) as the dependent variable and the percentage of college graduates (college) as the independent variable. It superimposed the best-fitting OLS line on the scatterplot and labeled the equation with this text:

Percent of state legislators who are women = 3.01 + 0.74*college.

The constant, 3.01, is the Y-intercept, the estimated value of Y when X equals 0. If you were using this equation to estimate the percentage of women legislators for a state, you would start with 3.01 percent and then add .74 for each percentage of the state's population with a college degree. So your estimate for a state with, say, 10 percent college graduates would be 3.01 + .74 * 10, or about 10.4 percent female legislators. The main statistic of interest, then, is the regression coefficient, .74, which estimates the average change in the dependent variable for each unit change in the independent variable. A regression coefficient of .74 tells us that, for each 1-unit increase in the percentage of college graduates, there is a .74-unit increase in the percentage of female legislators. So a 1-percentage-point increase in college is associated with a .74-percentage-point increase in womleg.[3]

Now take a step back from the regression equation and contemplate the overall pattern of dots. You can discern the positive relationship reported by the regression coefficient. By and large, states toward the lower end of the X-axis have lower percentages of female lawmakers than do states at the upper end of the X-axis. But clearly this relationship is not terribly systematic. After all, many states have lower percentages of women legislators than the regression would predict, and many have higher percentages of women legislators than the regression would predict. Our earlier correlation analysis revealed a Pearson's r of .410, a modestly positive association. The R-square statistic, which accompanies the regression analysis, provides a more precise measure of strength. According to SPSS, R-square is equal to .17. What does this mean? R-square communicates the proportion of the variation in the dependent variable that is explained by the independent variable. Like any proportion, R-square can assume any value between 0 and 1. Thus, of all the variation in womleg between states, .17, or 17 percent, is explained by college. The rest of the variation in womleg, 83 percent, remains unexplained by the independent variable.

Before moving on to a more detailed discussion of regression, let's edit the scatterplot to make it more presentable. To invoke the editing functions, double-click on the graphic. We will make several appearance-enhancing changes. As we did before, we will make the dots solid and larger. Go ahead and do this. And, as before, we will modify the Y-axis title to read "State legislators: % women." Go ahead and make this change, too. (The X-axis title is all right, so we'll leave it alone.)

Let's make some further changes. First, we will move the intrusive regression equation label to the top of the graphic, just above the upper border. Click and "hold" anywhere on the equation label "Percent of state legislators who are women = 3.01 + 0.74*college." Drag it up, off of the scatterplot, and bring it to rest just above the upper border, as shown in Figure 8-12. Next we will improve the regression line's appearance. Place the cursor anywhere on the equation label and double-click. The Regression Parameters window opens (see Figure 8-12). In the Regression Parameters window, click Options, which opens the Regression Options window (Figure 8-13). There are two tabs here: an Appearance tab and a Key tab. In the Line panel of the Appearance tab, click Weight and select a heavier weight, such as 1½ point. In the Label panel, click Connector and select None, eliminating the reference line SPSS uses to connect the regression label and the regression line. Now click on the Key tab and uncheck the Display Key box. Click Apply, and then click OK. Return to the SPSS Viewer by clicking anywhere outside the editing toolbars. Your finished product should now look similar to Figure 8-14. A scatterplot like this one would provide professional-quality graphic support to a research report or article. Nicely done.

USING REGRESSION → LINEAR

When you request a regression fit from Interactive Scatterplot, you end up with useful—but very basic—regression statistics: the Y-intercept, the regression coefficient, and R-square. The SPSS Regression routine provides a much more detailed array of information about the exact nature of the relationship between the independent and dependent variables. In addition to other essential statistics, SPSS Regression will give you the information you need to test hypotheses about the effect of the independent variable on the dependent variable. In this section we first will demonstrate how to obtain and interpret regression output for bivariate

Figure 8–12 Moving the Equation Label and Opening the Regression Parameters Window

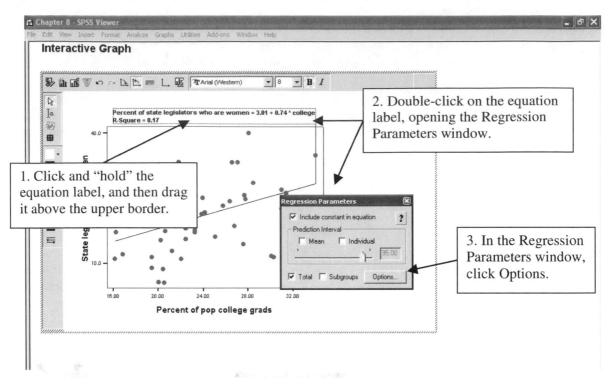

Figure 8–13 Regressions Options Window

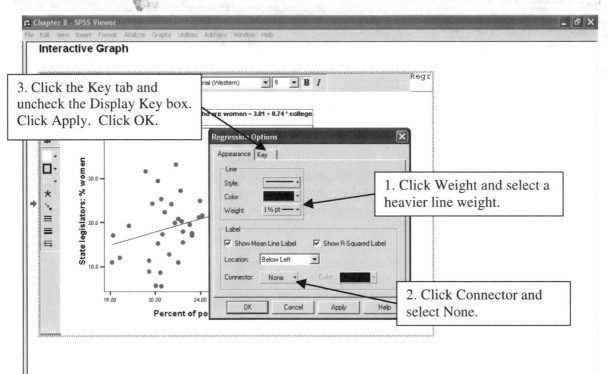

regression. We then will run a multiple regression analysis, one that uses more than one independent variable to predict a dependent variable.

Suppose a policy researcher is investigating factors causally related to motor vehicle deaths in the states. One such factor might be a simple characteristic of states: their population density. Residents of sparsely populated states, the policy researcher reasons, would typically drive longer distances at higher speeds than would residents of more densely populated states. Plus, a car accident in a thinly populated state would be

Figure 8–14 Edited Interactive Scatterplot with Regression Fit

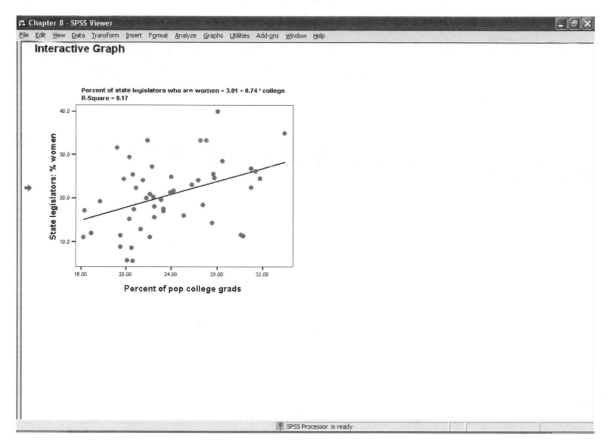

more likely to be fatal, because "both Good Samaritans and hospitals are more scattered in thinly populated states compared to the denser states."[4] So as density goes up, we should find that fatalities go down. Another variable might be demographic: the proportion of young people in the population. As every insurance agent knows—and as many premium-paying parents will attest—younger drivers are more likely to be involved in automobile accidents than are older drivers. Thus, as the proportion of younger people goes up, fatalities should be found to go up, too.

States.sav contains three variables: carfatal, the number of motor vehicle deaths per 100,000 residents; density, state population per square mile; and under20, the percentage of the population 19 years of age or younger. A preliminary correlation analysis of these three variables (which, of course, you are welcome to repeat) produced this correlation matrix:

	Carfatal Motor vehicle fatalities (per 100,000 pop.)	Density Pop. per square mile	Under20 Percentage of pop. age 19 or younger
Motor vehicle fatalities (per 100,000 pop.)	1	−.619	.440
Pop. per square mile	−.619	1	−.496
Percentage of pop. age 19 or younger	.440	−.496	1

Note the correlation between each independent variable and the dependent variable. The correlation between density and carfatal is negative, indicating that as density increases, motor vehicle fatalities decrease (r = −.619). The relationship between under20 and carfatal, as the policy researcher suspected, is positive: As the percentage of young people increases, fatalities also increase (r = .440). But notice, too, that the two

Figure 8–15 Linear Regression Window

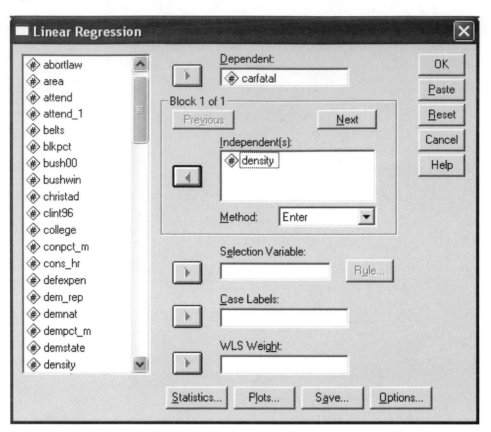

independent variables are themselves moderately related (r = –.496). This correlation is negative, suggesting that densely populated states have lower percentages of young people than do sparsely populated states. (This relationship may become important later on.)

Let's run a simple regression, using carfatal as the dependent variable and density as the independent variable. Click Analyze → Regression → Linear. The Linear Regression window appears. Click carfatal into the Dependent box. Find density in the variable list and click it into the Independent(s) box, as shown in Figure 8-15. Click OK.

SPSS regression output includes four tables: "Variables Entered/Removed," "Model Summary," "ANOVA" (which stands for "analysis of variance"), and "Coefficients." For the regression analyses you will perform in this book, the Model Summary table and the Coefficients table contain the most important information. The regression output for these tables is pictured in Figure 8-16. First, consider the Coefficients table. The leftmost column, under the heading "Model," contains the names of the key elements in the regression equation. "Constant" is the Y-intercept of the regression line, and "Population per square mile" is the label of the independent variable. The numbers along the "Constant" row report statistics about the Y-intercept, and the numbers along the "Population per square mile" row report statistics about the independent variable. Now look at the first column of numbers, which shows the regression coefficient for each parameter. According to these values, the Y-intercept is equal to 20.278, and the regression coefficient is –.014. (If you are running SPSS 11.5 or earlier, SPSS may have expressed the regression coefficient using scientific notation, –1.4E–02, meaning "move the decimal point two places to the left.") The regression equation for the effect of density on carfatal, therefore, is

Motor vehicle fatalities per 100,000 pop. = 20.278 –.014*pop. per square mile.

What do these coefficients mean? In terms of its magnitude, for example, the regression coefficient seems to be an incredibly small number, and its meaning is not intuitively obvious. Remember to keep the substantive relationship in mind—and focus on the units of measurement. Very thinly populated states will have an estimated fatality rate close to the intercept, or about 20 fatalities per 100,000 population. Alaska, for exam-

Figure 8–16   Bivariate Regression Output

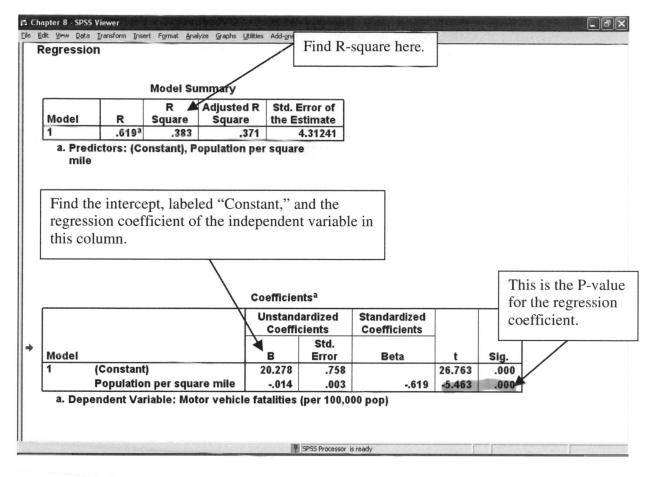

a. Predictors: (Constant), Population per square mile

a. Dependent Variable: Motor vehicle fatalities (per 100,000 pop)

ple, has a population density of just more than 1 person per square mile. So its estimated fatality rate would be close to the intercept of 20. The regression coefficient tells us that, for each additional *person* per square mile, the motor vehicle fatality rate drops by .014. New Jersey, for instance, is a very densely populated state, with a density of about 1,000 people per square mile. So New Jersey's estimated fatality rate would be 20 − .014 * 1000, which is equal to 20 − 14, or about 6 fatalities per 100,000 population. Thus, as density increases, by one person at a time, fatalities decrease by .014 of a fatality per 100,000 population.

What would the null hypothesis have to say about all this? Of course, we are not analyzing a random sample here, because we have information on the entire population of 50 states. But let's assume, for illustrative purposes, that we have just analyzed a random sample and that we have obtained a sample estimate of the effect of density on carfatal. The null hypothesis would say what it always says: In the population from which the sample was drawn, no relationship exists between the independent variable (in this case, population density) and the dependent variable (automobile fatalities). In the population the true regression coefficient is equal to 0. Furthermore, the regression coefficient that we obtained, −.014, occurred by chance. In SPSS Regression output, you test the null hypothesis by examining the last two columns of the Coefficients table: "t," which reports t-ratios, and "Sig.," which reports P-values. Informally, in order to safely reject the null hypothesis, the researcher generally looks for t-ratios with magnitudes (absolute values) of 2 or greater. According to the results of our analysis, the regression coefficient for density has a t-ratio of −5.463, well above the informal 2-or-greater rule. A P-value, which tells you the probability of obtaining the results if the null hypothesis is correct, helps you to make more precise inferences about the relationship between the independent variable and the dependent variable. If "Sig." is greater than .05, then the observed results would occur too frequently by chance, and you must not reject the null hypothesis. By contrast, if "Sig." is equal to or less than .05, then the null hypothesis represents an unlikely occurrence and may be rejected. The t-ratio for density has a corresponding P-value of .000. If the null is correct, it is highly unlikely that we would obtain these results.[5] Reject the null hypothesis. It depends on the research problem at hand, of course, but for most applications you can ignore the t-ratio and P-value for the constant.[6]

Figure 8–17 Bivariate Regression Output (modified)

a. Dependent Variable: Motor vehicle fatalities (per 100,000 pop)

Now direct your attention to the Model Summary table. Here we find R-square, an overall measure of how well population density explains motor vehicle fatalities. According to the Model Summary table, R-square is equal to .383. Thus, of all the variation among states in automobile fatality rates, about 38 percent is explained by population density. As bivariate regression models go, that's not too bad.

Now let's run another bivariate regression. We will keep carfatal as the dependent variable, but this time we'll use the percentage of the population 19 years old or younger (under20) as the independent variable. Because you now know how to use SPSS Regression, this will be an abbreviated example. Return to the Linear Regression window. Click density back into the variable list. Locate under20 and click it into the Independent(s) panel. Click OK.

Examine the Coefficients table and the Model Summary table (Figure 8-17). What is the regression line for the effect of under20 on carfatal? It is

Motor vehicle fatalities per 100,000 pop. = −13.174 + 1.07*percentage of pop. age 19 or younger.

As is sometimes the case with regression, the constant, −13.174, represents an "unreal" situation. The estimated value of carfatal for states with a value of 0 on the independent variable is a *minus* 13.174 motor vehicle deaths per 100,000 residents. Of course, the smallest value of under20 in the actual data is substantially higher than 0.[7] However, for the regression line to produce the best estimates for real data, SPSS Regression has anchored the line at a Y-intercept. The regression coefficient, 1.070, says that for each percentage-point increase in under20, there is a bit more than a one-unit increase in the motor vehicle fatality rate—one additional fatality per 100,000 population. As the percentage of younger people in the population increases, so too does the fatality rate. In the population, could the true value of the regression coefficient be 0? Probably not, according to the t-ratio (3.395) and the P-value (.001). And, according to R-square, the independent variable does a fair amount of work in explaining the dependent variable. About 19 percent of the variation in carfatal is explained by under20.

Figure 8–18 Multiple Regression Output

```
┌─ Chapter 8 - SPSS Viewer ──────────────────────────────────── _ ⊡ ✕ ┐
File  Edit  View  Data  Transform  Insert  Format  Analyze  Graphs  Utilities  Add-ons  Window  Help
```

Regression

Model Summary

Model	R	R Square	Adjusted R Square	Std. Error of the Estimate
1	.008ᵃ	.407	.381	4.27479

a. Predictors: (Constant), Population per square mile, Percent of pop age 19 or younger

Coefficientsᵃ

Model		Unstandardized Coefficients		Standardized Coefficients	t	Sig.
		B	Std. Error	Beta		
1	(Constant)	7.535	9.403		.801	.427
	Percent of pop age 19 or younger	.428	.315	.176	1.360	.180
	Population per square mile	-.012	.003	-.532	-4.109	.000

a. Dependent Variable: Motor vehicle fatalities (per 100,000 pop)

```
                                    SPSS Processor is ready
```

Note: ANOVA table not shown.

Let's review what we have found so far. In the first bivariate regression, we found that population density has a statistically significant negative effect on motor vehicle fatalities. Low-density states have higher fatality rates than do high-density states. In the second bivariate regression, we found that the percentage of younger people has a significant positive effect on motor vehicle fatalities. States with lower percentages of young people have lower fatality rates than do states with higher percentages of young people. But recall the initial correlation matrix. There we found that the two independent variables are related: As density goes up, the percentage of younger people goes down. So when we compare states with lower percentages of young people with states with higher percentages of young people, we are also comparing high-density states with low-density states. Perhaps states with higher percentages of young people have higher fatality rates not because they have more young people, but because they have lower population densities. Thus the relationship between under20 and carfatal might be spurious. Then again, it might not be. Unless we reexamine the under20-carfatal relationship, controlling for density, there is no way to tell.

Multiple regression is designed to estimate the partial effect of an independent variable on a dependent variable, controlling for the effects of other independent variables. SPSS Regression easily allows the researcher to run multiple regression analysis. Let's do such an analysis, again using carfatal as the dependent variable and entering *both* density and under20 as independent variables. Click Analyze → Regression → Linear. Under20 should still be in the Independent(s) panel. We will leave it there. Find density in the variable list and click it into the Independent(s) panel. Now SPSS will use both variables, under20 and density, to estimate carfatal. Click OK.

The Coefficients table and the Model Summary table provide the information we need to isolate the partial effect of each independent variable on the dependent variable (Figure 8-18). The multiple regression equation is

Motor vehicle fatalities per 100,000 pop. =
7.535 + .428*percentage of pop. age 19 or younger −.012*pop. per square mile.

Let's focus on the regression coefficients for each of the independent variables. The coefficient for under20, .428, tells us the effect of under20 on carfatal, controlling for density. Recall that in the bivariate analysis, a 1-percentage-point increase in under20 was associated with about a one-unit increase in the fatality rate. When we control for density, however, we find a substantial reduction in this effect—to less than a half-unit-increase in the fatality rate. What is more, the regression coefficient for under20, with a P-value of .180, is not statistically significant. Density, by contrast, retains much of its predictive power. The regression coefficient, –.012, is very close to the effect we found earlier when we investigated the bivariate relationship between carfatal and density. With a P-value of .000, we can say that, controlling for the percentage of young residents, population density is significantly related to motor vehicle fatalities. It would appear, then, that the carfatal-under20 relationship is a spurious artifact of differences between states in population density.

In multiple regression, R-square communicates how well all of the independent variables explain the dependent variable. So by knowing two things about states—the percentage of younger people and the population density—we can account for about 40 percent of the variation in motor vehicle death rates. But notice that this value of R-square is only slightly higher than the R-square we found before, using density by itself to explain carfatal. Clearly, density does the lion's share of explanatory work in accounting for the dependent variable.

EXERCISES

For the exercises in this chapter, you will analyze States.sav.

1. Consider a plausible scenario for the relationships between three variables: the percentages of a state's U.S. House and U.S. Senate delegations who are Democrats, the percentage of state legislators who are Democrats, and the percentage of workers in the state who are unionized. We could hypothesize that, compared with states with fewer Democrats in the state legislatures, states having larger percentages of Democratic legislators would also have greater proportions of Democrats in their U.S. congressional delegations. Furthermore, because unions tend to support Democratic candidates, we would also expect more heavily unionized states to have higher percentages of Democratic legislators at the state and national levels. States.sav contains three variables: demnat, the percentage of House and Senate members who are Democrats; demstate, the percentage of state legislators who are Democrats; and union, the percentage of workers who are union members.

   A. Run SPSS Correlate to find the Pearson correlation coefficients among demnat, demstate, and union. Fill in the four empty cells of this correlation matrix:

		Percent U.S. House and Senate Democratic	Percent state legislators Democratic	Percent workers who are union members
Percent U.S. House and Senate Democratic	Pearson Correlation	1	.559	
Percent state legislators Democratic	Pearson Correlation	.559	1	
Percent workers who are union members	Pearson Correlation			1

   B. According to the correlation coefficient, as the percentage of unionized workers increases, the percentage of Democratic U.S. representatives and U.S. senators (circle one)

   increases.   decreases.

   C. According to the correlation coefficient, as the percentage of unionized workers decreases, the percentage of Democratic U.S. representatives and U.S. senators (circle one)

   increases.   decreases.

_−1,848_

incorrect because _____

_____ _____ .

D. Run Regression → Linear to obtain multiple regression estimates for the partial effects of dempct_m and libpct_m on demstate. Demstate is the dependent variable, and dempct_m and libpct_m are the independent variables. Based on your results, the multiple regression for estimating the percentage of Democratic state legislators is

−27.143 + _____ * dempct_m + _____ * libpct_m.

E. The P-value for the regression coefficient on dempct_m is _____, and the P-value for the regression coefficient on libpct_m is _____.

F. As you may know, Nebraska's state legislature is unique in two ways: It is unicameral (all other state legislatures are bicameral), and it is nonpartisan. Candidates do not run for the state legislature using party labels, and the legislature is not organized on the basis of party. Thus Nebraska has a missing value on the variable demstate, and it was not included in the regression analysis you just performed. However, if you were to peruse States.sav, you would find that 29.03 percent of Nebraskans are Democrats and 16.44 percent are self-described liberals. For the sake of speculation, assume that Nebraska decided that all members of the state legislature should declare a partisan allegiance. Based on your regression model, about what percentage of state legislators would be Democrats (circle one)?

About 24 percent   About 36 percent   About 60 percent

G. Based on your interpretation of the multiple regression output, you can conclude that (check all that apply)

❑ controlling for the percentage of the mass public who are liberal, a 1-percentage-point increase in the percentage of Democrats in the mass public is associated with about a 5.8-percentage-point increase in the percentage of Democratic state legislators.

❑ controlling for the percentage of the mass public who are Democratic, a 1-percentage-point increase in the percentage of liberals in the mass public is associated with about a 1.5-percentage-point increase in the percentage of Democratic state legislators.

❑ both independent variables are significantly related to the dependent variable.

❑ the relationship between dempct_m and demstate is spurious.

❑ taken together, both independent variables explain about one-half of the variation in the dependent variable.

That concludes the exercises for this chapter. Before exiting SPSS, be sure to save your output file.

NOTES

1. The icon next to each variable in the variable list indicates that variable's level of measurement. The ruler icon denotes an interval-level, or "scale," measurement.
2. A graphic layout is characterized by its aspect ratio, the ratio of its length to its height. An aspect ratio of 4:3 (or 1.33:1) is a common and visually pleasing layout. Television screens—non-HDTV screens, anyway—have a 1.33:1 aspect ratio.
3. Regression analysis on variables measured by percentages can be confusing. Always stay focused on the exact units of measurement. One percentage point would be 1.00. So if college increases by 1.00, then womleg increases, on average, by .74, or .74 of a percentage point.
4. Edward R. Tufte, _Data Analysis for Politics and Policy_ (Englewood Cliffs, N.J.: Prentice Hall, 1974), 21. Tufte uses regression analysis to evaluate the effectiveness of motor vehicle inspections, controlling for population density.

5. SPSS Regression → Linear reports two-tailed P-values, not one-tailed P-values. Strictly speaking, then, you may correctly apply the .05 standard by rejecting the null hypothesis for any reported P-value of equal to or less than .10. However, in this book we follow the more conservative practice of rejecting the null hypothesis for P-values of equal to or less than .05.

6. The t-ratio for the Y-intercept permits you to test the null hypothesis that, in the population, the Y-intercept is 0. In this case it would be nonsensical to test the hypothesis that states having 0 population density have 0 car fatalities per 100,000 population.

7. If you do a quick Descriptives run, you will find that the lowest value of under20 is 25 percent.

9

Dummy Variables and Interaction Effects

You can adapt regression analysis to different research situations. In one situation you might have nominal or ordinal independent variables. Provided that these variables are dummy variables, you can run a regression analysis, using categorical variables to predict values of an interval-level dependent variable. In this chapter you will learn how to construct dummy variables and how to use them in regression analysis. In a second research situation you might suspect that the effect of one independent variable on the dependent variable is not the same for all values of another independent variable—in other words, that interaction is going on in the data. Provided that you have created an interaction variable, you can use multiple regression to estimate the size and statistical significance of interaction effects. In this chapter you will learn how to create an interaction variable and how to perform and interpret multiple regression with interaction effects.

REGRESSION WITH DUMMY VARIABLES

A dummy variable can take on only two values, 1 or 0. Each case being analyzed either has the characteristic being measured (a code of 1) or does not have it (a code of 0). For example, a dummy variable for gender might code females as 1 and males as 0. Everybody who is coded 1 has the characteristic of being female, and everybody who is coded 0 does not have that characteristic. An easy way to create a dummy variable in SPSS is to use the Transform → Recode → Into Different Variables transformation. In fact, one of the variables you created in Chapter 4, married, is a dummy variable. You created married by recoding the original variable, marital, into two categories: married (coded 1) and unmarried (coded 0). In this chapter's first guided example, you will create another dummy variable in NES2000.sav and run a dummy variable regression. Before beginning the example, open NES2000.sav.

In several examples of political analysis in this book, you have investigated the role of gender in shaping political attitudes and behavior. Let's figure out how to use gender as an independent variable in regression analysis. Gender is a nominal variable, coded 1 for males and 2 for females. Because of the way gender is currently coded, it cannot be used in regression analysis. But we can use gender to define a dummy variable named female. We want female to take on the values of 1 for females and 0 for males. We could assign these values by using Transform → Recode → Into Different Variables and applying this recoding scheme:

Respondent's gender	Old value (gender)	New value (female)
Male	1	0
Female	2	1
	Missing	Missing

You know how to use Transform → Recode → Into Different Variables, so go ahead and create female, which you can label "Female dummy." (Figure 9-1 helps to reacquaint you with the recode procedure.) To check

Figure 9–1 Recoding to Create a Dummy Variable

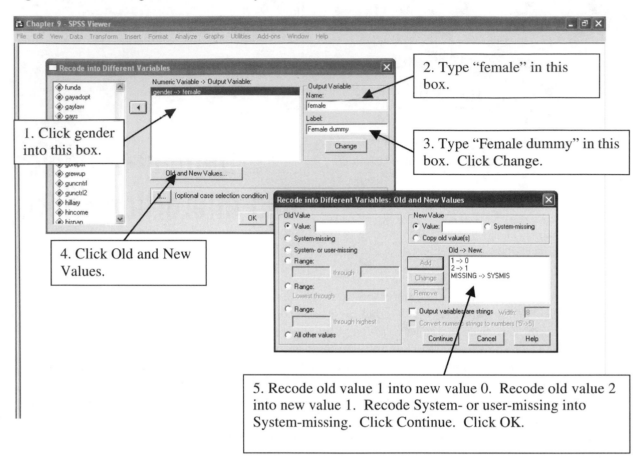

your work, run Frequencies on gender and female to ensure that the distributions are the same. If every-thing checks out, return to the Variable View, change Decimals to 0, and assign value labels to the dummy variable you have created ("Male" for value 0, "Female" for value 1).

Now let's run linear regression, using the Al Gore feeling thermometer (gorepre) as the dependent variable and female as the independent variable. Click Analyze → Regression → Linear. Click gorepre into the Dependent box, and click female into the Independent(s) box. Click OK. According to the Coefficients table (Figure 9-2), the regression equation is as follows:

$$\text{Al Gore thermometer rating} = 53.919 + 6.522 * \text{Female dummy}.$$

How would we interpret these estimates? Just as in any regression, the constant estimates the value of the dependent variable when the independent variable is 0. Because males have a value of 0 on the female dummy variable, the mean thermometer rating of Al Gore for males is 53.919, the Y-intercept. The regression coefficient on female tells us the mean change in the dependent variable for each unit change in the independent variable. So when female switches from 0 to 1, the Gore rating goes up, on average, about 6.5 degrees. Remember that the coefficient, 6.522, is not the mean for women. Rather, it is the mean difference between women and men. We can arrive at the estimated mean rating for females, of course, by adding 53.919 and 6.522, which is equal to 60.441. So men rated Gore at about 54 and women rated him at about 60. Was this gender difference produced by random sampling error? Not according to the P-value, which equals .000. Do gender differences account for a big chunk of the variation in Al Gore thermometer ratings? Not exactly. According to R-square, gender alone accounts for less than 2 percent of the variation in the dependent variable. Clearly, other variables must contribute to the explanation of Gore's ratings. Let's expand the model.

We would expect partisanship to have a big effect on the Gore thermometer scale. Democrats should score higher on the dependent variable than do independents or Republicans. Plus, we know that women are more likely than men to be Democrats, so the gorepre-female relationship might be the spurious result of par-

Figure 9–2 Bivariate Regression Output with Dummy Variable

Model Summary

Model	R	R Square	Adjusted R Square	Std. Error of the Estimate
1	.126a	.016	.015	25.455

a. Predictors: (Constant), Female dummy

Coefficientsa

Model		Unstandardized Coefficients		Standardized Coefficients	t	Sig.
		B	Std. Error	Beta		
1	(Constant)	53.919	.911		59.196	.000
	Female dummy	6.522	1.217	.126	5.357	.000

a. Dependent Variable: Pre:Thermometer Al Gore

Note: ANOVA table not shown.

tisan differences, not gender differences. NES2000.sav contains partyid3, which codes Democrats as 1, independents as 2, and Republicans as 3. Because partyid3 is a categorical variable, we cannot use it in a regression—not in its present form, anyway. But we can use partyid3 to create a dummy variable for partisanship.

Actually, we need to create not one but two dummy variables from partyid3. Why two? Here is a general rule about dummy variables: If the variable you want to "dummy-ize" has K categories, then you need K − 1 dummies to measure the variable. Because partyid3 has three categories, we need two dummy variables. One of these variables, which we will call demdum, is equal to 1 for Democrats and 0 for independents and Republicans. The second dummy variable, repdum, is equal to 1 for Republicans and 0 for Democrats and independents. Independents, then, are uniquely identified by their exclusion from both dummies. Independents have values of 0 on demdum and 0 on repdum. Consider this recoding protocol:

Party ID: 3 Categories	Old value (partyid3)	New value (demdum)	New value (repdum)
Democrat	1	1	0
Independent	2	0	0
Republican	3	0	1
	Missing	Missing	Missing

We will create demdum and repdum one at a time. To create demdum, click Transform → Recode → Into Different Variables. (If the gender recode is still in the window, then click Reset.) Follow these steps:

1. Click partyid3 into the Numeric Variable → Output Variable panel.
2. Click in the Name box and type "demdum."
3. Click in the Label box and type "Democrat dummy." Click Change.
4. Click Old and New Values.

In the Recode Into Different Variables: Old and New Values window, recode old value 1, the partyid3 code for Democrats, into new value 1, the code for Democrats on demdum. Old values 2 and 3, the partyid3 codes for independents and Republicans, are equal to new value 0, the code for independents and Republicans on demdum. You can use the Range boxes in the Old Value panel to accomplish this change. Make sure that you recode missing values on partyid3 into missing values on demdum. The Old and New Values window should now look like Figure 9-3.

Figure 9–3 Creating a Dummy Variable from a Categorical Variable

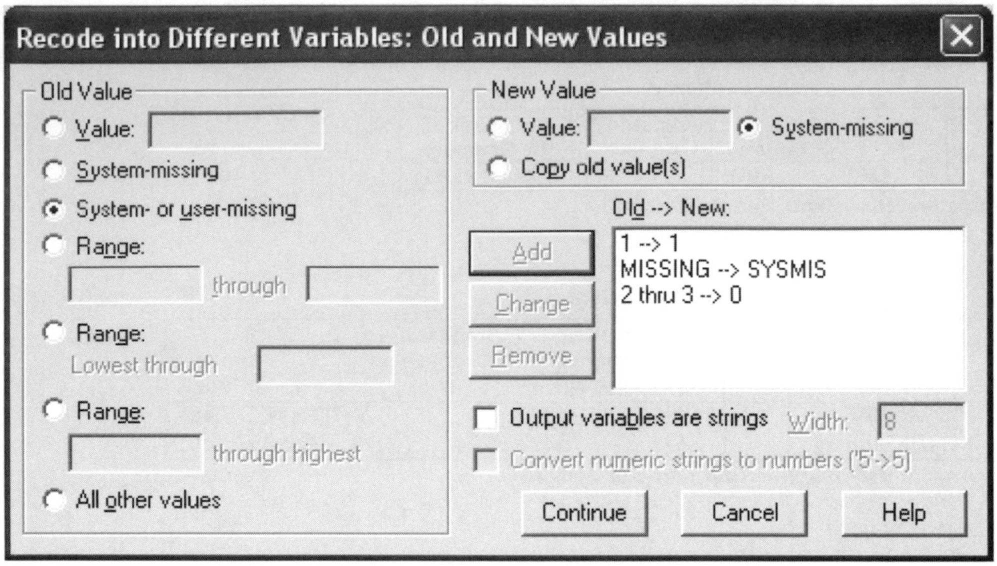

Figure 9–4 Creating a Dummy Variable from a Categorical Variable (modified)

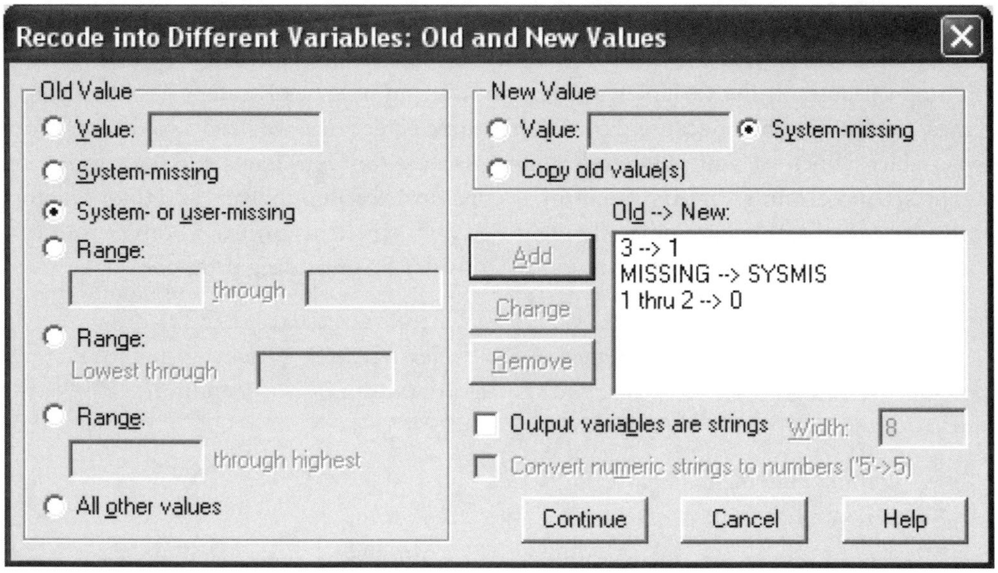

Repeat the recoding procedure, using partyid3 to create repdum. Return to the Transform → Recode → Into Different Variables window. To avoid confusion, click the Reset button. Click partyid3 into the Numeric Variable → Output Variable panel. Type "repdum" in the Name box. Type "Republican dummy" in the Label box and click Change. This time recode old value 3 on partyid3 into new value 1 on repdum. Old values 1 and 2 become 0 in the new values of repdum. Again, make sure to recode missing values on partyid3 into missing values on repdum (Figure 9-4).

Before analyzing these new variables, it would be prudent to check your work. Run a quick Frequencies on partyid3, demdum, and repdum. Your output should look like Figure 9-5. According to the distribution of partyid3, NES2000.sav has 620 Democrats, 451 Republicans, and 705 independents. According to the distribution of demdum, 620 respondents are coded 1.00 on the Democrat dummy. And according to the distribution of repdum, 451 respondents are coded 1.00 on the Republican dummy. So these codes check out. Notice, too, that the number of people coded .00 on the Democrat dummy (1,156) is equal to the number of Republicans (451) plus the number of independents (705); and the number of respondents coded .00 on

Figure 9–5 Using Frequencies to Check Dummy Variables

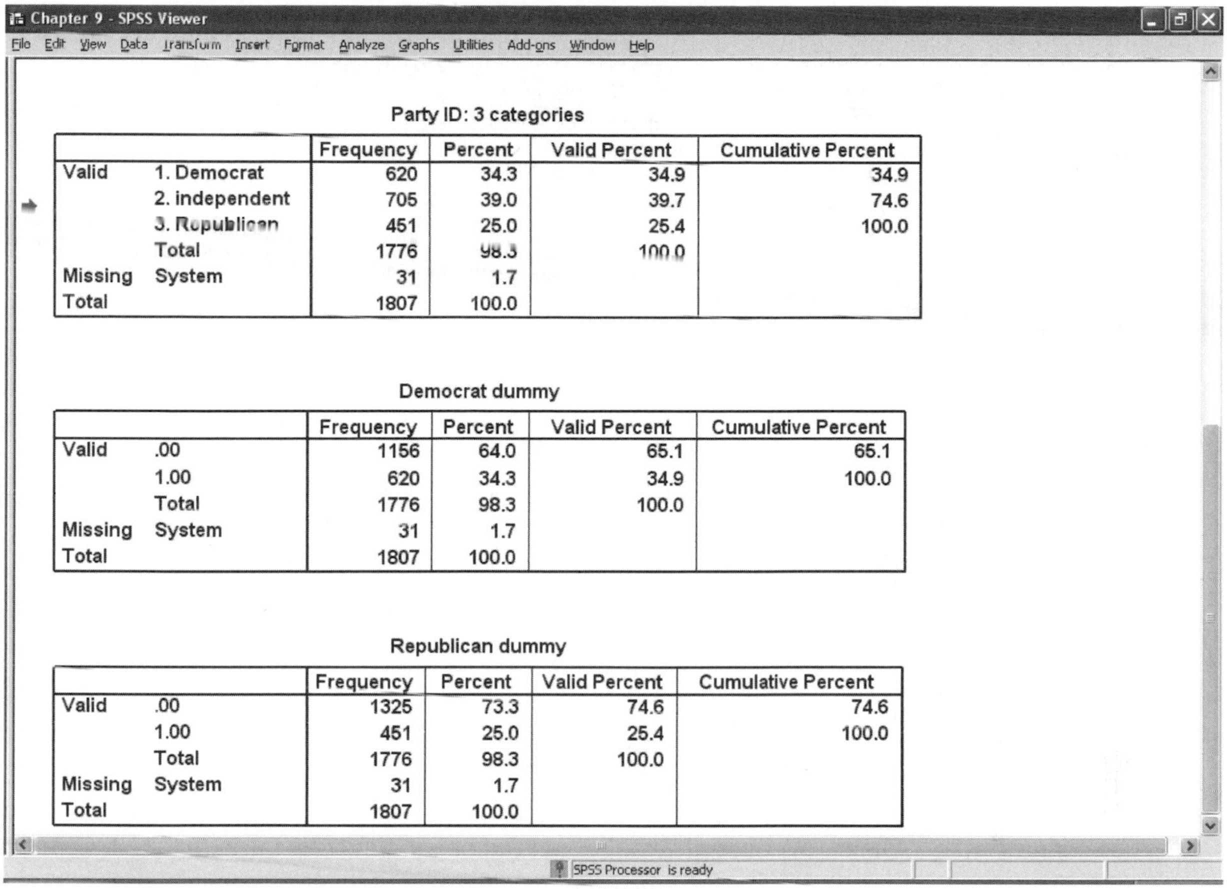

Party ID: 3 categories

		Frequency	Percent	Valid Percent	Cumulative Percent
Valid	1. Democrat	620	34.3	34.9	34.9
	2. independent	705	39.0	39.7	74.6
	3. Republican	451	25.0	25.4	100.0
	Total	1776	98.3	100.0	
Missing	System	31	1.7		
Total		1807	100.0		

Democrat dummy

		Frequency	Percent	Valid Percent	Cumulative Percent
Valid	.00	1156	64.0	65.1	65.1
	1.00	620	34.3	34.9	100.0
	Total	1776	98.3	100.0	
Missing	System	31	1.7		
Total		1807	100.0		

Republican dummy

		Frequency	Percent	Valid Percent	Cumulative Percent
Valid	.00	1325	73.3	74.6	74.6
	1.00	451	25.0	25.4	100.0
	Total	1776	98.3	100.0	
Missing	System	31	1.7		
Total		1807	100.0		

the Republican dummy (1,325) is equal to the number of Democrats (620) plus the number of independents (705). Everything checks. Before proceeding, return to the Variable View, change Decimals to 0 for demdum and repdum, and label the values for each of these new variables.

At last we are ready to run a multiple regression analysis of gorepre, using female, demdum, and repdum as independent variables. Click Analyze → Regression → Linear. Gorepre should still be in the Dependent panel and female in the Independent(s) panel. Fine. Click both of the partisanship dummies, demdum and repdum, into the Independent(s) panel. Click OK. Let's see what we have (Figure 9-6). The regression equation is as follows:

Al Gore thermometer rating =
52.110 + 3.552*Female dummy + 20.783*Democrat dummy – 14.469*Republican dummy.

First, get oriented by using the constant, 52.110, as a point of reference. Again, because this value estimates the dependent variable when all the independent variables are 0, 52.110 is the mean Gore rating for males who are independents. Why? Because all the dummies are switched to 0: female is 0 (that's the "male" part of the intercept) and both demdum and repdum are 0 (that's the "independent" part of the intercept). The regression coefficient on female tells us how much to adjust the "male" part of the intercept, controlling for partisanship. The regression coefficients on the partisanship dummies tell us how much to adjust the "independent" part of the intercept, controlling for gender. Thus, compared with independents, Democrats average nearly 21 degrees higher—and Republicans score more than 14 degrees lower—on the Gore thermometer. What about the effect of gender? The coefficient on the female dummy, 3.552, tells us that women, on average, score about 3.6 degrees higher on the Gore scale, controlling for partisanship. In the earlier regression, using the female dummy alone, we found a gender difference of more than 6.5 degrees. That regression, of course, didn't account for the fact that women are more likely than men to be Democrats. After we account for party differences, women still score about 3.6 degrees warmer on the thermometer than do men.

Figure 9–6 Multiple Regression Output with Dummy Variables

Chapter 9 - SPSS Viewer
File Edit View Data Transform Insert Format Analyze Graphs Utilities Add-ons Window Help

Model Summary

Model	R	R Square	Adjusted R Square	Std. Error of the Estimate
1	.550[a]	.303	.302	21.469

a. Predictors: (Constant), Republican dummy, Female dummy, Democrat dummy

Coefficients[a]

Model		Unstandardized Coefficients		Standardized Coefficients		
		B	Std. Error	Beta	t	Sig.
1	(Constant)	52.110	.994		52.433	.000
	Female dummy	3.552	1.040	.069	3.415	.001
	Democrat dummy	20.783	1.195	.386	17.398	.000
	Republican dummy	-14.469	1.306	-.245	-11.08	.000

a. Dependent Variable: Pre:Thermometer Al Gore

Note: ANOVA table not shown.

Multiple regression with dummy variables easily accommodates mean comparison analysis. Suppose you wanted to obtain and compare mean ratings of Al Gore for female Republicans and female Democrats. For Republican women you would start with the constant, 52, and then subtract the effect of being Republican, 14.5, leaving you with about 37.5. You would then add to 37.5 the effect of being female, 3.6. Thus the estimated mean for Republican women is about 41 degrees. Similarly, the estimated mean for Democratic women would be 52 plus the effect of being Democratic, 21, plus the effect of being female, 3.6, which is roughly equal to 77 degrees.

Let's interpret the rest of the information in the Coefficients table and the Model Summary table. Because all of the regression coefficients have P-values of less than .05, all of the effects pass muster with the null hypothesis. Note how much better we can explain the Al Gore variable by adding partisanship to the model. The R-square value of .303 tells us that all of the independent variables, taken together, account for about 30 percent of the variation in the dependent variable. So, in a manner of speaking, the glass is 30-percent full. A skeptic would point out, of course, that the glass is still 70-percent empty. You may want to exercise your new skills by constructing new variables and further expanding the model. In any event, you have just created three new variables in NES2000.sav. Before proceeding, be sure to save the dataset.

INTERACTION EFFECTS IN MULTIPLE REGRESSION

Multiple regression is a linear and additive technique. It assumes a linear relationship between the independent variables and the dependent variable. It also assumes that the effect of one independent variable on the dependent variable is the same for all values of the other independent variables in the model. In the regression we just estimated, for example, multiple regression assumed that the effect of being female is the same for all values of partisanship—that Democratic females are 3.6 degrees warmer toward Al Gore than are Democratic males and that Republican females and independent females also are 3.6 degrees warmer than are their male counterparts. This assumption works fine for additive relationships. However, if the effect of one independent variable depends on the value of another independent variable—if interaction is taking place—then multiple regression will not capture this effect. Before researchers attempt to model interaction effects by using multiple regression, they usually have performed preliminary analyses that suggest such effects are occurring in the data.

Consider an interesting theory in U.S. public opinion. According to this perspective, which we will call the polarization perspective, political disagreements are often more intense among people who are more

Figure 9–7 Setting Up a Multiple Line Chart

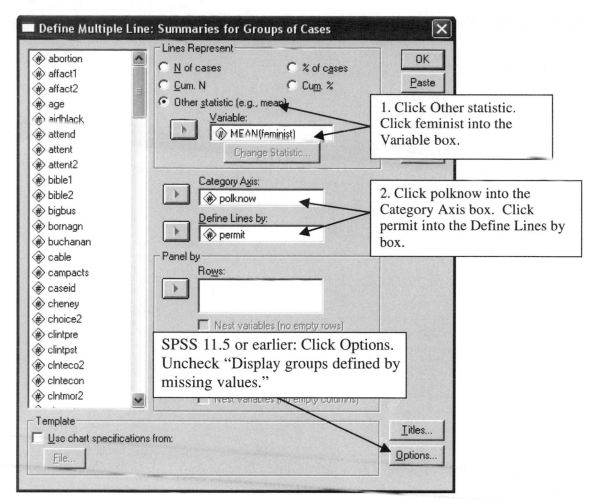

interested in and knowledgeable about public affairs than they are among people who are disengaged or who lack political knowledge. For example, it could be reasonably hypothesized that individuals who take a pro-choice position on abortion rights would view the feminist movement more favorably than would people who do not express a pro-choice position. So if we were to compare ratings on a feminist feeling thermometer for pro-choice and non-pro-choice respondents, we should find a higher mean among those who support abortion rights. According to the polarization perspective, however, this mean difference will not be the same at all levels of political knowledge. Among people with lower political knowledge, those who support abortion rights might give the feminist movement only slightly higher ratings than might those who oppose abortion rights. As political knowledge increases, however, the relationship should become stronger, with pro-choice individuals giving the feminist movement much higher ratings than do non-pro-choice individuals. Thus the strength of the relationship between abortion opinions and evaluations of feminists will depend on the level of political knowledge.

NES2000.sav contains feminist, which records respondents' feeling thermometer ratings of feminists. Another variable, permit, is a dummy variable, coded 1 for respondents who said abortion should "always" be permitted and coded 0 for all other responses.[1] A third variable, polknow, measures each respondent's political knowledge, based on how many of six political personalities or terms they could identify accurately. Scores range from 0 (the respondent could identify none of the personalities or terms) to 6 (the respondent could identify all six of the personalities or terms).

First, let's do a preliminary analysis and find out if the polarization perspective has merit. We will obtain a multiple line chart that records mean values of feminist on the vertical axis for each value of polknow on the horizontal axis. The chart will contain two lines: a line for respondents coded 0 on permit and a separate line for respondents coded 1 on permit. Go ahead and set up the chart. Click Graphs → Line, select Multiple, and then click Define (Figure 9-7). In the Lines Represent panel, click the Other statistic radio button and

Figure 9–8 Multiple Line Chart with Dummy Variable

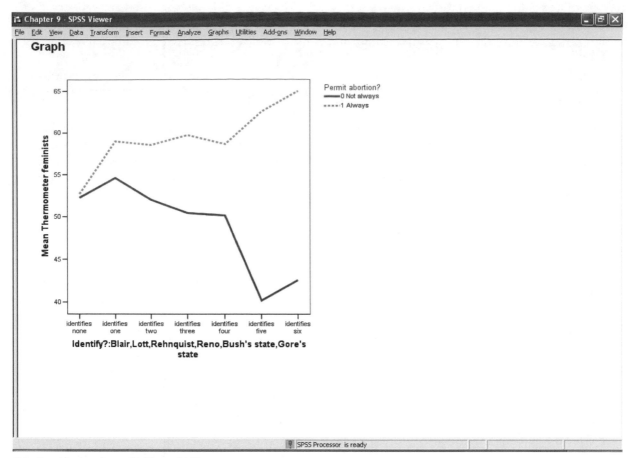

Note: Line styles have been edited for readability.

click feminist into the Variable box. Click polknow into the Category Axis box. Click permit into the box labeled "Define Lines by." (If you are running SPSS 11.5 or earlier, be sure to click Options and uncheck the box next to "Display groups defined by missing values.") Click Continue, and then click OK.

Now, this is a really interesting set of relationships (Figure 9-8). Notice that, for people with very low levels of political knowledge, little difference is evident between pro-choice and non-pro-choice respondents in their mean ratings of feminists. Those coded 1 on permit ("always") and those coded 0 ("not always") have virtually the same mean on the dependent variable. As political knowledge increases, however, the two lines begin to part company. At higher values of polknow a much larger difference—more polarization—is seen between pro-choice and non-pro-choice respondents on the mean of the dependent variable. It looks like the feminist-permit relationship strengthens as political knowledge increases. How would we use regression analysis to estimate the size and statistical significance of these relationships?

We want to specify a regression model that does three things. First, we want to estimate the mean difference on feminist between people with pro-choice opinions and those with non-pro-choice opinions. Second, we want to estimate the effect of political knowledge on the dependent variable. So our regression model would begin in a familiar way:

$$\text{Feminist thermometer rating} = a + b1*\text{permit} + b2*\text{polknow}.$$

These parameters—a, b1, and b2—are the additive building blocks of the model. We can use these parameters to estimate the mean of the dependent variable for different combinations of the independent variables. Much as we did in the Gore thermometer regression, we will be able to add the effect of being, say, pro-choice to the effect of scoring a 2 on the knowledge variable. The Y-intercept will estimate feminist for respondents who have a value of 0 on both independent variables—non-pro-choice respondents who score

0 on the political knowledge variable. Third, however, we want to adjust this additive estimate, depending on "where we are" on the political knowledge variable. For low values of knowledge, we want a modest adjustment to the additive effects. But as knowledge values increase, we want a larger and larger adjustment, because the mean difference between pro-choice and non-pro-choice respondents increases as political knowledge increases.

In multiple regression you accomplish the third goal by including an interaction variable as an independent variable. To create an interaction variable, you multiply one independent variable by the other independent variable. Consider how we would create an interaction variable for the problem at hand: permit*polknow. All respondents who are coded 0 on permit will, of course, have a value of 0 on the interaction variable. For respondents coded 1 on permit, however, the magnitude of the interaction variable will increase as political knowledge increases—from 0 for pro-choice individuals scoring 0 on polknow to 6 for pro-choice individuals scoring 6 on polknow. Let's include this term in the model just discussed and see what it looks like:

$$\text{Feminist thermometer rating} = a + b1*\text{permit} + b2*\text{polknow} + b3*(\text{permit}*\text{polknow}).$$

We would estimate the mean feminist rating for respondents having a value of 0 on permit by using the additive building blocks. We would start with the intercept and add the political knowledge effect, which would be b2 times a respondent's political knowledge score. What happens when permit switches to 1? We would start with the intercept, add the effect of being pro-choice (b1), and add the political knowledge effect, b2 times the respondent's political knowledge score. But we would also add the interaction effect, b3 times the value of the interaction variable (permit*polknow). This coefficient, b3, tells us how much to adjust our additive estimate for each 1-unit increase in political knowledge among pro-choice respondents.

Let's work through the research problem and get SPSS to estimate the model for us. NES2000.sav contains feminist, permit, and polknow, but it does not contain a variable that measures the interaction effect. We will use the Compute transformation feature to calculate this variable. Click Transform → Compute. Let's name the new variable interact. Type "interact" in the Target Variable box (Figure 9-9). In the Numeric Expression box type "permit*polknow." Next, click Type & Label. In the Compute Variable: Type and Label window, type "permit*polknow," in the Label box. Click Continue, and then click OK. Now we're set to estimate our model.

Click Analyze → Regression → Linear. Click Reset to clear the panels for our new analysis. Click feminist into the Dependent box. Click permit, polknow, and interact into the Independent(s) box, as shown in Figure 9-10. Click OK. Figure 9-11 shows the Coefficients table. Let's plug the estimates into our model (we'll use the variables' names instead of their lengthy labels):

$$\text{feminist} = 55.692 + .233*\text{permit} - 1.950*\text{polknow} + 3.095*\text{interact}.$$

Again use the constant, 55.692, to get oriented. This is the estimated mean of feminist for respondents who have values of 0 on all the independent variables: non-pro-choice individuals (coded 0 on permit) who accurately identified none of the political figures or terms (a value of 0 on polknow). So this group averages a bit less than 56 on the dependent variable. Now notice the puny coefficient on the abortion dummy, .233, which has a P-value of .926. This value communicates the same thing we saw in the line graph: When political knowledge is 0, switching permit from 0 to 1 has very little effect on the feminist thermometer scale. So pro-choice people with a value of 0 on the knowledge variable average 55.692 + .233, or also about 56, on the dependent variable. No polarization there.

What happens as political knowledge increases? According to the regression coefficient on polknow, −1.950, each 1-unit increase in knowledge is associated with a 1.950-point decline on the feminist scale. So as knowledge goes up, mean feminist ratings go down. But is this what happens for all respondents as polknow increases in value? Not according to the large coefficient on the interaction variable, 3.095. This coefficient tells us how much to adjust that 1.950-point decline for each 1-unit increase in knowledge among pro-choice respondents. For people coded 0 on permit, we make no adjustment because these respondents are all 0 on the interaction variable. But for people coded 1 on permit, we need to adjust our estimate upward by about 3 units for each 1-unit increase in polknow. At low levels of knowledge, this

Figure 9–9 Computing an Interaction Variable

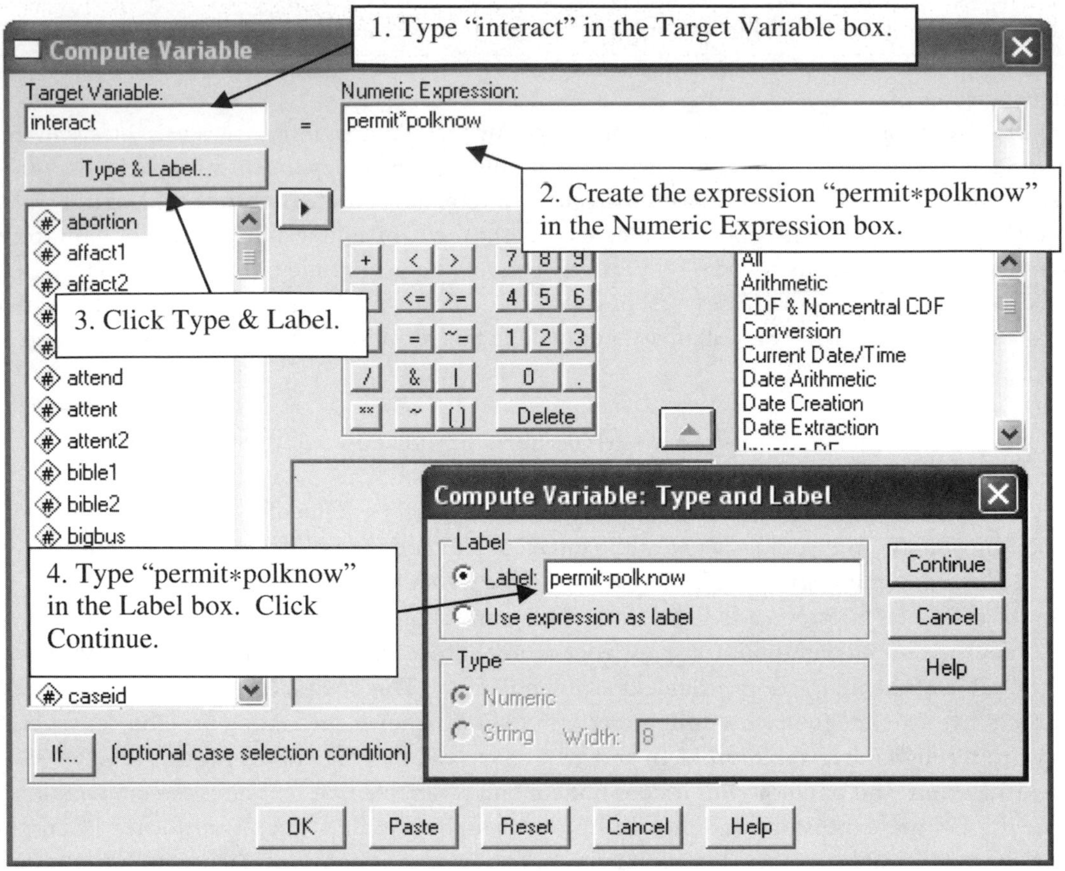

1. Type "interact" in the Target Variable box.

2. Create the expression "permit∗polknow" in the Numeric Expression box.

3. Click Type & Label.

4. Type "permit∗polknow" in the Label box. Click Continue.

Figure 9–10 Requesting Multiple Regression with Dummy and Interaction Variables

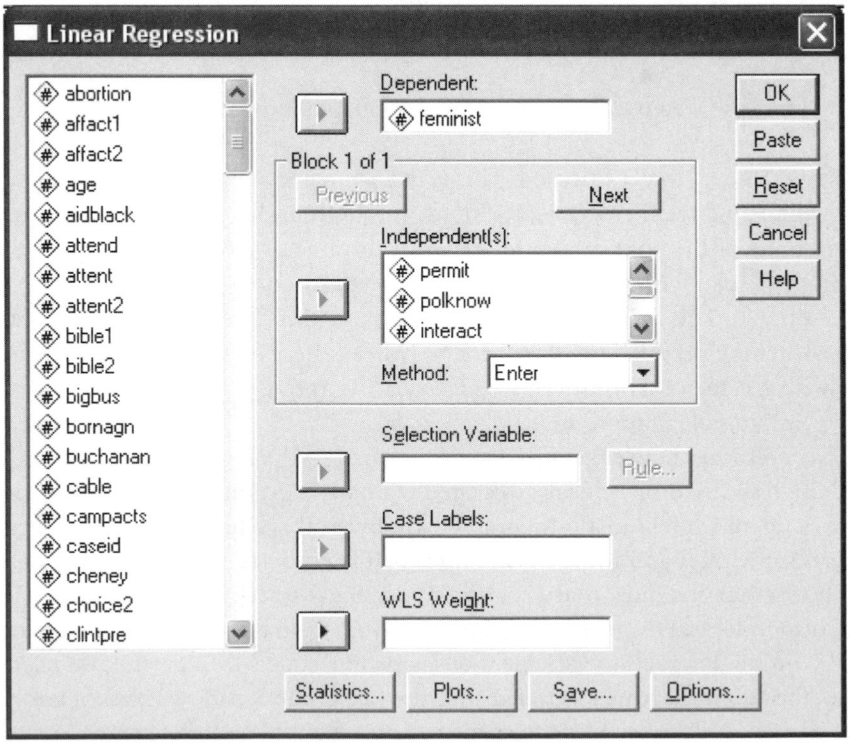

Figure 9–11 Multiple Regression Output with Dummy and Interaction Variables

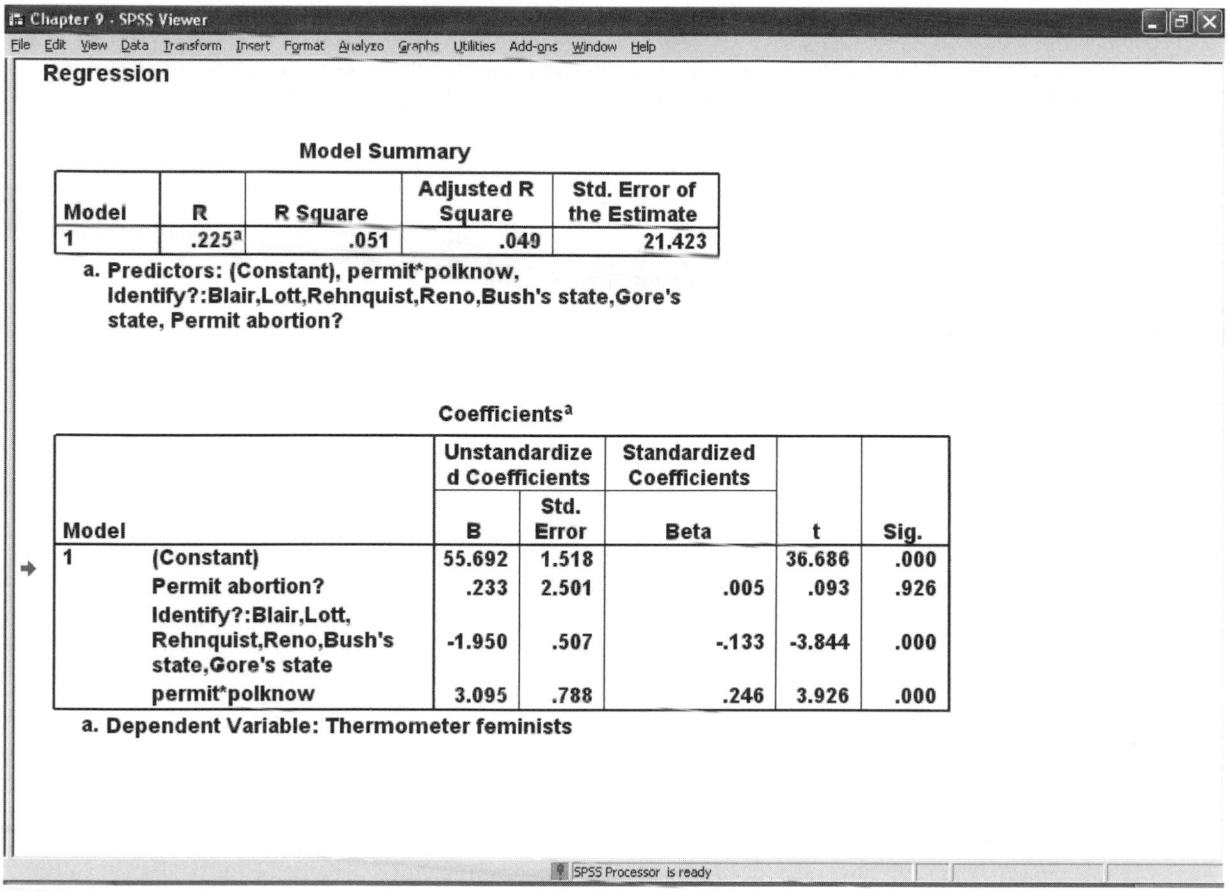

Regression

Model Summary

Model	R	R Square	Adjusted R Square	Std. Error of the Estimate
1	.225[a]	.051	.049	21.423

a. Predictors: (Constant), permit*polknow, Identify?:Blair,Lott,Rehnquist,Reno,Bush's state,Gore's state, Permit abortion?

Coefficients[a]

Model		Unstandardized Coefficients B	Unstandardized Coefficients Std. Error	Standardized Coefficients Beta	t	Sig.
1	(Constant)	55.692	1.518		36.686	.000
	Permit abortion?	.233	2.501	.005	.093	.926
	Identify?:Blair,Lott, Rehnquist,Reno,Bush's state,Gore's state	-1.950	.507	-.133	-3.844	.000
	permit*polknow	3.095	.788	.246	3.926	.000

a. Dependent Variable: Thermometer feminists

adjustment results in small mean differences between respondents who hold different opinions about abortion. For people scoring 1 on political knowledge, for example, the mean feminist rating for non-pro-choice respondents would be 55.692 – 1.950, which is about 54. The mean for pro-choice people who score 1 on knowledge would be 55.692 + .233 – 1.950 + 3.095, which is about 57. So we have a mean of 54 compared with a mean of 57. At a low knowledge level, polarization is only faintly discernible. As polknow increases, however, the mean difference widens. For individuals at the highest level of knowledge—they accurately identified all six items—the estimated mean rating for non-pro-choice respondents is about 44, compared with a mean of 63 for pro-choice respondents. You can do the math!

According to their P-values, the political knowledge variable and the interaction variable achieved significance in the model. But an R-square of .051 is nothing to write home about. Before you save the changes you have made to NES2000.sav and put your output file safely on disk, you might want to expand the model and crank out some more regressions. Who knows? An interesting relationship might turn up.

EXERCISES

In Exercises 1, 2, and 3 you will analyze World.sav. In Exercises 4 and 5 you will analyze GSS2002.sav.

1. In the first exercise in Chapter 5, you used World.sav to investigate the relationship between economic development and democracy. In this exercise and in the next exercise, you will use multiple regression to analyze a similar relationship—one between economic development and political rights. In this exercise you will create dummy variables from the World.sav variable econdev3. In Exercise 2 you will perform and interpret a regression analysis, using polrts as the dependent variable and your new dummies as the independent variables.

   A. World.sav contains econdev3, which is coded 1 for the "least" developed countries, 2 for "middle," and 3 for the "most" developed. Use econdev3 to create two dummy variables, one named devmid and labeled "mid-devel dummy," and the other named devmost and labeled "most-devel dummy." Follow this recoding scheme:

Economic development 3 Categories	Old value (econdev3)	New value (devmid)	New value (devmost)
Least	1	0	0
Middle	2	1	0
Most	3	0	1
	Missing	Missing	Missing

Check your recoding work by running Frequencies on econdev3, devmid, and devmost. In the table that follows, write the number of cases (raw frequencies) in the cells that have question marks.

Economic development: 3 Categories	Frequency	devmid	Frequency	devmost	Frequency
Least	22	.00	?	.00	?
Middle	?	1.00	?	1.00	?
Most	?				
Valid total	106				

B. Imagine running a regression using devmid and devmost to estimate a dependent variable: Dependent variable = Constant + b1*devmid + b2*devmost. Complete the matching exercise below by drawing a line connecting the desired estimate on the left to the appropriate coefficient (or combination of coefficients) on the right.

Your estimate of the . . .	Would be provided by (the) . . .
mean difference between the least developed and the most developed . . .	constant
mean of the dependent variable for the most developed . . .	b1
mean of the dependent variable for the least developed . . .	constant + b2
mean difference between the least developed and the middle developed . . .	b2

2. World.sav contains polrts, each country's political rights score. Polrts measures countries on a scale from 1 (the country has the fewest rights) to 7 (the country has the most rights). Run Regression → Linear, using polrts as the dependent variable and devmid and devmost as independent variables.

A. The regression equation for estimating polrts is as follows (fill in the blanks, putting the constant in the first blank):

Polrts = _____ + _____ * devmid + _____ * devmost.

B. Use the regression coefficients to arrive at estimated mean values of polrts for countries at each level of economic development. Write the estimates in the table that follows.

Level of economic development	Estimated mean on political rights scale
Least	
Middle	
Most	

C. Which of the following conclusions are supported by your analysis (check all that apply)?

❑ Countries with middle levels of economic development do not have significantly higher values on the political rights scale than do countries with the least economic development.

❑ As economic development increases, political rights increase.

❑ Countries with the highest levels of economic development have significantly higher values on the political rights scale than do countries with the least economic development.

❑ Level of economic development explains less than half of the variation in the political rights scale.

3. As a country becomes richer, do more of its citizens benefit economically? Or do economic resources become inequitably distributed across society? The answer may depend on the type of regime in power. Democratic regimes, which need to appeal broadly for votes, may adopt policies that redistribute wealth. Dictatorships, by contrast, are less concerned with popular accountability, and so might hoard economic resources among the ruling elite, creating a less equitable distribution of wealth. This explanation suggests a set of interaction relationships. It suggests that, when we compare poorer democracies with richer democracies, richer democracies will have a more equitable distribution of wealth. However, it also suggests that, when we compare poorer dictatorships with richer dictatorships, richer dictatorships will have a less equitable distribution of wealth. In this exercise you will investigate this set of relationships.

World.sav contains the variable gini, which measures the extent to which wealth is inequitably distributed in society. The variable can take on any value between 0 (equal distribution of wealth) and 100 (unequal distribution of wealth). So, lower values of gini denote less economic inequality and higher values of gini denote greater economic inequality. Gini is the dependent variable. World.sav also has a dummy variable, hi_gdp, that classifies each country as low-gdp (coded 0) or high-gdp (coded 1). Hi_gdp will serve as the measure of the independent variable, level of wealth. Another dummy, regime, which categorizes each country as a democracy (coded 0 on regime) or dictatorship (coded 1 on regime), is the control variable.

A. Before running a regression analysis, obtain a multiple line chart to see whether interaction is occurring. Click Graphs → Line → Multiple. Select Other statistic and click gini into the Variable box in the Lines Represent panel. The independent variable, high_gdp, will go in the Category Axis box, and the control variable, regime, will go in the Define Lines by box. Edit the line styles to clearly distinguish between dictatorships and democracies. Print the multiple line chart you created.

B. World.sav contains interact, an interaction variable computed by the expression regime*hi_gdp. Think about how regime and hi_gdp are coded. The interaction variable takes on a value of 1 for (check one)

❑ all high-gdp countries.

❑ high-gdp dictatorships.

❑ high-gdp democracies.

C. Run Regression → Linear, using gini as the dependent variable and hi_gdp, regime, and interact as independent variables. The regression equation for estimating gini is as follows (fill in the blanks, putting the constant in the first blank):

Gini = _____ + _____ * hi_gdp + _____ * regime + _____ * interact.

D. Use the regression to arrive at estimated mean values of gini for low-gdp and high-gdp democracies and dictatorships. Write your estimates in the table that follows.

Country gdp and regime	Estimated mean of gini
Low-gdp democracies	
Low-gdp dictatorships	
High-gdp democracies	
High-gdp dictatorships	

E. Suppose someone were to claim that, from the standpoint of statistical significance, low-gdp dictatorships have a significantly more equitable distribution of wealth than do low-gdp democracies. This claim is (circle one)

correct.   incorrect.

Explain your answer. _____

_____

_____

_____

F. Suppose someone were to claim that, as gdp increases, wealth becomes significantly more equitably distributed in democracies but not in dictatorships. This claim is (circle one)

correct.   incorrect.

Explain your answer. _____

_____

_____

_____

In Exercise 1 you added two useful variables to World.sav. Before proceeding to the next exercise, be sure to save the dataset.

4. The abortion issue is a perennially conflictual debate in U.S. politics. What factors divide people on this issue? Because opposition to abortion is often deeply rooted in religious convictions, you could hypothesize that individuals having strong religious ties will be more likely to oppose abortion than will those with weaker affiliations. (If this hypothesis seems too commonplace to test, be patient. It gets more interesting below.) GSS2002.sav contains the variable abortion, a scale that records the number of conditions under which respondents believe an abortion should be allowed. Scores can range from 0 (abortion should be allowed under none of the conditions) to 6 (abortion should be allowed under all conditions). So higher scale scores denote a stronger pro-abortion stance. GSS2002.sav also has the dummy variable relint2, scored 0 for respondents with weak (or no) religious affiliations and 1 for those with strong ties. If the relint2-abortion hypothesis is correct, then respondents who are coded 0 on relint2 will have higher scores on the abortion variable than will respondents who are coded 1 on relint2.

A. Run Regression to test the hypothesis that people with strong religious affiliations will be more likely to oppose abortion than will those with weak religious affiliations. Abortion is the dependent variable and relint2 is the independent variable. Examine the output, and fill in the blanks below.

The constant (or intercept) is equal to _____, and relint2's regression coefficient is equal to _____. Relint2s regression coefficient has a P-value of _____, and R-square is equal to _____.

B. Based on your analysis, you can conclude that (check all that apply)

❑ people with weaker religious affiliations score about 4 on the abortion scale.

❑ people with stronger religious affiliations score about 1 on the abortion scale.

❑ relint2 is not significantly related to abortion opinions.

❑ relint2 explains about 6 percent of the variation in abortion scores.

C. A critic, upon examining your results, might reasonably ask, "Did you control for education? It could be that individuals with strong religious ties have lower levels of education than do the weakly affiliated. If education is also related to abortion opinions, then you might be confusing the effect of religious attachment with the effect of education."

GSS2002.sav contains educ, which measures the number of years of formal education for each respondent, from 0 (no formal schooling) to 20 (20 years of formal schooling). Run the regression again, using abortion as the dependent variable and relint2 and educ as independent variables. Based on your results, you may conclude that (check all that apply)

❑ controlling for education, the relationship between relint2 and abortion is spurious.

❑ controlling for education, individuals with strong religious ties score about 1 point lower on the abortion scale than do individuals with weaker religious ties.

❑ according to the regression estimates, strongly affiliated individuals with no formal schooling would score about 4 on the abortion scale.

❑ controlling for strength of religious affiliation, each 1-year increase in education is associated with an increase of about one-tenth of a point on the abortion scale.

❑ education is significantly related to abortion opinions.

❑ both independent variables together explain more than 25 percent of the variation in the dependent variable.

5. One of the examples in this chapter discussed the polarization perspective—the idea that political conflict is more pronounced among people who are more knowledgeable about politics than it is among less knowledgeable people. Perhaps the same pattern applies to the relationship between strength of religious attachment and abortion opinions. That is, it could be that religious commitment has a strong effect on abortion attitudes among politically knowledgeable people but that this effect is weaker for people who have lower knowledge about politics. We can use respondents' years of education (educ) as a surrogate for political knowledge because we can reasonably assume that people with more education will be more politically knowledgeable than will less-educated people. In this exercise you will compute an interaction variable. You will then run and interpret a multiple regression that includes the interaction variable you created.

A. Use Transform → Compute to create a new variable, interact, by multiplying relint2 by educ. (The numeric expression will be relint2*educ.) Give interact the label "relint2*educ." Run Frequencies on interact. Print and examine the frequencies output.

B. Think about the interaction variable you computed. A respondent with a weak religious affiliation (coded 0 on relint2) has what value on the interaction variable (circle one)?

a value of 0   a value of 1   a value equal to his or her years of education

A respondent with a strong religious affiliation (coded 1 on relint2) has what value on the interaction variable (circle one)?

a value of 0   a value of 1   a value equal to his or her years of education

C. Run a multiple regression, using abortion as the dependent variable and relint2, educ, and interact as the independent variables. According to the Coefficients table, the multiple regression equation for estimating scores on the abortion scale is as follows (fill in the blanks, putting the constant in the first blank):

_____ + _____ * relint2 + _____ * educ + _____ * interact.

D. Consider the regression coefficients and the P-values. Suppose you were to use this regression to estimate the effect of religious commitment on abortion opinions among people with no formal education, that is, for people with a value of 0 on educ. Your estimates would show that (check one)

❑ people with stronger religious commitment score significantly lower on the abortion scale than do people with weaker religious commitment.

❑ strength of religious commitment is not significantly related to abortion opinions.

❑ people with stronger religious commitment score significantly higher on the abortion scale than do people with weaker religious commitment.

E. Now suppose you were to use this regression to estimate the effect of religious commitment on abortion opinions among people with 20 years of education, that is, for people with a value of 20 on educ. First use the regression to estimate the mean abortion score for respondents who have 20 years of education and weak religious affiliations (coded 0 on relint2). These respondents score about (circle one)

3 on the abortion scale.   4 on the abortion scale.   5 on the abortion scale.

Now use the regression to estimate the mean abortion score for respondents who have 20 years of education and strong religious affiliations (coded 1 on relint2). These respondents score about (circle one)

3 on the abortion scale.   4 on the abortion scale.   5 on the abortion scale.

F. Think about the polarization perspective. Does the analysis support the idea that, as education increases, religious commitment plays a larger role in defining conflict on the abortion issue?

Yes   No

Briefly explain your reasoning. _____

_____

_____

_____

That concludes the exercises for this chapter. Before exiting SPSS, be sure to save your output file.

NOTES

1. Permit is based on abortion, a variable in NES2000.sav. Respondents coded 1, 2, or 3 on abortion are coded 0 on permit; respondents coded 4 on abortion are coded 1 on permit.

10

Logistic Regression*

You now have an array of SPSS skills that enable you to perform the appropriate analysis for just about any situation you will encounter. To analyze the relationship between two categorical variables—variables measured at the nominal or ordinal level—you would enlist SPSS Crosstabs. If the dependent variable is an interval-level scale and the independent variable is categorical, then mean comparison analysis would be one way to go. Alternatively, you might create a dummy variable (or variables), specify a linear regression model, and run Regression → Linear to estimate the effects of the categorical variable(s) on the dependent variable. Finally, if both the independent and dependent variables are interval level, then Regression → Linear or Interactive Scatterplot would be appropriate techniques. There is, however, a common research situation that you are not yet equipped to tackle.

In its most specialized application, logistic regression is designed to analyze the relationship between an interval-level independent variable and a binary dependent variable. A binary variable, as its name suggests, can assume only two values. Binary variables are just like the dummy variables you created and analyzed earlier in this book. Either a case has the attribute or behavior being measured or it does not. Voted/did not vote, married/not married, favor/oppose gay marriage, and South/non-South are all examples of binary variables.

Consider a binary dependent variable of keen interest to students of political behavior: whether people voted in an election. This variable, of course, has only two values: Either individuals voted (coded 1 on the binary variable) or they did not vote (coded 0). Now think about an interval-level independent variable often linked to turnout, years of education. As measured by the General Social Survey, this variable ranges from 0 (no formal schooling) to 20 (20 years of education). We would expect a positive relationship between the independent and dependent variables. As years of education increase, the probability of voting should increase as well. So people with fewer years of schooling should have a relatively low probability of voting, and this probability should increase with each additional year of education. Now, we certainly can conceptualize this relationship as positive. However, for statistical and substantive reasons, we cannot assume that it is linear—that is, we cannot assume that a 1-year change in education occasions a consistent increase in the probability of voting. Because ordinary least squares (OLS) regression assumes linearity between the independent and dependent variables, we cannot use Regression → Linear to analyze this relationship. But as luck and statistics would have it, we can assume a linear relationship between education and the logged odds of voting. Let's put the relationship into logistic regression form and discuss its special properties:

$$\text{Logged odds (voting)} = a + b(\text{years of education}).$$

This logistic regression model is quite OLS-like in appearance. Just as in OLS regression, the constant or intercept, a, estimates the dependent variable (in this case, the logged odds of voting) when the independent

---

*For this chapter you will need access to a full-version SPSS installation that includes the SPSS Regression Models module. The full version of SPSS Base, by itself, does not permit the user to perform logistic regression. The SPSS Student Version does not contain the Regression Models module.

Figure 10–1 The Logistic Regression Window

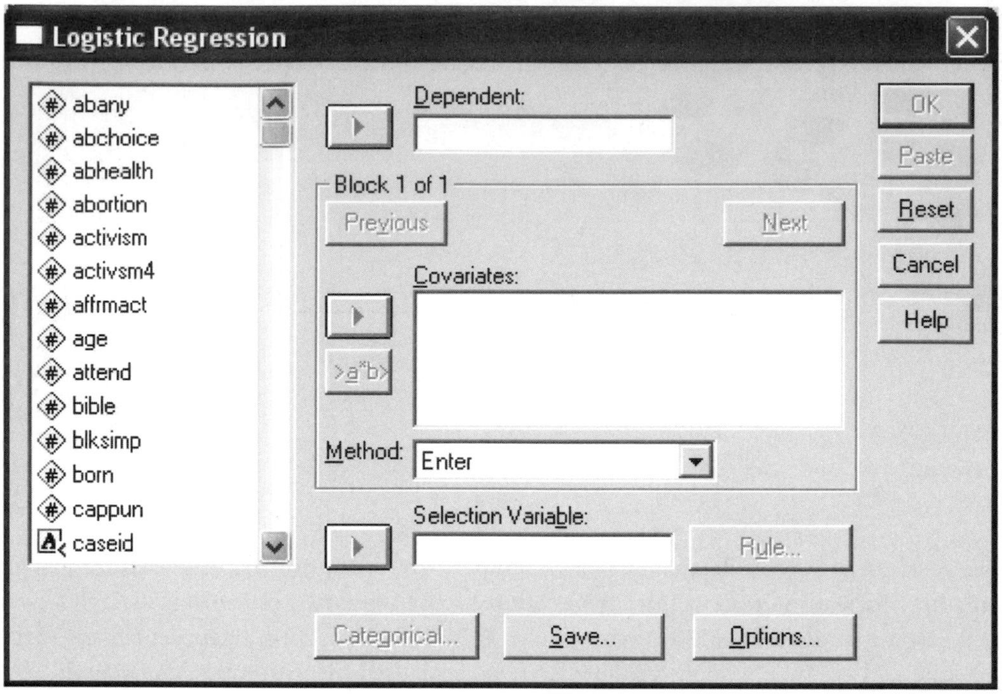

variable is equal to 0—that is, for people with no formal education. And the logistic regression coefficient, b, will estimate the change in the logged odds of voting for each 1-year increase in education. What is more, the analysis will produce a standard error for b, permitting us to test the null hypothesis that education has no effect on turnout. Finally, SPSS output for logistic regression will provide R-square-type measures, giving us an idea of the strength of the relationship between education and the likelihood of voting. In all of these ways, logistic regression is comfortably akin to linear regression.

However, logistic regression output is more difficult to interpret than are OLS results. In ordinary regression, the coefficients of interest, the constant (a) and the slope (b), are expressed in actual units of the dependent variable. If we were to use OLS to investigate the relationship between years of education (X) and income in dollars (Y), the regression coefficient on education would communicate the dollar-change in income for each 1-year increase in education. With OLS, what you see is what you get. With logistic regression, by contrast, the coefficients of interest are expressed in terms of the logged odds of the dependent variable. The constant (a) will tell us the logged odds of voting when education is 0, and the regression coefficient (b) will estimate the change in the logged odds for each unit change in education. Logged odds, truth be told, have no intuitive appeal. Thus we often must translate logistic regression results into language that makes better intuitive sense.

USING REGRESSION → BINARY LOGISTIC

Let's run the voting-education analysis and clarify these points. GSS2002.sav contains vote00, coded 0 for respondents who did not vote in the 2000 election and coded 1 for those who voted. GSS2002.sav also has educ, which records the number of years of schooling for each respondent. Click Analyze → Regression → Binary Logistic, opening the Logistic Regression window (Figure 10-1). Find vote00 in the variable list and click it into the Dependent box. Click educ into the Covariates box. (In logistic regression, independent variables are often called covariates.) For this run, we will do one additional thing. At the bottom of the Logistic Regression window, click Options. The Logistic Regression: Options window opens (Figure 10-2). Click the box next to "Iteration history." This option will produce output that helps to illustrate how logistic regression works. Click Continue, returning to the main Logistic Regression window. Click OK.

In typical fashion, SPSS has given us a wealth of information. Eleven tables now populate the SPSS Viewer. Happily, for the essential purposes of this book, you need to be conversant with only three or four of these tables. Scroll to the bottom of the output, to the table labeled "Variables in the Equation." Here you

Figure 10–2 Requesting Logistic Regression with Iteration History

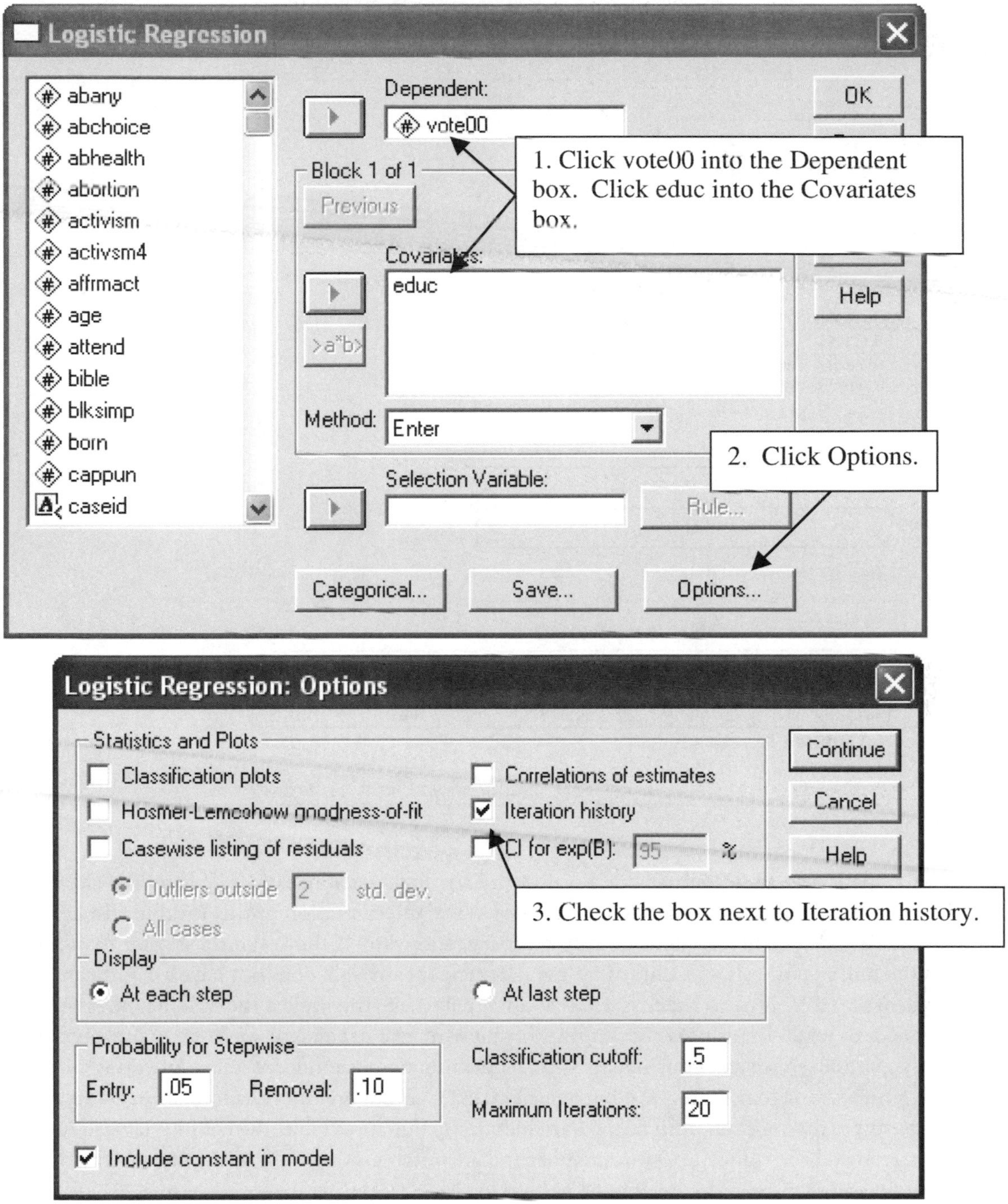

will find the main results of the vote00-educ analysis (Figure 10-3). Just as in Regression → Linear, the numbers in the column labeled "B" are the estimates for the constant and the regression coefficient. Plug these estimates into our model:

$$\text{Logged odds (voting)} = -2.154 + .223(educ)$$

What do these coefficients tell us? Again, the constant says that, for people with no education, the estimated logged odds of voting is equal to –2.154. And the logistic regression coefficient on educ says that the logged odds of voting increases by .223 for each 1-year increase in education. So, as expected, as the independent variable increases, the likelihood of voting increases, too. Does education have a statistically significant effect on the likelihood of voting? In OLS regression, SPSS determines statistical significance by

Figure 10–3 Logistic Regression Output with One Independent Variable: Variables in the Equation and Model Summary

Omnibus Tests of Model Coefficients

		Chi-square	df	Sig.
Step 1	Step	206.979	1	.000
	Block	206.979	1	.000
	Model	206.979	1	.000

Model Summary

Step	-2 Log likelihood	Cox & Snell R Square	Nagelkerke R Square
1	3037.490[a]	.077	.107

a. Estimation terminated at iteration number 4 because parameter estimates changed by less than .001.

Classification Table[a]

			Predicted		
			Did R vote in the 2000 election?		
	Observed		Did not vote	Voted	Percentage Correct
Step 1	Did R vote in the 2000 election?	Did not vote	110	712	13.4
		Voted	74	1704	95.8
	Overall Percentage				69.8

a. The cut value is .500

Variables in the Equation

		B	S.E.	Wald	df	Sig.	Exp(B)
Step 1[a]	educ	.223	.017	174.64	1	.000	1.250
	Constant	-2.154	.222	94.079	1	.000	.116

a. Variable(s) entered on step 1: educ.

calculating a t-statistic and an accompanying P-value. In logistic regression, SPSS calculates a Wald statistic (which is based on chi-square) and reports a P-value for Wald. Interpretation of this P-value, displayed in the column labeled "Sig.," is directly analogous to ordinary regression. If the P-value is greater than .05, then do not reject the null hypothesis. Conclude that the independent variable does not have a significant effect on the dependent variable. If the P-value is less than or equal to .05, then reject the null hypothesis and infer that the independent variable has a significant relationship with the dependent variable. In our output, the P-value for educ is .000, so we can conclude that, yes, education has a significant effect on voting turnout.

Now let's return to the logistic regression coefficient, .223, and figure out how to make it more meaningful. Consider the right-most column of the Variables in the Equation table, the column labeled "Exp(B)." Here SPSS has reported the value 1.250 for the independent variable, educ. Where did this number originate? SPSS obtained this number by raising the natural log base *e* (approximately equal to 2.72) to the power of the logistic regression coefficient, .223. This procedure translates the logged odds regression coefficient into an *odds ratio*. An odds ratio tells you by how much the odds of the dependent variable change for each unit change in the independent variable. An odds ratio of less than 1 says that the odds decrease as the independent variable increases (a negative relationship). An odds ratio equal to 1 says that the odds do not change as the independent variable increases (no relationship). And an odds ratio of greater than 1 says that the odds of the dependent variable increase as the independent variable increases (a positive relationship). An odds ratio of 1.250 means that respondents at a given level of education are 1.25 times more likely to have voted than are respondents at the next lower level of education. So people with, say, 10 years of education are 1.25 times more likely to have voted than are people with 9 years of education, people with 14 years are 1.25 times more likely to have voted than people with 13 years, and so on.

The value of Exp(B) is often used to obtain an even more understandable estimate, the *percentage change in the odds* for each unit change in the independent variable. Mercifully, simple arithmetic accomplishes this task. Subtract 1 from Exp(B) and multiply by 100. In our current example: (1.25 − 1) * 100 = 25.

Figure 10–4 Logistic Regression Output with One Independent Variable: Model Summary, Omnibus Tests of Model Coefficients, and Iteration History

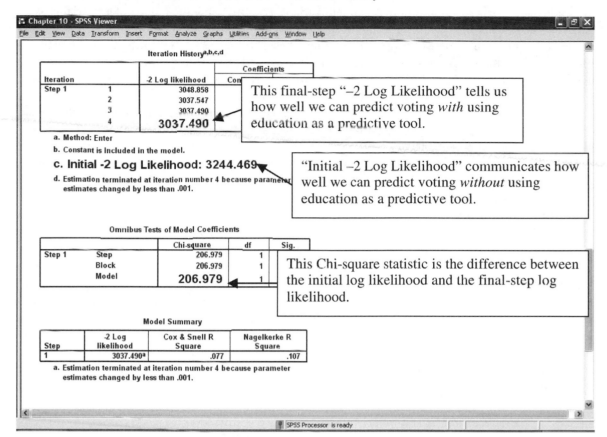

We can now say that each 1-year increment in education increases the odds of voting by 25 percent. As you can see, when the relationship is positive—that is, when the logistic regression coefficient is greater than 0 and the odds ratio is greater than 1—figuring out the percentage change in the odds requires almost no thought. Just subtract 1 from Exp(B) and move the decimal point two places to the right. But be alert for negative relationships, when the odds ratio is less than 1. (In one of the exercises at the end of this chapter you will interpret a negative relationship.) Suppose, for example, that Exp(B) were equal to .25, communicating a negative relationship between the independent variable and the probability of the dependent variable. The percentage change in the odds would be equal to $(.25 - 1) * 100 = -75.0$, indicating that a one-unit change in the independent variable decreases the odds of the dependent variable by 75 percent.

How strong is the relationship between years of education and the likelihood of voting? Consider the table labeled "Model Summary," also shown in Figure 10-3. OLS researchers are quite fond of R-square, the overall measure of strength that gauges the amount of variation in the dependent variable that is explained by the independent variable(s). For statistical reasons, however, the notion of "explained variation" has no direct analog in logistic regression. Even so, methodologists have proposed various "pseudo R-square" measures that seek to communicate the strength of association between the dependent and independent variables. SPSS reports two of these: the Cox and Snell R-square and the Nagelkerke R-square. These measures are designed to return a value of between 0 (no relationship) and 1 (perfect relationship). However, Cox-Snell can be rather conservative. The Nagelkerke measure adjusts for this, and so it generally reports a higher pseudo R-square than Cox-Snell. These two measures are never wildly different, and they do give the researcher a ballpark feel for the strength of the relationship. With values in the .077 to .107 range, you could conclude that education, though related to voting, by itself provides a less-than-complete explanation of it.

There is one other measure reported in the Model Summary table, "–2 Log likelihood," equal to 3037.490. In some ways this is the most important measure of strength produced by logistic regression. By itself, however, the magnitude of –2 Log likelihood doesn't mean very much. But scroll up a bit, so that you can view the tables labeled "Model Summary," "Omnibus Tests of Model Coefficients," and "Iteration History" together on your screen (Figure 10-4).[1]

In figuring out the most accurate estimates for the model's coefficients, logistic regression uses a technique called maximum likelihood estimation (MLE). When it begins the analysis, MLE finds out how well it can predict the observed values of the dependent variable without using the independent variable as a predictive tool. So MLE first determined how accurately it could predict whether individuals voted by not knowing how much education they have. The number labeled "Initial –2 Log Likelihood" (equal to 3244.469 and found beneath the Iteration History table) summarizes this "know-nothing" prediction. MLE then brings the independent variable into its calculations, running the analysis again—and again and again—to find the best possible predictive fit between years of education and the likelihood of voting.

According to the Iteration History table, SPSS ran through four iterations, finally deciding that it had maximized its ability to predict voting by using education as a predictive instrument. This final-step log likelihood, 3037.490, is recorded in the Iteration History table and it appears, as well, in the Model Summary table. The amount of explanatory leverage gained by including education as a predictor is determined by subtracting the final-step –2 log likelihood (3037.490) from the initial –2 log likelihood (3244.469). If you performed this calculation by hand, you would end up with 206.979, which appears in the Omnibus Tests of Model Coefficients table next to "Model." This number, which could be more accurately labeled "Change in –2 log likelihood," is a chi-square test statistic. In the "Sig." column of the Omnibus Tests of Model Coefficients table, SPSS has reported a P-value of .000 for this chi-square statistic. Conclusion: Compared with how well we can predict voting without knowing education, including education as a predictor significantly enhances the performance of the model.

By now you are aware of the interpretive challenges presented by logistic regression analysis. In running good old Regression → Linear, you had a mere handful of statistics to report and discuss: the constant, the regression coefficient(s) and accompanying P-value(s), and R-square. That's about it. With Regression → Binary Logistic, there are more statistics to record and interpret. Below is a tabular summary of the results of the vote00-educ analysis. You could use this tabular format to report the results of any logistic regressions you perform:

Model estimates and model summary: Logged odds (voting) = a + b (educ)

Model estimates	Coefficient	Significance	Exp(B)*	Percentage change in odds
Constant	–2.154			
Education	.223	.000	1.25	25.0

Model summary	Value	Significance		
Chi-square**	206.979	.000		
Cox-Snell R-square	.077			
Nagelkerke R-square	.107			

  * Alternatively, this column could be labeled "Odds ratio."
** Alternatively, this row could be labeled "Change in –2 Log likelihood."

LOGISTIC REGRESSION WITH MULTIPLE INDEPENDENT VARIABLES

The act of voting might seem simple, but we know that it isn't. Certainly, education is not the only characteristic that shapes the individual's decision whether to vote or to stay home. Indeed, we have just seen that years of schooling, although clearly an important predictor of turnout, returned so-so pseudo-R square statistics, indicating that other factors might also contribute to the explanation. Age, race, marital status, strength of partisanship, political efficacy—all of these variables are known predictors of turnout. What is more, education might itself be related to other independent variables of interest, such as age or race. Thus you might reasonably want to know the partial effect of education on turnout, controlling for the effects of these other independent variables. When performing OLS regression, you can enter multiple independent variables into the model and estimate the partial effects of each one on the dependent variable. Logistic regression, like OLS regression, can accommodate multiple predictors of a binary dependent variable. Consider this logistic regression model:

$$\text{Logged odds (voting)} = a + b_1(\text{educ}) + b_2(\text{age})$$

Figure 10–5 Logistic Regression Output with Two Independent Variables: Variables in the Equation and Model Summary

Chapter 10 - SPSS Viewer

Model Summary

Step	-2 Log likelihood	Cox & Snell R Square	Nagelkerke R Square
1	2755.332[a]	.169	.237

a. Estimation terminated at iteration number 5 because parameter estimates changed by less than .001.

Classification Table[a]

Observed			Predicted: Did R vote in the 2000 election? Did not vote	Predicted: Did R vote in the 2000 election? Voted	Percentage Correct
Step 1	Did R vote in the 2000 election?	Did not vote	322	498	39.3
		Voted	190	1581	89.3
	Overall Percentage				73.4

a. The cut value is .500

Variables in the Equation

		B	S.E.	Wald	df	Sig.	Exp(B)
Step 1[a]	educ	.293	.019	236.19	1	.000	1.341
	age	.047	.003	231.33	1	.000	1.048
	Constant	-5.153	.316	266.40	1	.000	.006

a. Variable(s) entered on step 1: educ, age.

SPSS Processor is ready

Again we are in an OLS-like environment. As before, educ measures number of years of formal education. The variable age measures each respondent's age in years, from 18 to 89. From a substantive standpoint, we would again expect b_1, the coefficient on educ, to be positive: As education increases, so too should the logged odds of voting. We also know that older people are more likely to vote than are younger people. Thus we should find a positive sign on b_2, the coefficient on age. Just as in OLS, b_1 will estimate the effect of education on voting, controlling for age, and b_2 will estimate the effect of age on the dependent variable, controlling for the effect of education. Finally, the various measures of strength—Cox-Snell, Nagelkerke, –2 Log likelihood—will give us an idea of how well both independent variables explain turnout.

Let's see what happens when we add age to our model. Click Analyze → Regression → Binary Logistic. Everything is still in place from our previous run: vote00 is in the Dependent box and educ is in the Covariates box. Good. Now locate age in the variable list and click it into the Covariates box. Click OK to run the analysis. Now scroll to the bottom of the output and view the results displayed in the Variables in the Equation table (Figure 10-5). Plug these estimates into our model:

$$\text{Logged odds (voting)} = -5.153 + .293(\text{educ}) + .047(\text{age}).$$

Interpretation of these coefficients follows a straightforward multiple regression protocol. The coefficient on educ, .293, tells us that, controlling for age, each additional year of education increases the logged odds of voting by .293. And notice that, controlling for education, age is positively related to the likelihood of voting. Each 1-year increment in age produces an increase of .047 in the logged odds of voting. According to Wald and accompanying P-values, each independent variable is significantly related to the dependent variable.

Now consider SPSS's helpful translations of the coefficients, from logged odds to odds ratios, which are displayed in the "Exp(B)" column. Interestingly, after controlling for age, the effect of education is noticeably stronger than its uncontrolled effect, which we analyzed earlier. Taking respondents' age differences into

Figure 10–6 Logistic Regression Output with Two Independent Variables: Model Summary, Omnibus Tests of Model Coefficients, and Iteration History

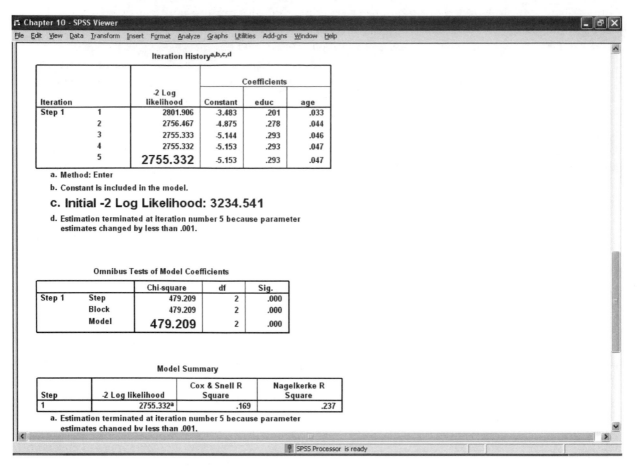

account, we find that each additional year of schooling increases the odds ratio by 1.341 and boosts the odds of voting by 34 percent: $(1.341 - 1) * 100 = 34.1$.[2] For age, too, the value of Exp(B), 1.048, is greater than 1, again communicating the positive relationship between age and the likelihood of voting. If you were to compare two individuals having the same number of years of education but who differed by 1 year in age, the older person would be 1.048 times more likely to vote than the younger person. Translating 1.048 into a percentage change in the odds: $(1.048 - 1) * 100 = 4.8$. Conclusion: Each additional year in age increases the odds of voting by about 5 percent.[3]

According to Cox-Snell (.169) and Nagelkerke (.237), adding age to the model increased its explanatory power, at least when compared with the simple analysis using education as the sole predictor. The value of –2 Log likelihood, 2755.332, is best viewed through the lens of the chi-square test, which you will find by scrolling up to the tables labeled "Omnibus Tests of Model Coefficients" and "Iteration History" (Figure 10-6). MLE's initial know-nothing model—estimating the likelihood of voting without using education or age as predictors—returned a –2 Log likelihood of 3234.541. After bringing the independent variables into play and running through five iterations, MLE settled on a –2 Log likelihood of 2755.332, an improvement of 479.209. This value, which is a chi-square test statistic, is statistically significant ("Sig." = .000). This tells us that, compared with the know-nothing model, both independent variables significantly improve our ability to predict the likelihood of voting.

WORKING WITH PREDICTED PROBABILITIES

You now know how to perform basic logistic regression analysis, and you know how to interpret the logistic regression coefficient in terms of an odds ratio and in terms of a percentage change in the odds. No doubt, odds ratios are easier to comprehend than are logged odds. And percentage change in the odds seems more understandable still. Having said this, most researchers prefer to think in terms of probabilities. One might reasonably ask, "What is the effect of a 1-year increase in education on the probability of voting?" Inconveniently, with logistic regression the answer is always, "It depends."

In the first analysis we ran, which examined the voting-education relationship, logistic regression assumed that a linear relationship exists between years of education and the logged odds of voting. This linearity assumption permitted us to arrive at an estimated effect that best fits the data. However, the technique also assumed a nonlinear relationship between years of education and the probability of voting. That is, it assumed that for people who lie near the extremes of the independent variable—respondents with either low or high levels of education—a 1-year increase in education will have a weaker effect on the probability of voting than will a 1 year increase for respondents in the middle range of the independent variable. Because people with low education are unlikely to vote, a 1-year change should not have a huge effect on this likelihood. Ditto for people with many years of schooling. They are already quite likely to vote, and a one-unit increase should not greatly enhance this probability. It is in the middle range of the independent variable that education should have its most potent marginal impact, pushing individuals over the decision threshold from "do not vote" to "vote." So the effect of a 1-year change in education is either weaker or stronger, depending on where respondents "are" on the education variable.

In logistic regression models having more than one independent variable, such as the vote00-educ-age analysis, working with probabilities becomes even more problematic. The technique assumes that the independent variables have additive effects on the logged odds of the dependent variable. Thus for any combination of values of the independent variables, we arrive at an estimated value of the logged odds of the dependent variable by adding up the partial effects the predictor variables. However, logistic regression also assumes that the independent variables have interactive effects on the probability of the dependent variable. For example, in the case of younger respondents (who have a lower probability of voting), the technique might estimate a large effect of education on the probability of voting. For older respondents (who have a higher probability of voting), logistic regression might find a weaker effect of education on the probability of voting. So the effect of each independent variable on the probability of the dependent variable will depend on the values of the other predictors in the model.

Let's explore these issues one at a time, beginning with the simple model that used education alone to predict voting. Even though we cannot identify a single coefficient that summarizes the effect of education on the probability of voting, we can use SPSS to calculate a predicted probability of voting for respondents at each level of education. How does this work? Recall the logistic regression equation SPSS estimated in our first analysis:

$$\text{Logged odds (voting)} = -2.154 + .223(\text{educ}).$$

SPSS would use this logistic regression model to obtain an estimated logged odds of voting for each respondent. It would plug in each respondent's education level, do the math, and calculate an estimated value of the dependent variable, the logged odds of voting. SPSS would then use the following formula to convert the estimated logged odds of voting into a predicted probability of voting:

$$\text{Probability of voting} = \text{Exp(Logged odds of voting)} / (1 + \text{Exp(Logged odds of voting)}).$$

According to this formula, we retrieve the probability of voting by first raising the natural log base e to the power of the logged odds of voting. We then divide this number by the quantity one plus e raised to the power of the logged odds of voting.[4] Clear as mud.

To get an idea of how SPSS calculates predicted probabilities, let's work through an example. Consider respondents who have a high school education, 12 years of schooling. Using the logistic regression equation obtained in the first guided example, we find the logged odds of voting for this group to be $-2.154 + .223$ (12) $= -2.154 + 2.676 = .522$. What is the predicted probability of voting for people with 12 years of education? It would be Exp(.522) / (1 + Exp(.522)) = 1.685 / 2.685 = .628. So for respondents with a high school education, the estimated probability of voting is .628. At the user's request, SPSS will follow this procedure to calculate predicted probabilities for individuals at all values of education, and it will save these predicted probabilities as a new variable in the dataset.

Let's run the vote00-educ analysis again and request that SPSS calculate and save the predicted probability of voting for each respondent. Click Analyze → Regression → Binary Logistic. All of the variables are still

Figure 10–7 Requesting Predicted Probabilities

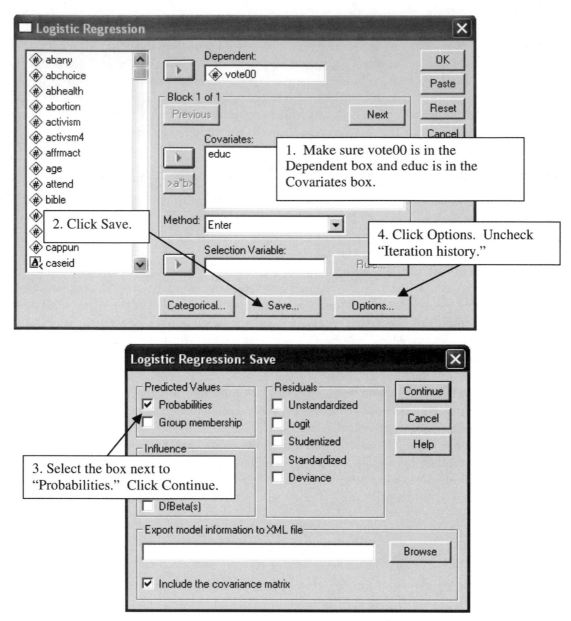

in place from our previous run. This time, however, we want to use only one independent variable, educ. Select age with the mouse and click it back into the variable list, leaving educ in the Covariates box and vote00 in the Dependent box. Now click the Save button, which you will find at the bottom of the Logistic Regression window. This opens the Logistic Regression: Save window (Figure 10-7). In the Predicted Values panel, click the Probabilities box. Click Continue, which returns you to the Logistic Regression window. One more thing. We won't be discussing iteration history on this run, so click Options and uncheck the Iteration history box. Click Continue. Ready to go. Click OK.

SPSS generates output that is identical (except for the iteration history) to our earlier run. So where are the predicted probabilities that we requested? Because we just ran the analysis, SPSS has taken us to the SPSS Viewer. Return to the Variable View of the Data Editor. Scroll to the bottom of the Variable View. As you know, this is where SPSS puts the new variables that you create using Recode or Compute. There you will find a new variable bearing the innocuous name "PRE_1" and the equally bland label "Predicted probability" (Figure 10-8). SPSS has performed just as requested. It ran the analysis, generated the logistic regression output, and discreetly saved a new variable, the predicted probability of voting for each case in the data set. We will want to have a look at PRE_1. But first we need to give it a more descriptive label. Click in the Label cell and type a more informative variable label, such as "Pred prob: educ-vote00."

Figure 10–8 Predicted Probability Saved as a New Variable in the Data Editor

	Name	Type	Width	Decimals	Label	Va
184	vote96	Numeric	8	0	Did R vote in the 1996 election?	{0, Dic
185	educ2	Numeric	8	2		{.00, <
186	income2	Numeric	8	2		None
187	in				income, 2 cats	{.00, <
188	w					None
189	w					None
190	er					None
191	cohort3	Numeric	8	0	Year born: 3 categories	{1, Be
192	intoler	Numeric	8	2	intolerance	None
193	interact	Numeric	8	2	relint2*educ	None
194	PRE_1	Numeric	11	5	Pred prob: educ-vote00	None
195						

> Click in the Label cell and type a more informative variable label, such as "Pred prob: educ-vote00."

In what ways can this new variable, PRE_1, help us to describe changes in the estimated probability of voting as education increases? Remember, SPSS now has a predicted probability of voting for respondents at each value of the education variable, from 0 years to 20 years. So there are two complementary ways to describe the relationship between education and PRE_1, the predicted probability of voting. First, we can perform Analyze → Compare Means → Means, asking SPSS to calculate the mean values of PRE_1 (dependent variable) for each value of educ (independent variable). This would show us by how much the estimated probability of voting increases between groups of respondents having different numbers of years of schooling. Second, we can obtain a line chart of the same information. To obtain a line chart, click Graphs → Line → Simple and click educ into the "Category Axis" box. Then select "Other statistic," and click PRE_1 into the Line Represents panel. This allows us to visualize the nonlinear relationship between education and the predicted probability of voting.

To you, both of these modes of analysis are old hat, so go ahead and perform the analyses. In the mean comparison results (Figure 10-9), the values of educ appear in ascending order down the left-hand column, and mean predicted probabilities (somewhat distractingly, to 7-decimal point precision) are reported in the column labeled "Mean." The line chart (Figure 10-10) adds clarity and elegance to the relationship. To get a feel for what is going on, scroll back and forth between the tabular analysis and the graphic output. What happens to the predicted probability of voting as education increases? Notice that, in the lower range of the independent variable, between 0 years and about 6 years, the predicted probabilities are quite low (between .10 and about .31) and these probabilities increase on the order of .02 to .04 for each increment in education. Now shift your focus to the upper reaches of education and note much the same thing. Beginning at about 13 years of schooling, the estimated probability of voting is at or above about .68—a high likelihood of turning out—and so increments in this range have weaker effects on the probability of voting. In the middle range, from 7 to 12 years, the probabilities increase at a "faster" marginal rate, and within this range the graphic curve shows its steepest slope.

Although most political researchers like to get a handle on predicted probabilities, as we have just done, there is no agreed-upon format for succinctly summarizing logistic regression results in terms of probabilities. One commonly used approach is to report the so-called full effect of the independent variable on the probability of the dependent variable. The full effect is calculated by subtracting the probability associated with the lowest value of the independent variable from the probability associated with the highest value of the independent variable. According to our Compare Means analysis, the predicted probability of voting for people with no formal schooling is about .10, and the predicted probability for those with 20 years of education is .91. The full effect would be .91 − .10 = .81. So, measured across its full range of observed values, education boosts the probability of voting by a healthy .81.

Another way of summarizing a relationship in terms of probabilities is to report the interval of the independent variable that has the biggest impact on the probability of the dependent variable. Suppose that you had to pick the 1-year increment in education that has the largest impact on the probability of voting.

Figure 10–9 Mean Comparison Table for Predicted Probabilities

Chapter 10 - SPSS Viewer

File Edit View Data Transform Insert Format Analyze Graphs Utilities Add-ons Window Help

Report

Pred prob: educ-vote00

Highest year	Mean	N
0	.1039430	5
1	.1266338	2
2	.1534299	15
3	.1846970	2
4	.2206750	6
5	.2614142	8
6	.3067143	25
7	.3560800	14
8	.4087070	66
9	.4635132	60
10	.5192152	88
11	.5744437	137
12	.6278749	818
13	.6783538	265
14	.7249845	374
15	.7671752	157
16	.8046375	377
17	.8373500	93
18	.8655005	128
19	.8894223	43
20	.9095341	70
Total	.6820058	2753

SPSS Processor is ready

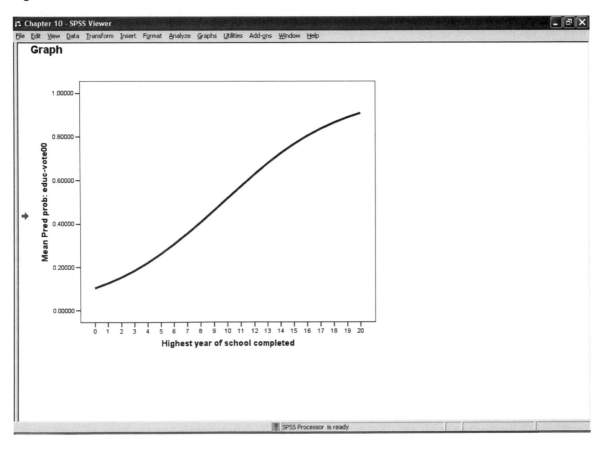

Figure 10–10 Line Chart for Predicted Probabilities

What would that increment be? Study the output and think about the phenomenon you are analyzing. Remember that voting is an up or down decision. A person either decides to vote or decides not to vote. But between which two values of education does a "vote" decision become more likely than a "do not vote" decision? You may have noticed that, between 9 years and 10 years, the predicted probabilities increase from .46 to .52, a difference of .06 and the largest marginal increase in the data. And it is between these two values of education that, according to the analysis, the binary decision shifts in favor of voting—from a probability of less than .50 to a probability of greater than .50. So the interval between 9 years and 10 years is the "sweet spot"—the interval with the largest impact on the probability of voting, and the interval in which the predicted probability switches from less than .50 to more than .50.[5]

Saving predicted probabilities using the Logistic Regression: Save option works fine for simple models with one independent variable. By examining these predicted probabilities, you are able to summarize the full effect of the independent variable on the dependent variable. Furthermore, you can describe the interval of the independent variable having the largest impact on the probability of the dependent variable. Of course, SPSS also will gladly save predicted probabilities for logistic regression models having more than one independent variable. With some specialized exceptions, however, these predicted probabilities are not very useful for summarizing the effect of each independent variable on the probability of the dependent variable, controlling for the other independent variables in the model. As noted earlier, although logistic regression assumes that the independent variables have an additive effect on the logged odds of the dependent variable, the technique also assumes that the independent variables have an interactive effect on the probability of the dependent variable. Thus the effect of, say, education on the probability of voting will be different for younger people than for older people. And the effect of age will vary, depending on the level of education being analyzed. How can we summarize these interaction effects?

In dealing with logistic regression models with multiple independent variables, many researchers use the *sample averages method* for presenting and interpreting probabilities. In the sample averages approach, the analyst presents the full effect of each independent variable while holding the other independent variables constant at their sample means. For example, we would ask and answer these questions: "For people of 'average' age, what effect does education have on the probability of voting?" "For respondents with 'average' levels of education, what effect does age have on the probability of voting?" In this way, we can get an idea of the effect of each variable on individuals who are "average" on all the other variables being studied. Unfortunately, Regression → Binary Logistic will not calculate the predicted probabilities associated with each value of an independent variable, while holding the other variables constant at their sample means.[6] That's the bad news. The good news is that the desired probabilities are easily obtained using Transform → Compute, and they are readily analyzed using Compare Means.

THE SAMPLE AVERAGES METHOD USING COMPUTE AND COMPARE MEANS

Here is the logistic regression model that SPSS estimated for the vote00-educ-age relationships:

$$\text{Logged odds (voting)} = -5.153 + .293(\text{educ}) + .047(\text{age}).$$

We can enlist this equation for two tasks. First, we can plug in the sample mean of age and calculate the full effect of educ on the probability of voting. Second, we can plug in the sample mean of educ and calculate the full effect of age on the probability of voting. Here we will work through the first task only—figuring out the full effect of education on the probability of voting for people of average age. Before proceeding, of course, we need to obtain the sample mean of age. A quick Descriptives run (which you are invited to replicate) reveals that age has a mean value of 46.28 years. The following equation would permit us to estimate the logged odds of voting at any value of educ, holding age constant at its mean:

$$\text{Logged odds (voting)} = -5.153 + .293(\text{educ}) + .047(46.28).$$

We have already seen that probabilities may be retrieved from logged odds via this conversion:

$$\text{Probability of voting} = \text{Exp(Logged odds of voting)} / (1 + \text{Exp(Logged odds of voting)}).$$

Figure 10–11 Computing a Predicted Probability for Different Values of an Independent Variable at the Mean Value of Another Independent Variable

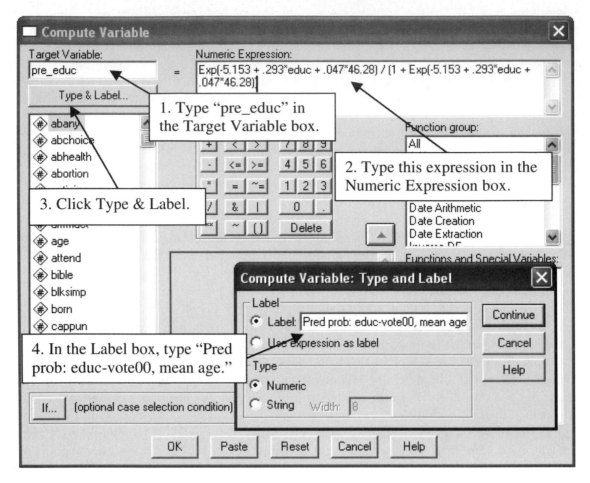

The following equation, therefore, would convert a logged odds of voting into a predicted probability of voting for any plugged-in value of educ, holding age constant at its mean of 46.28:

$$\text{Probability of voting} = \text{Exp}(-5.153 + .293*educ + .047*46.28) /$$
$$(1 + \text{Exp}(-5.153 + .293*educ + .047*46.28)).$$

Of course, we could figure all this out using a hand calculator—first finding the predicted probability of voting for individuals having no formal schooling (educ = 0) and then calculating the predicted probability of people with 20 years of education (educ = 20). By subtracting the first probability (when educ = 0) from the second probability (when educ = 20), we would arrive at the full effect of educ at the mean value of age. But let's ask SPSS to do the work for us. Click Transform → Compute. What do we want SPSS to do? We want it to calculate the predicted probability of voting for respondents at each level of education, holding age constant at its sample mean. Because we are holding age constant but allowing educ to vary, we will name this variable "pre_educ." Type "pre_educ" in the Target Variable box. In the Numeric Expression box type this expression: "Exp(−5.153 + .293*educ + .047*46.28) / (1 + Exp(−5.153 + .293*educ + .047*46.28))," as shown in Figure 10-11.[7] Click Type & Label. In the Label box, give pre_educ the descriptive label "Pred prob: educ-vote00, mean age." Click OK. SPSS computes a new variable, pre_educ, and enters this variable into the dataset.

Finally we have the estimates that permit us to examine the effect of education on the probability of voting for respondents of average age. Click Analyze → Compare Means → Means. Click our newly computed variable, pre_educ, into the Dependent List, and click educ into the Independent List. Click OK. Examine the output (Figure 10-12). What is the full effect of education? Notice that people with 0 years of

Figure 10–12 Mean Comparison Table for Predicted Probabilities (modified)

Report

Pred prob: educ-vote00, mean age

Highest year of	Mean	N
0	.0484	5
1	.0639	2
2	.0838	15
3	.1092	2
4	.1411	6
5	.1805	8
6	.2280	25
7	.2836	14
8	.3466	66
9	.4156	60
10	.4880	88
11	.5610	137
12	.6314	818
13	.6966	265
14	.7548	374
15	.8049	157
16	.8469	377
17	.8811	93
18	.9086	128
19	.9302	43
20	.9470	70
Total	.6956	2753

education have a probability of voting equal to about .05 (5 chances in 100 that the individual voted), compared with a probability of about .95 for individuals with 20 years of education (95 chances in 100 that the individual voted). Thus, holding age constant at its sample mean, the full effect of education is equal to .95 – .05 = .90. You might also note that the largest marginal effect of education, a boost of more than .07 in the probability of voting, occurs between 10 and 11 years of schooling.

EXERCISES

In Exercise 1 you will analyze States.sav. In Exercise 2 you will analyze World.sav.

1. As you know, presidential elections in the United States take place within an unusual institutional context. Naturally, candidates seek as many votes as they can get, but the real electoral prizes come in winner-take-all, state-sized chunks: The plurality-vote winner in each state receives all the electoral college votes from that state. Cast in logistic regression terms, each state represents a binary outcome—it goes either Republican or Democratic. What variables shape this outcome? What factors make states more likely to end up in the Republican column than in the Democratic column? Given the Republican Party's reputation for conservative positions on social issues, the following hypothesis seems plausible: In comparing states, those with higher percentages of residents who frequently attend religious services will be more likely to be won by the Republican candidate than will states having lower percentages of residents who frequently attend religious services.

   States.sav contains gb_win04, a binary variable coded 1 if the state's electoral vote went to Republican George W. Bush in 2004, and coded 0 if the state went to Democrat John Kerry. This is the dependent variable. States.sav also has attend, the percentage of state residents who frequently attend religious services. Attend, which displays interesting variation across states, is the independent variable.[8] Run Regression → Binary Logistic, clicking gb_win04 into the Dependent box and clicking attend into the Covariates box. In Options, request

Iteration history. Click Save. In the Predicted Values panel of the Logistic Regression: Save window, select Probabilities.

A. The following table contains seven question marks (?). Fill in the correct value next to each question mark.

Model estimates	Coefficient	Significance
Constant	?	
Attend	?	?

Model summary	Value	Significance
Chi-square	?	?
Cox-Snell R-square	?	
Nagelkerke R-square	?	

B. For the variable attend, Exp(B) is equal to _____. After converting this number to a percentage change in the odds of a Bush win, you could say that a one-unit increase in attend increases the odds of a Bush win by _____ percent.

C. Run Analyze → Compare Means → Means, obtaining mean values of the predicted probability of gb_win04 (dependent variable, which SPSS saved as PRE_1) for each value of attend (independent variable). Print the mean comparison table. Use the results to answer parts D, E, and F.

D. The full effect of attend on the probability of gb_win04 is equal to _____.

E. A Republican strategist must decide in which states to concentrate her limited campaign resources. She calculates that, with an all-out effort, her team can increase the probability of a Republican win by about .03 in one state. To achieve maximum effect, this strategist should concentrate her campaign on (check one)

❏ a state in which about 24 percent of its residents frequently attend religious services.

❏ a state in which about 34 percent of its residents frequently attend religious services.

❏ a state in which about 44 percent of its residents frequently attend religious services.

F. Briefly explain your reasoning in part E. _____

_____

_____

_____

2. For one of the exercises in Chapter 5, you used SPSS Crosstabs and World.sav to investigate the relationship between ethnic heterogeneity and democracy. You tested this hypothesis: In comparing countries, those having lower levels of ethnic heterogeneity will be more likely to be democracies than will those having higher levels of ethnic heterogeneity. This hypothesis says that, as heterogeneity goes up, the probability of democracy goes down. You then reran the analysis, controlling for a measure of countries' economic development, gross domestic product per capita. For this independent variable, the relationship is thought to be positive: As economic development increases, so does the likelihood that a country will be democratic. In Chapter 5 you used less precise ordinal-level measures of the independent variables to test these hypotheses. In the current exercise, you will reexamine this set of relationships, using interval-level independent variables and a more powerful method of analysis, logistic regression.

World.sav contains these three variables: democ, eth_het, and gdp_1000. The variable democ is coded 1 if the country is a democracy and coded 0 if it is not a democracy. This is the dependent variable. One of the independent variables, eth_het, can vary between .00 (denoting low heterogeneity) and 1.00 (high heterogeneity). The other independent variable, gdp_1000, measures gross domestic product per capita in units of $1,000.

A. Run Regression → Binary Logistic, clicking democ into the Dependent box and clicking eth_het and gdp_1000 into the Covariates box. In Options, request Iteration history. (For this exercise, you will not be saving predicted probabilities.) Click OK to run the analysis. The following table contains eight question marks (?). Fill in the correct value next to each question mark.

Model estimates	Coefficient	Significance	Exp(B)
Constant	−.414		
Eth_het	−2.334	?	?
Gdp_1000	.351	?	?

Model summary	Value	Significance
Chi-square	?	?
Cox-Snell R-square	?	
Nagelkerke R-square	?	

B. Use each value of Exp(B) to calculate a percentage change in the odds. Controlling for gdp_1000, a one-unit change in eth_het, from low heterogeneity to high heterogeneity (check one)

❑ increases the odds of democracy by about 10 percent.

❑ decreases the odds of democracy by about 10 percent.

❑ decreases the odds of democracy by about 90 percent.

Controlling for eth_het, each $1,000 increase in per capita gross domestic product (check one)

❑ increases the odds of democracy by about 142 percent.

❑ increases the odds of democracy by about 42 percent.

❑ increases the odds of democracy by about 14 percent.

To respond to parts C, D, E, and F, you will need to use Compute to calculate a new variable. This new variable, which you will name "pre_eth," will estimate the probability of democracy for each value of eth_het, holding gdp_1000 constant at its mean. *Useful fact:* The mean of gdp_1000 is equal to 4.80. *Helpful hint:* The numeric expression for computing the predicted probability of democracy for each value of eth_het is "Exp(−.414 −2.334*eth_het + .351*4.80) / (1 + Exp(−.414 −2.334*eth_het + .351*4.80))". After computing pre_eth, run Compare Means → Means, entering pre_eth as the dependent variable and eth_het as the independent variable.

C. Print the output from the Analyze → Compare Means → Means analysis you just did. You will use it to answer parts D, E, and F of this exercise.

D. As an empirical matter, the most homogeneous country in World.sav has a value of .00 on eth_het, and the most heterogeneous country has a value of .90 on eth_het. The predicted probability of democracy for a highly homogeneous country (eth_het = .00) with an average level of gdp_1000 is equal to _____. The predicted probability of democracy for a highly heterogeneous country (eth_het = .90) with an average level of gdp_1000 is equal to _____.

E. As eth_het increases, from low heterogeneity to high heterogeneity, the predicted probability of democracy (circle one)

decreases.   does not change.   increases.

F. At mean levels of gdp_1000, the full effect of eth_het (from .00 to .90) on the probability of democracy is equal to _____.

That concludes the exercises for this chapter. Before exiting SPSS, be sure to save your output file.

NOTES

1. When you request Iteration history, SPSS will by default produce two histories—one appearing near the beginning of the output beneath the label "Block 0: Beginning Block" and one appearing later beneath the label "Block 1: Method = Enter." In most situations, all of the information you will need can be found under the Block 1 entry. Figure 10-4 portrays the information contained in the Block 1 entry.

2. Why is the controlled effect of education (a 34-percent increase in the odds of voting) greater than its uncontrolled effect (a 25-percent increase in the odds of voting)? Running Analyze → Correlate → Bivariate for educ and age provides an important clue: educ and age are negatively correlated ($r = -.116$). Thus in the earlier analysis, in which we compared respondents having less education with respondents having more education (but in which we did not control for age), we were also comparing older respondents (who, on average, have fewer years of schooling) with younger respondents (who, on average, have more years of schooling). Because younger people are less likely to vote than are older people, the uncontrolled effect of age weakens the zero-order relationship between educ and vote00. In a situation like this, age is said to be a *suppressor variable,* because it suppresses or attenuates the true effect of education on turnout.

3. When using interval-level independent variables with many values, you will often obtain logistic regression coefficients and odds ratios that appear to be quite close to null hypothesis territory (coefficients close to 0 and odds ratios close to 1) but that nonetheless trump the null hypothesis. Remember that logistic regression, like OLS, estimates the marginal effect of a one-unit increment on the logged odds of the dependent variable. In the current example, logistic regression estimated the effect of a 1-year change in age (from, say, an age of 20 years to 21 years) on the logged odds of voting. The researcher may describe the relationship in terms of larger increments. Thus, if a 1-year increase in age (from 20 years to 21 years) increases the odds of voting by an estimated 5 percent, then a 10-year increase in age (from 20 years to 30 years) would produce a 50-percent increase in the odds of voting.

4. The expression "Exp(Logged odds of voting)" translates logged odds into odds: Exp(Logged odds of voting) = Odds of voting. One gets from an odds to a probability by dividing the odds by the quantity one plus the odds: Probability of voting = Odds of voting / (1 + Odds of voting). Thus the formula for the probability of voting, "Exp(Logged odds of voting) / (1 + Exp(Logged odds of voting))," is equivalent to the formula "Odds of voting / (1 + Odds of voting)."

5. The largest marginal effect of the independent variable on the probability of the dependent variable is sometimes called the *instantaneous effect.* In our example, the instantaneous effect is equal to .06, and this effect occurs between 9 years and 10 years of education. The effect of a one-unit change in the independent variable on the probability of the dependent variable is always greatest for the interval containing a probability equal to .5. The instantaneous effect, calculated by hand, is equal to b * .5 * (1 − .5), in which b is the value of the logistic regression coefficient. For a discussion of the instantaneous effect, see Fred C. Pampel, *Logistic Regression: A Primer,* Sage University Papers Series on Quantitative Applications in the Social Sciences, series no. 07-132 (Thousand Oaks, CA: Sage Publications, 2000), 24–26.

6. In calculating predicted probabilities for multivariate logistic regression models, SPSS returns estimated probabilities for subjects having each combination of values on the independent variables. It does not calculate the probabilities associated with each value of a given independent variable, while holding the other predictors constant.

7. SPSS has a large repertoire of canned statistical functions. The function Exp(numerical expression) returns the natural log base *e* raised to the power of the numerical expression. This is precisely what we want here, because the estimated probability of voting is equal to Exp(Logged odds of voting) / (1 + Exp(Logged odds of voting)).

8. Attend varies between 24.28 percent (Washington) and 60.95 percent (Louisiana). A total of 13 states lack sufficient information on attend and have been set to missing on this variable. The remaining 37 states are analyzed in this exercise.

11

Doing Your Own Political Analysis

In working through the guided examples in this book, and in performing the exercises, you have developed some solid analytic skills. The datasets you have analyzed throughout this book could, of course, become the raw material for your own research. You would not be disappointed, however, if you were to look elsewhere for excellent data. High-quality social science data on a variety of phenomena and units of analysis—individuals, census tracts, states, countries—are increasingly accessible via the Internet and might serve as the centerpiece for your own research. Your school, for example, may be a member of the Inter-university Consortium for Political and Social Research (ICPSR), the premier organizational clearinghouse for datasets of all kinds.[1] You will find that the expertise you have gained can be productively applied to any number of research questions that interest you.

Even so, there is much to be said for striking out on your own—observing an interesting fact or behavior, developing an explanation and hypothesis, and collecting and analyzing your own original dataset. Doing original research from the ground up can yield large intellectual dividends. (And besides, your instructor may require it.) In this chapter we explore the do-it-yourself route. We begin by laying out the stages of the research process and by offering some manageable ideas for original analysis. We illustrate how the raw dataset included with this book, senate2003.txt, was created from information collected from an Internet site. By following the steps described in this chapter, you will learn how to get SPSS to read the raw data. Finally, we describe a serviceable format for an organized and presentable research paper.

FIVE DOABLE IDEAS

Let's begin by describing an ideal research procedure and then discuss some practical considerations and constraints. In an ideal world you would

1. observe an interesting behavior or relationship and frame a research question about it;
2. develop a causal explanation for what you have observed and construct a hypothesis;
3. read and learn from the work of other researchers who have tackled similar questions;
4. collect and analyze the data that will address the hypothesis; and
5. write a research paper or article in which you present and interpret your findings.

In this scenario the phenomenon that you observe in stage 1 drives the whole process. First think up a question, and then research it and obtain the data that will address it. As a practical matter, the process is almost never this clear cut. Often someone else's idea or assertion may pique your interest. For example, you might read articles or attend lectures on a variety of topics—democratization in developing countries, global environmental issues, ideological change in the Democratic or Republican Party, the effect of election laws on turnout and party competition, and so on—that suggest hypotheses you would like to examine. So you may begin the process at stage 3, and then return to stage 1 and refine your own ideas. Furthermore, the availability of relevant data, considered in stage 4, almost always plays a role in the sorts of questions we address. Suppose, for example, that you want to assess the organizational efforts to mobilize African Americans in your state in the last presidential election. You want precinct-level registration data, and you need to compare these numbers with the figures from previous elections. You would soon become an expert in the bureaucratic hassles and expense involved in dealing with county governments, and you might have to revise your research agenda. Indeed, for professional researchers and academics, data collection in itself can be a full-time job. For students who wish to produce a competent and manageable project, the so-called law of available data can be a source of frustration and discouragement.

A doable project often requires a compromise between stage 1 and stage 4. What interesting question can you ask, given the available data? Fortunately, this compromise need not be as restrictive as it sounds. Consider five possibilities: political knowledge, economic performance and election outcomes, state courts and criminal procedure, electoral turnout in comparative perspective, and the U.S. Congress.

Political Knowledge

As you may have learned in other political science courses, scholars continue to debate the levels of knowledge and political awareness among ordinary citizens. Do citizens know the length of a U.S. senator's term of office? Do they know what constitutional protections are guaranteed by the First Amendment? Do people tend to know more about some things—Internet privacy or abortion policy, for example—and less about other things, such as foreign policy or international politics? Political knowledge is a promising variable because you are likely to find some people who know a lot about politics, some who know a fair amount, and others who know very little. You could ask, "What causes this variation?" Imagine constructing a brief questionnaire that asks 8 or 10 multiple-choice questions about basic facts and is tailored to the aspects of political knowledge you find most thought provoking. After including questions that gauge some potentially important independent variables (partisanship, gender, liberalism/conservatism, college major, class standing), you could conduct an exploratory survey among perhaps 50 or 100 of your fellow students. (Your sample would not be random, but you would still get some compelling results that could guide you toward a more ambitious study.)

Economic Performance and Election Outcomes

Here is one of the most widely discussed ideas in political science: The state of the economy before an election has a big effect on the election result. If the economy is strong, then the candidate of the incumbent party does well, probably winning. If the economy is performing poorly, then the incumbent party's nominee pays the price, probably losing. This idea has a couple of intriguing aspects. For one thing, it works well—but not perfectly. (The 2000 presidential election is a case in point.) Moreover, the economy-election relationship has several researchable layers. Focusing on presidential elections, you can imagine a simple two-category measure of the dependent variable—the incumbent party wins or the incumbent party loses. Now consider several stints in the reference section of the library, collecting information on some potential independent variables for each presidential election year: inflation rates, unemployment, economic growth, and so on. Alternatively, you could look at congressional or state-level elections, or elections in several different countries. Or you could modify and refine the basic idea, as many scholars have done, by adding additional noneconomic variables you believe to be important. Scandal? Foreign policy crises? With some hands-on data collection and guidance from your instructor, you can produce a well-crafted project.

State Courts and Criminal Procedure

To what extent does a justice's partisanship (or political ideology) affect his or her ruling in a case? This is a perennial question in the annals of judicial research. Again, the 2000 election comes to mind. The U.S. Supreme Court based its pivotal decision on judicial principles, but the Court split along partisan lines. And, given the level of partisan acrimony that accompanies the nominations of would-be federal judges, members of the U.S. Senate behave as if political ideology plays a role in judicial decision making. Original research on judicial proceedings, particularly at the federal level, is among the most difficult to conduct, even for seasoned scholars. But consider state judicial systems. Using an online resource available through most university servers, you could collect information about a large number of, say, criminal cases heard on appeal by the highest court in your state.[2] You could record whether the criminal defendant won or lost and then determine the party affiliations of the justices. Additionally, you could compare judicial decision making in two states—one in which judges are appointed and one in which they are elected. You could make this comparison at the individual justice level at one point in time. Or you could look at the same set of courts over time, using aggregate units of analysis.

Electoral Turnout in Comparative Perspective

The record of voter turnout in U.S. presidential elections, while showing an encouraging reversal in 2004, generally is pretty anemic. Despite the down-to-the-wire closeness of the 2000 contest, for example, just slightly more than half of the voting-age population went to the polls on the day of the election. The situation in other democratic countries is strikingly different. Turnouts in some Western European countries average well above 70 percent. Why? More generally, what causes turnout to vary between countries? Some scholars have focused on legal factors. Unlike the United States, some countries may not require their citizens to register beforehand, or they may penalize citizens for not voting. Other scholars look at institutional differences in electoral systems. Many countries, for example, have systems of proportional representation in which narrowly focused parties with relatively few supporters nonetheless can gain representation in the legislature. Are citizens more likely to be mobilized to vote under such institutional arrangements? Using sources available in the reference section of the library, you could gather information on 15 or 20 nations. You could then look to see if different legal requirements and institutional arrangements are associated with differences in turnout. This area of research might also open the door for some informed speculation on your part. What sort of electoral reforms, if instituted in the United States, might enhance electoral turnout? What other (perhaps unintended) consequences might such reforms have?

Congress

Political scholars have long taken considerable interest in questions about the U.S. Congress. Some researchers focus on internal dynamics: the role of leadership, the power of party ties versus the pull of constituency. Others pay attention to demographics: Has the number of women and minorities who serve in Congress increased in the recent past? Still others look at ideology: Are Republicans, on average, becoming more conservative and Democrats more liberal in their congressional voting? The great thing about Congress is the rich data that are available. The U.S. House and the U.S. Senate are among the most-studied institutions in the world. Several annual or biannual publications chronicle and report a large number of attributes of members of the House and Senate.[3] And the Internet is rife with information about current and past Congresses. Liberal groups, such as Americans for Democratic Action (ADA), and conservative groups, such as the American Conservative Union, regularly rate the voting records of elected officials and post these ratings on their Internet sites.

Each of these five possibilities represents a practical compromise between posing an interesting question and obtaining the data to address it. In the next section we take a closer look at one of these examples—research on the Senate. Using for illustration a dataset included with this book, we consider the nuts and bolts of the research: where to find worthwhile data, how to code the data, and how to get SPSS to read the data.

DOING RESEARCH ON THE U.S. SENATE

The Senate is an intriguing institution. Recall a seemingly insignificant historical event that illustrates the institution's complexity. Following the 2000 elections, the Senate was split right down the middle on partisanship: There were 50 Republicans and 50 Democrats. Republican vice president Dick Cheney, acting in his constitutional capacity, was the tie-breaker, giving the Republican Party a nominal majority. However, a few months after the elections, in May 2001, one of the Republicans, Sen. James Jeffords of Vermont, formally abandoned his party affiliation and became an independent, making the Democrats the majority party in the Senate.

This was a controversial event. But what *general* questions did it raise about Congress? For one thing, it underscored the fact that each house of Congress is formally organized on the basis of party. The party that holds a majority gains control of the leadership posts, and to be chosen to chair a committee or subcommittee, a member of Congress must be from the majority party. Thus, following the partisan shift of a solitary member, all of the leadership and committee chair positions in the Senate went to members of the Democratic Party—a situation that remained in place until after the 2002 elections, when Republicans reclaimed a majority. Yet Jeffords's shift also illustrated that individual members of Congress have a measure of autonomy and that the parties do not always behave as cohesive partisan blocs. Why?

Congress is, of course, charged with making laws that affect the entire country. Democratic and Republican leaders put forward agendas that often reflect philosophically different approaches to lawmaking and governance. The success or failure of these agendas often hinges on whether Democrats and Republicans vote together along party lines. So partisan affiliation exerts an influence on elected representatives. But Congress is also designed as a representative institution—a forum in which the disparate interests of districts and states are brought to bear on public policy. Because representatives and senators must be careful not to support policies that may displease their constituents, they must often weigh the views of their constituencies against the aims of their party leaders. Consider the hypothetical example of an antiabortion measure supported by the Republican leadership and opposed by the Democratic leadership. Would a Democrat from a traditionally conservative region, such as the South, follow the Democratic leadership and oppose such a measure? What about a Republican from a liberal region, such as the Northeast? More generally, one could ask whether partisan and regional interests are more likely to clash on certain types of issues, such as abortion or military spending, than on other issues, such as energy policy or tax cuts. Or do region and party reinforce one another? Is the United States becoming, as some analysts have said, "two political countries," with the interior South and mountain West aligned on the conservative side of issues and the Northeast, upper Midwest, and coastal West aligned on the liberal side? These are general questions. And they are questions worth asking. Where do we find the data?

Finding Raw Data

In this example we show how one of this book's datasets, senate2003.txt, was created from information that appears on an Internet site. This site, maintained by ADA, provides ratings of each member of Congress across a range of congressional votes.[4] Specifically, for each session of Congress the ADA selects a number of key votes, which reflect either a liberal position, supported by ADA, or a conservative position, opposed by ADA. The ADA selects these votes from different policy areas: abortion, taxes, health care, defense spending, and so on. Thus we can look for variations in voting patterns, depending on the type of policy being considered. Make no mistake—the ADA has an agenda to promote. Its members are down-the-line liberal on every issue. But this consistency works to our advantage in measuring congressional ideology because we can be reasonably certain that a "more favorable" ADA rating is a valid gauge of liberalism and that a "less favorable" rating is a valid measure of conservatism.

Figure 11-1 displays a partial Web page from ADA's site, which reports ratings of the 2003 Senate. The left-most column shows the state's name and the names of the senators from that state, and the next column displays party affiliation. The next 20 columns show how each senator voted on the 20 key votes, with a plus sign (+) denoting a liberal vote and a minus sign (−) denoting a conservative vote. If the senator did not vote, the ADA records this absence with a question mark (?). The substantive policy of each vote, appearing as unhelpful numbers 1 through 20 on the Web page shown in Figure 11-1, can be obtained elsewhere at the ADA site. For example, a little browsing reveals that vote number 1 dealt with President George W. Bush's judicial nomination of Miguel A. Estrada, which the ADA opposed. Senators who voted no on this measure got a plus and those supporting it received a minus. Vote number 2, which ADA supported, was an abortion measure expressing Senate support for the Supreme Court's decision in *Roe v. Wade*. Senators voting in favor of this measure were given a plus, and those voting against got a minus. On the right side of the page we find ADA's overall liberalism score for 2003, under the heading "LQ," which stands for Liberal Quotient. ADA arrives at the Liberal Quotient by determining the percentage of votes on which the senator supported ADA's position. Scores can range from 0% (most conservative) to 100% (most liberal). How would you take the information from this site and put it into a form that SPSS can analyze?

How to Code Raw Data

Coding raw data is the sweat equity phase of original research, the stage of tedious labor well invested. You must start with numbers or symbols that appear as text on a printed page—or pixels on a computer screen—and record them as numbers or codes that SPSS can interpret. This coding can be done in several ways. A popular approach is to type the data into a spreadsheet, such as Microsoft Excel. Excel, of course, has the advantages of being widely available and easy to use. Alternatively the data could simply be typed into a plain text file editor (like Wordpad) or a favorite word processor and converted to plain text. Another

Figure 11–1 Internet Site of Americans for Democratic Action: Ratings of the U.S. Senate (2003)

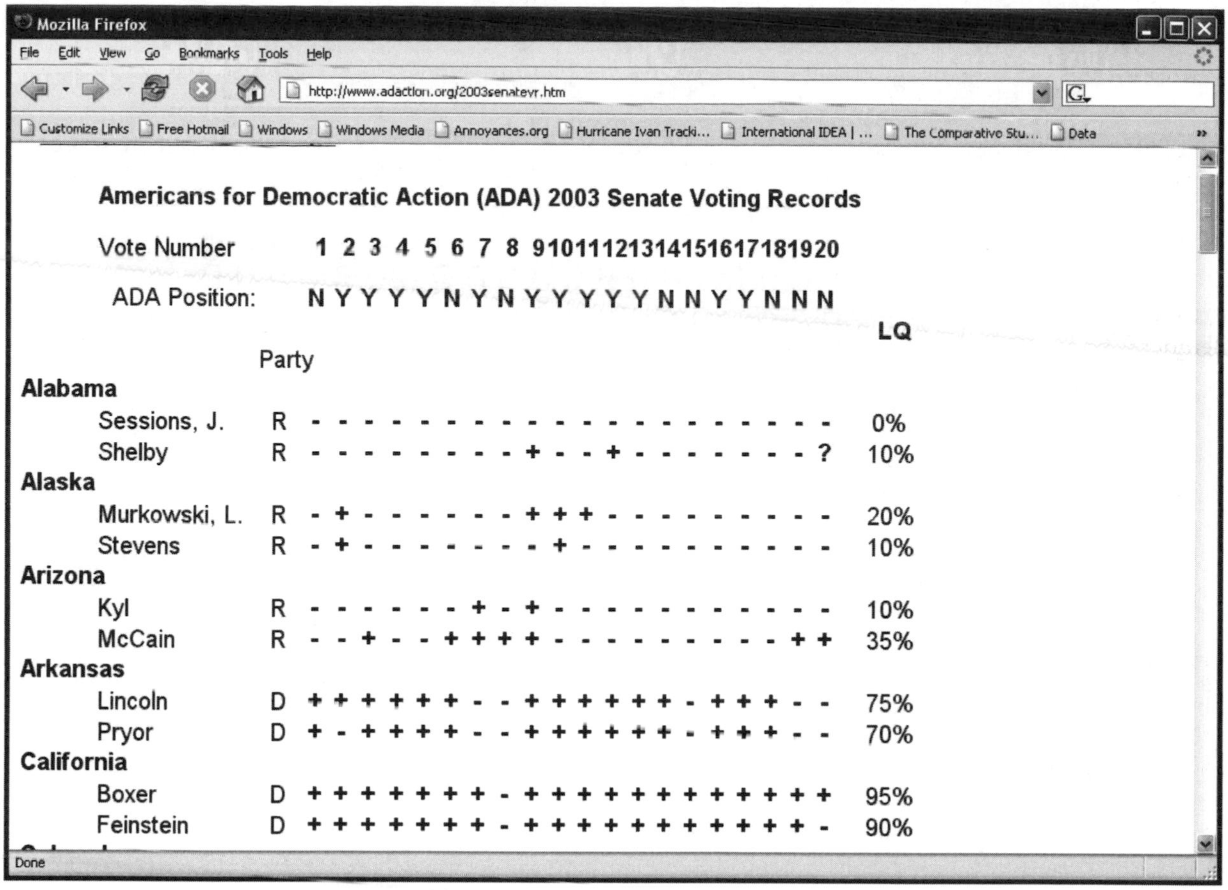

Americans for Democratic Action (ADA) 2003 Senate Voting Records

Vote Number		1 2 3 4 5 6 7 8 91011121314151617181920
ADA Position:		N Y Y Y Y N Y N Y Y Y Y Y N N Y Y N N N

	Party		LQ
Alabama			
Sessions, J.	R	- - - - - - - - - - - - - - - - - - - -	0%
Shelby	R	- - - - - - - - + - - + - - - - - - - ?	10%
Alaska			
Murkowski, L.	R	- + - - - - - - + + + - - - - - - - - -	20%
Stevens	R	- + - - - - - - - + - - - - - - - - - -	10%
Arizona			
Kyl	R	- - - - - - + - + - - - - - - - - - - -	10%
McCain	R	- - + - - + + + + - - - - - - - - - + +	35%
Arkansas			
Lincoln	D	+ + + + + + - - + + + + + + - + + + - -	75%
Pryor	D	+ - + + + + - - + + + + + + - + + + - -	70%
California			
Boxer	D	+ + + + + + + - + + + + + + + + + + + +	95%
Feinstein	D	+ + + + + + + - + + + + + + + + + + + -	90%

approach is to enter the information directly into the SPSS Data Editor and then proceed with the analysis. Fortunately, the choice of method doesn't really matter. SPSS will read a large variety of data formats, including Excel spreadsheets and plain text. What *does* matter is that the coded information be in a form that SPSS understands. So whether you are using a spreadsheet, a text editor, or the SPSS Data Editor, some coding rules are in order. To make sure that all contingencies are covered, we use the most accessible approach—typing data into a word processor or text file—to illustrate how to code the ADA data. We then describe some coding shortcuts.

To learn some coding essentials, consider the second line of information from the ADA page, data on Senator Shelby of Alabama:

Shelby R – – – – – – – – + – – + – – – – – – – ? 10%

Although SPSS would read this data line, it would have trouble analyzing it. SPSS recognizes two basic forms of data, string and numeric. String data are words or symbols, such as Senator Shelby's name, his party designation, the question mark denoting a missed vote, and the plus and minus signs. In fact, in the preceding data line, none of variables are numeric data. SPSS would encounter the percentage sign in "10%" and interpret the entire value as a string. It is a good practice to use numeric codes whenever possible. To convert this line of information into an SPSS-friendly form, we will code the pluses and minuses as 1s and 0s, with 1 representing a liberal vote and 0 representing a conservative vote. Because "?" represents a missed vote, we will replace it with a period (.), recognized as missing data by SPSS. Also, we will delete the "%," leaving the numeric value 10 as Senator Shelby's overall LQ score:

Shelby R 0 0 0 0 0 0 0 0 1 0 0 1 0 0 0 0 0 0 0 . 10

Now each liberal vote is coded 1, and each conservative vote is coded 0. Only the senator's name and his party affiliation ("R" for Republican) remain in nonnumeric form. Notice, too, that the codes are separated by

Figure 11–2 Coding Data in a Text Editor

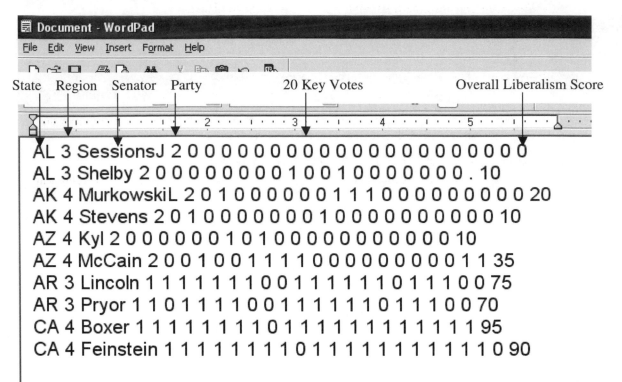

spaces. SPSS interprets spaces as delimiters, boundaries that separate the values of different variables. Alternatively, we can use commas, semicolons, or tabs, because SPSS also recognizes them as delimiters.[5]

We will want to add the state name and census region to each data line. And we also will replace the "D" and "R" party codes with a numeric code for the party affiliation of each senator. State names will be represented by two-character strings, but for region and party we will use numeric codes. For region, each senator from the Northeast will be coded 1; from the Midwest, 2; from the South, 3; and from the West, 4. For party, we'll code Democrats 1 and Republicans 2. (We will code Vermont's Senator Jeffords, the institution's lone independent, 3 on the party variable.) Here is Senator Shelby's complete typed data line:

AL   3   Shelby   2 0 0 0 0 0 0 0 0 1 0 0 1 0 0 0 0 0 0 0 . 10

Senator Shelby represents Alabama (clearly enough), which is in the South census region (coded 3), and he is a Republican (coded 2). We would follow the same coding scheme for each case in the ADA data, consistently typing the state, region code, senator's name, party code, codes for each of the 20 votes, and the overall ADA score. The first 10 cases, typed into a text editor, would look like Figure 11-2. (Notice that, to avoid potential confusion, spaces and commas have been removed from senators' names. So, "Sessions, J." becomes "SessionsJ," and "Murkowski, L." becomes "MurkowskiL.")

Thus far, all of our coding efforts have been aimed at making the data SPSS-friendly—using numeric codes when possible, leaving spaces between the values of different variables, and using periods for missing data. Before we read the data into SPSS, however, we will want to invent a brief but descriptive name for each variable—a word or abbreviation that communicates what the variable is measuring.

Keep in mind two goals when you invent variable names. The first goal is to follow SPSS's variable-naming rules. If you are running SPSS 11.5 or earlier, these rules are rather restrictive. An SPSS variable name must be no longer than eight characters, must begin with a letter, and must not contain any blanks or special characters, such as dashes or commas. If you are running SPSS 12.0 or later, life is easier. Although variable names must begin with a letter and cannot contain special characters, they can be up to 64 characters in length. But to keep the presentation general, here we will use 11.5-compatible variable names. The variable-naming rules are easily followed for the first four variables, which we'll call state, region, senator, and party.

Table 11-1 Key Votes in the U.S. Senate (2003), as Identified by the Americans for Democratic Action (ADA), with Corresponding Variable Names and Variable Labels

Key Vote	Vote Description	Outcome of a yes vote	ADA's position	Winning position	Variable name	Variable label
1	Estrada judicial nomination	Limit debate and vote on nomination	No	No	estrada	Cloture on Estrada
2	Amendment to abortion bill	Express support for *Roe v. Wade*	Yes	Yes	abort1	Support Roe
3	ANWR oil drilling	Kill language authorizing oil drilling	Yes	Yes	energy1	ANWR drilling
4	Budget resolution on childcare	Increase mandatory childcare spending	Yes	No	daycare	Childcare spending
5	Unemployment insurance extension	Waive Budget Act and extend unemployment benefits	Yes	No	employ1	Unemployment insurance
6	Tax reduction	Reduce taxes by $350 billion over 11 years	No	Yes	tax	Tax cuts
7	Nuclear power plants	Kill loan guarantees for seven new nuclear power plants	Yes	No	energy2	Nuclear power
8	Prescription drug benefit	Authorize creation of prescription drug benefit	No	Yes	rxplan1	Rx benefit
9	State Department reauthorization, HIV/AIDS	Support full funding of global HIV/AIDS bill	Yes	Yes	aids	AIDS funding
10	Overtime pay regulations	Prohibit regulations taking away overtime pay	Yes	Yes	employ2	Overtime pay
11	Student financial aid eligibility	Prohibit change in student loan formulas	Yes	Yes	govloan	Student loans
12	FCC media ownership rule	Disapprove allowing media companies to own more television stations	Yes	Yes	fcc_rule	FCC media rule
13	Iraq reconstruction funding	Eliminate money allocated for reconstruction of Iraq	Yes	No	iraq1	Iraq reconstruction
14	Supplemental funds for Iraq and Afghanistan	Kill above amendment (see key vote number 13)	No	Yes	iraq2	Iraq/Afghanistan
15	Late term abortion ban	Ban medical procedure known as partial birth abortion	No	Yes	abort2	Partial birth abortion
16	Competitive sourcing, government/private	Prohibit competition between government and private sources	Yes	No	sourcing	Competitive sourcing
17	Election systems overhaul	Add grants to states for improving election technology	Yes	Yes	vot_tech	Voting technology
18	Pickering judicial nomination	Limit debate and vote on nomination	No	No	pickerin	Cloture on Pickering
19	Bush energy policy	End debate on energy bill	No	No	energy3	Energy policy
20	Prescription drug benefit conference report	End debate on bill that would create a prescription drug benefit	No	Yes	rxplan2	Rx benefit, conference report

Source: For key vote descriptions, ADA positions, and winning positions, see the Internet site of Americans for Democratic Action, www.adaction.org.

Note: SPSS variable names and variable labels are author's suggestions.

The second goal is to give similar names to variables that measure similar characteristics. According to the ADA site, for example, key votes 2 and 15 dealt with abortion, and key votes 3, 7, and 19 had to do with energy policy. We would keep such similarities in mind when devising names for the key votes. As noted earlier, a measure involving the Estrada nomination was the first key vote, which we can name estrada. We'll call the second and third votes, abort1 and energy1, respectively. (See Table 11-1 for a description of every

Figure 11–3 Typing Variable Names in a Text Editor

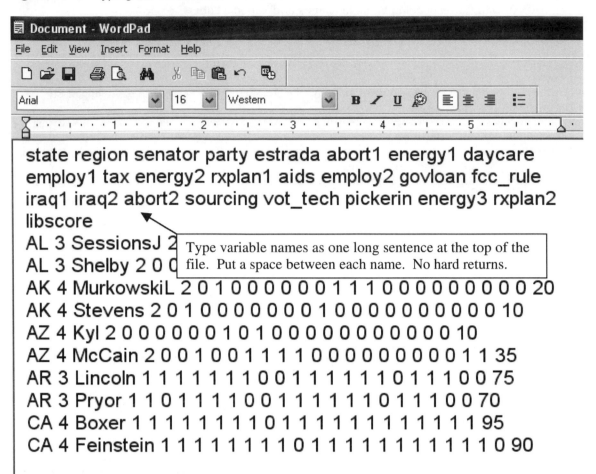

key vote.) We type these names at the top of the text data file in precisely the order in which they appear for each case. We type them as if they were one long sentence, with a space between each name and no hard returns. So the variable names—including state, region, senator, party, the 20 key votes, and the overall liberalism score (named "libscore")—and the first 10 cases in the Senate data would look like Figure 11-3.

Two Possible Coding Shortcuts

Typing a raw data file, line by line, can be tedious work. If you want to code data that you find in printed sources, there is no other option. You've got to hand-code the numbers. However, if you want to retrieve data from an Internet site, there are two ways in which you might cut your coding time. First, most browsers allow you to save a Web page in a format that can be accessed by other applications. Mozilla Firefox, for example, permits you to save the ADA page as a file with the *.htm extension, which Microsoft Excel will gladly open. To be sure, once the data are in Excel, much editing and labeling are required, but at least the data are in the spreadsheet and in workable form. The second method is somewhat more mundane: Select the desired text on the Web page, copy it to the clipboard, and then paste it into your word processor. Once it is in the word processor, you can make abundant use of the Find and Replace editing functions to alter the form of the data—replacing all the plus signs with 1s and all the minus signs with 0s, for example. The Senate dataset used in this illustration was created in just this way, although a fair amount of hand-typing— the state abbreviations and the region codes—was still required. The data were edited using Microsoft Word, and then the file was saved as a plain text file, with the *.txt extension.

You have seen how senate2003.txt was created. Now you will read the data file into SPSS.

Using the SPSS Text Import Wizard

Open SPSS. In the Data View of the Data Editor, click File → Read Text Data. Browse the file directory and locate the text data file, senate2003.txt. Select the data file and click Open. Step 1 of the Text Import Wizard

Figure 11–4 Step 1 of the Text Import Wizard

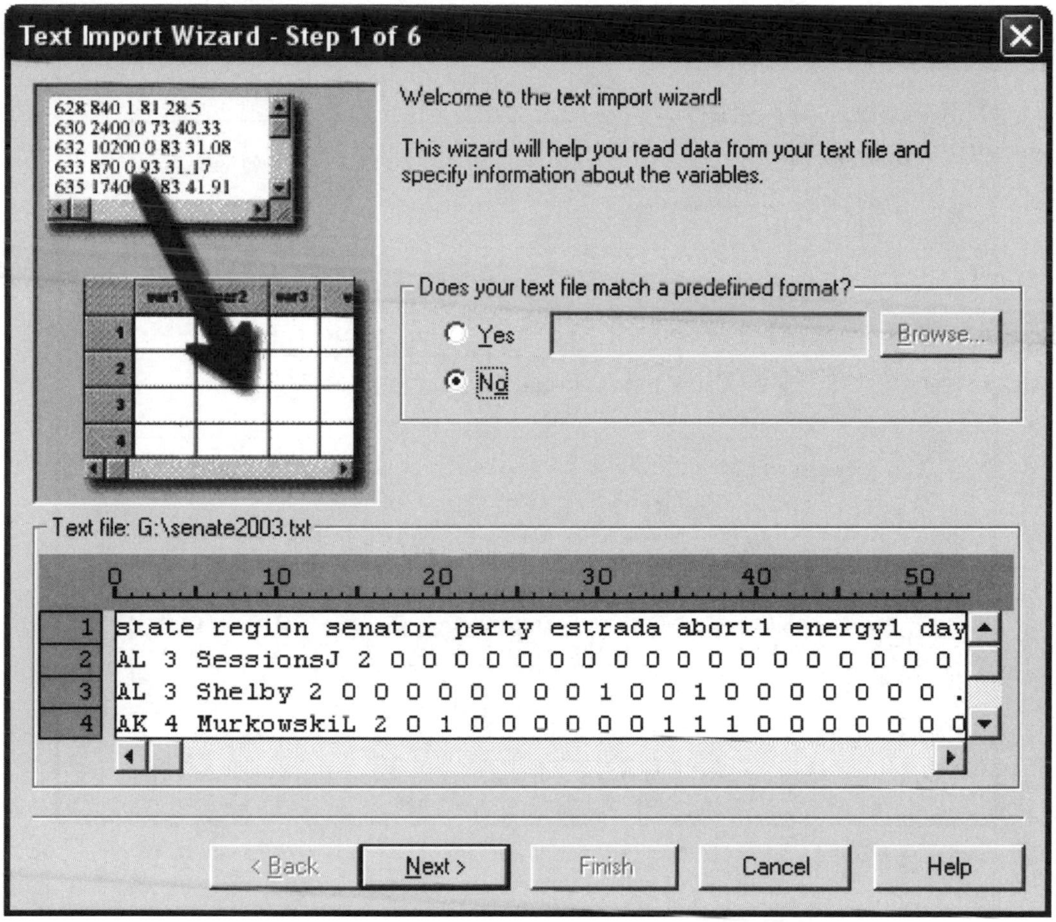

appears (Figure 11-4). SPSS asks one question about the data: "Does your text file match a predetermined format?" Make sure that the radio button next to "No" is clicked. At the bottom of the Step 1 window, SPSS offers a preview window. You can scroll through the preview and see if everything checks out. If all is well, click Next. Step 2 opens (Figure 11-5). Because the ADA variables are separated by spaces, in Step 2 you will answer "Delimited" to the question "How are your variables arranged?" and "Yes" to "Are variable names included at the top of your file?" Each succeeding step in the Text Import Wizard follows in this vein as SPSS elicits more specific information about the text data.

In Step 3 (Figure 11-6) you will tell SPSS that the first case of data begins on line 2 (because line 1 of the dataset contains the variable names), that each line represents a case, and that you want SPSS to import all the cases. In Step 4 (Figure 11-7) you will make sure that "Space" is selected because spaces—not tabs, commas, or semicolons—define the boundaries between variables. In Step 5 (Figure 11-8) you will make a minor change to the SPSS defaults. With the sort of text data you are importing in this example, SPSS sets a default of 10 characters for string variables. This limit works fine for the state abbreviation, but it won't accommodate the full text of all senators' names. To remedy this problem, click on the variable name "senator." In the Characters box, change the value to 12. In Step 6 (Figure 11-9), answer no to both questions, and click Finish. The dataset appears in the SPSS Data Editor (Figure 11-10). Data for the by-now familiar Senator Sessions appear along the first data row, data for his fellow Alabaman, Senator Shelby, in the second row, and so on. Naturally, you can scroll through the data to ensure that you imported the text file correctly. If so, you will want to save your data file in SPSS format. Click File → Save and choose a name and location. Save the Senate data as Senate2003.sav.

This is an eminently analyzable dataset. You may want to explore it. You can create new variables using Recode or Compute.[6] You can perform mean comparison analyses, comparing scores on the liberalism scale for Democrats and Republicans from different regions of the country. You can create liberalism scales for different policy areas. For example, you could sum the abortion votes (abort1 and abort2) and the drug benefit votes (rxplan1 and rxplan2) and then use Correlate to see how strongly these two new variables are related.

Figure 11–5   Step 2 of the Text Import Wizard

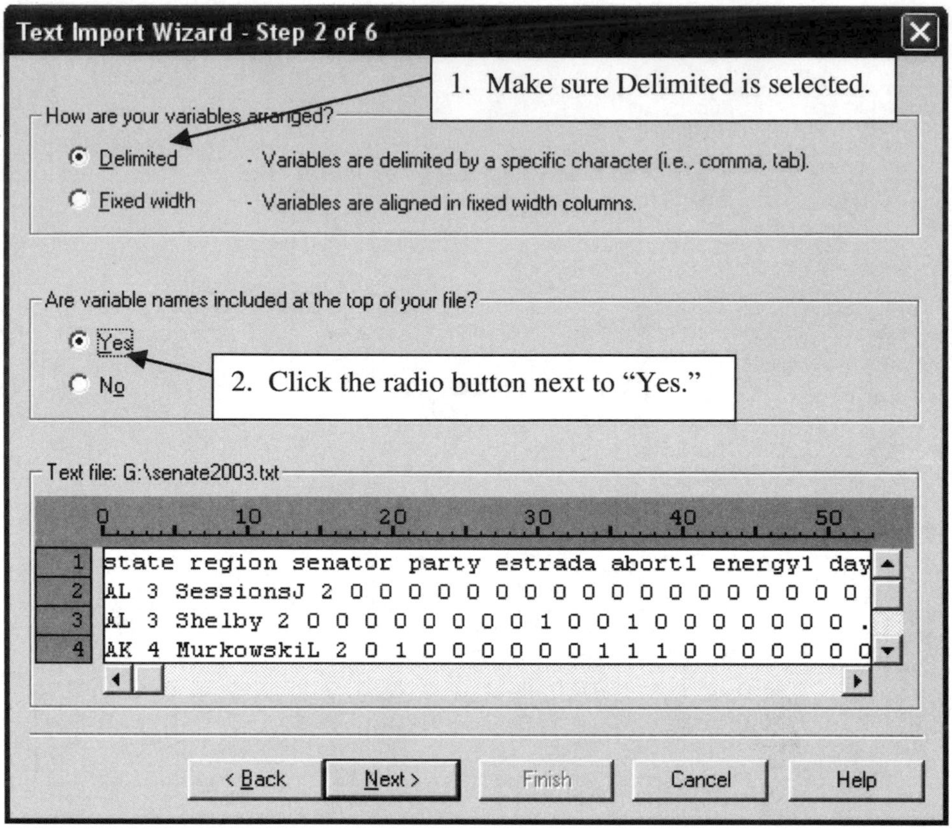

Figure 11–6   Step 3 of the Text Import Wizard

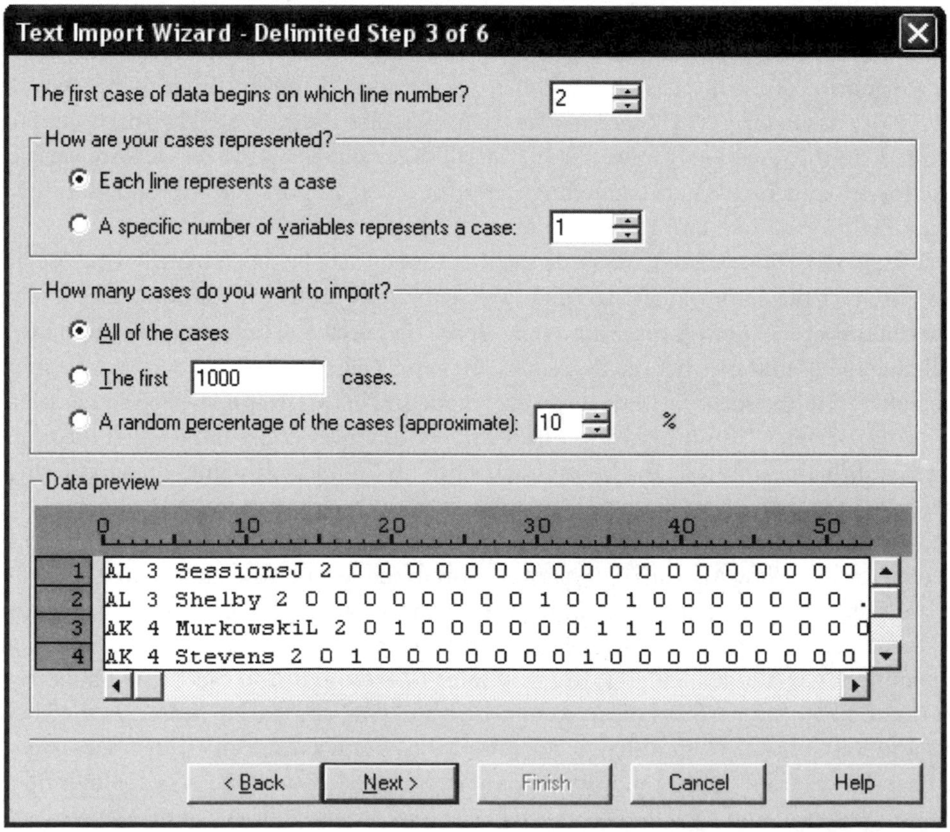

Figure 11–7   Step 4 of the Text Import Wizard

Text Import Wizard - Delimited Step 4 of 6   ☒

Which delimiters appear between variables?   What is the text qualifier?

☐ Tab   ☑ Space   ⦿ None

☐ Comma   ☐ Semicolon   ○ Single quote

☐ Other: [   ]   ○ Double quote

                                              ○ Other: [   ]

Data preview

state	region	senator	party	estrada	abort1	ene
AL	3	SessionsJ	2	0	0	0
AL	3	Shelby	2	0	0	0
AK	4	MurkowskiL	2	0	1	0
AK	4	Stevens	2	0	1	0

[< Back]   [Next >]   [Finish]   [Cancel]   [Help]

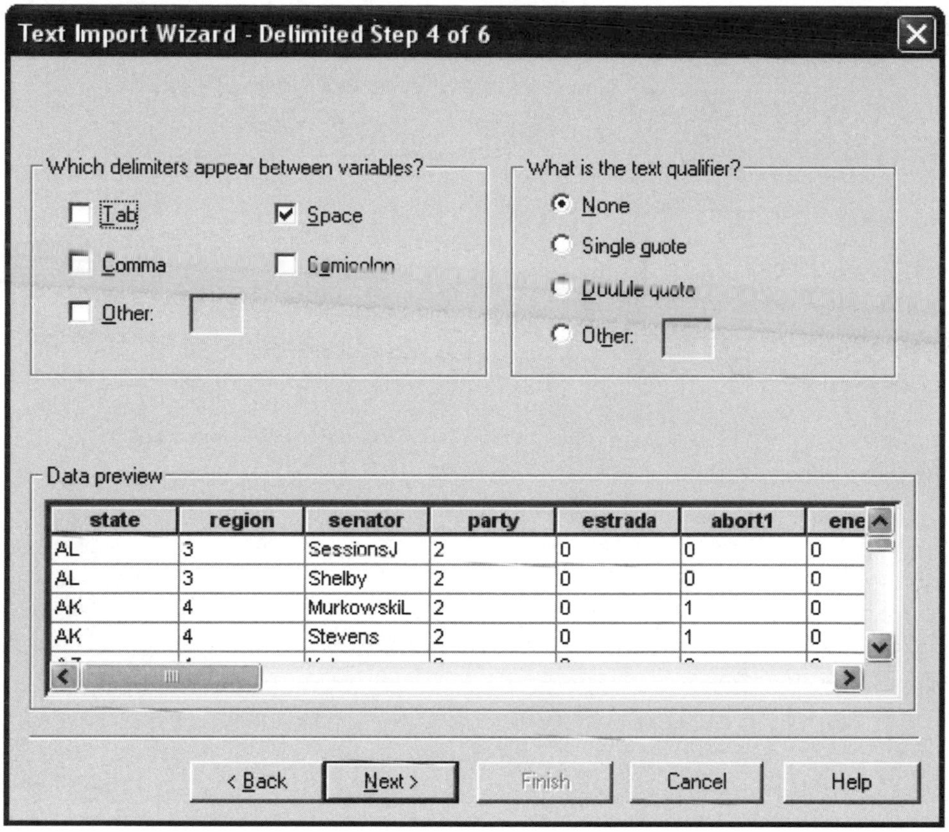

Figure 11–8   Step 5 of the Text Import Wizard

Text Import Wizard - Step 5 of 6   ☒

Specifications for variable(s) selected in the data preview

Variable name: Original Name:

[senator]   senator

2. Change Characters to "12."

Data format:

[String ▼]   Characters: [12 ⇅]

1. Click on the variable name "senator." This selects the column.

Data preview

state	region	senator	party	estrada	abort1	ene
AL	3	SessionsJ	2	0	0	0
AL	3	Shelby	2	0	0	0
AK	4	MurkowskiL	2	0	1	0
AK	4	Stevens	2	0	1	0

[< Back]   [Next >]   [Finish]   [Cancel]   [Help]

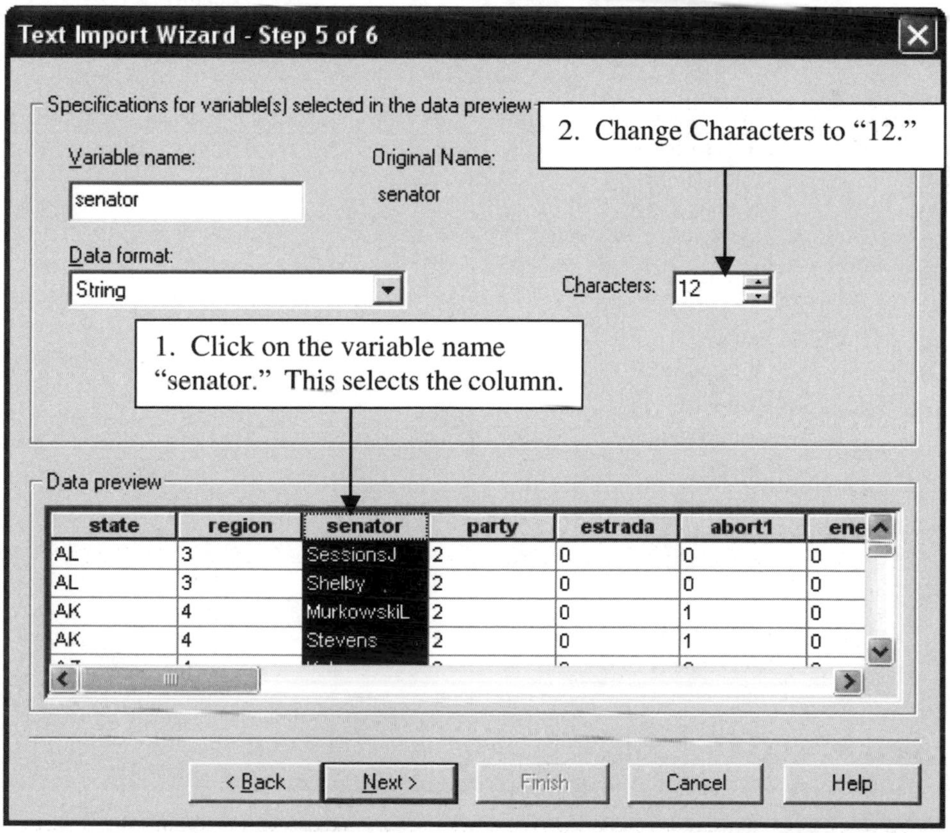

Figure 11–9 Step 6 of the Text Import Wizard

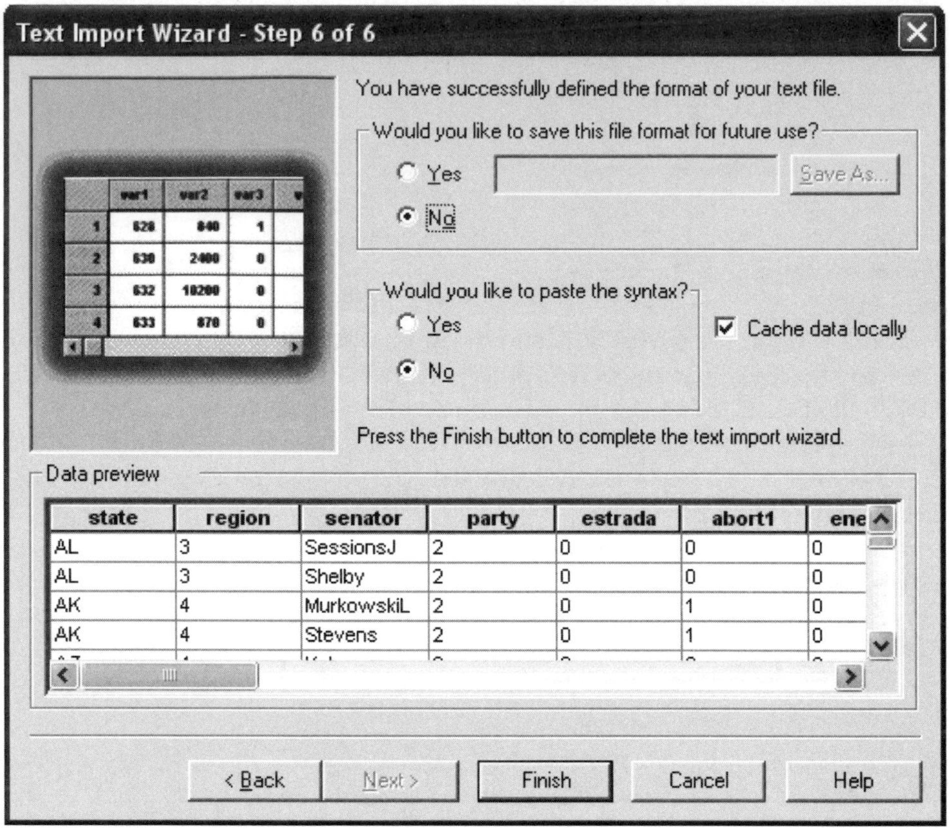

Figure 11–10 Senate Data in the Data Editor

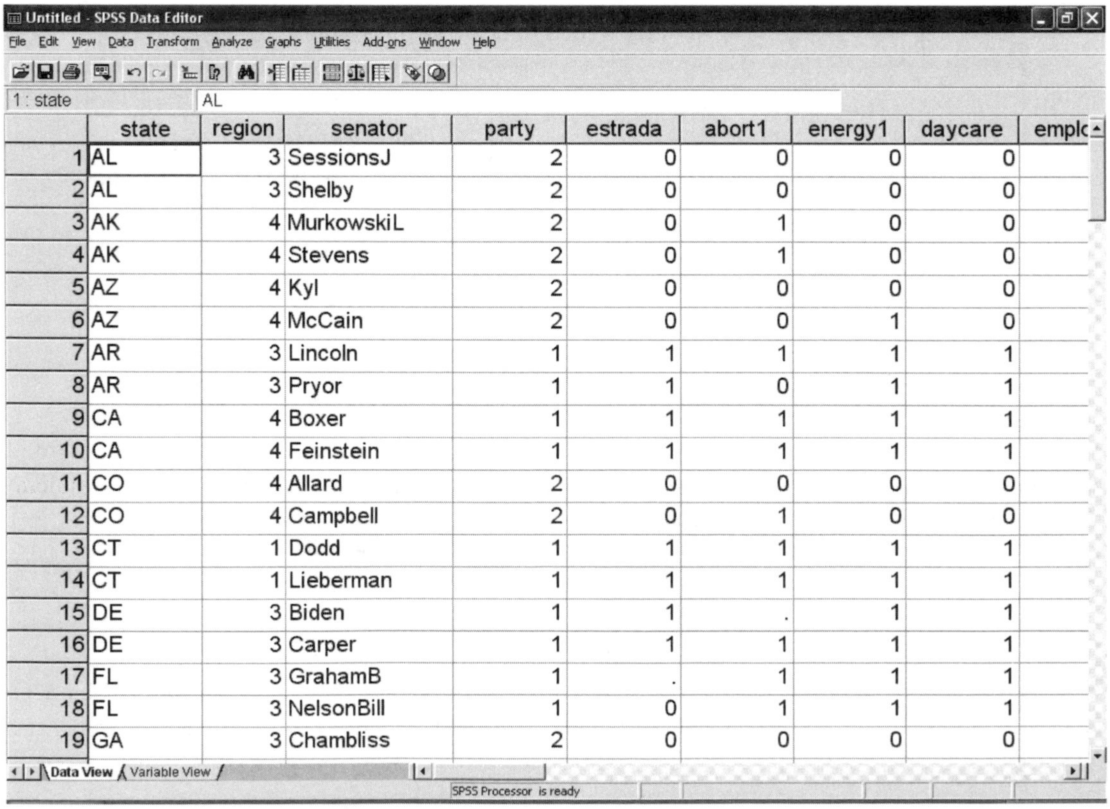

You can find additional information on each senator—the percentage of the vote they received in their most recent elections, the amount of money they spent on their campaigns, the number of years they have served in the Senate—and augment the dataset with this new information.[7] If you wanted to write a research paper on party, regionalism, and ideology in the Senate, Senate2003.sav would give you a good place to start.[8] Rewarding findings are guaranteed.

WRITING IT UP

At some point the analysis ends and the writing must begin. At this point, two contradictory considerations often collide. On one hand, you have an embarrassment of riches. You have worked on your research for several weeks, and you know the topic well—better, perhaps, than does anyone who will read the paper. You know the ins and outs of the data analysis. You know the inconsistencies in others' research on the topic. You know which variables and relationships yield notable measurements and outcomes and which do not. You want to include all of these things in your paper. On the other hand, you want to get it written, and you do not want to write a book. Viewed from an instructor's perspective, the two questions most frequently asked by students are "How should my paper be organized?" and "How long should it be?" (The questions are not necessarily asked in this order.)

Of course, different projects and instructors might call for different requirements. But here is a rough outline for a well-organized paper of 16 to 24 double-spaced pages (in a 12-point font).

I. The research question (3–4 pages)
    A. Introduction to the problem (1 page)
    B. Theory and process (1–2 pages)
    C. Propositions (1 page)
II. Previous research (2–4 pages)
    A. Descriptive review (1–2 pages)
    B. Critical review (1–2 pages)
III. Data and hypotheses (3–4 pages)
    A. Data and variables (1–2 pages)
    B. Measurement (1 page)
    C. Hypotheses (1 page)
IV. Analysis (5–8 pages, including tables)
    A. Descriptive statistics (1–2 pages)
    B. Bivariate comparisons (2–3 pages)
    C. Controlled comparisons (2–3 pages)
V. Conclusions and implications (3–4 pages)
    A. Summary of findings (1 page)
    B. Implications for theory (1–2 pages)
    C. New issues or questions (1 page)

The Research Question

Because of its rhetorical challenges, the opening section of a paper is often the most difficult to write. In this section you must both engage the reader's interest and describe the purpose of the research. Here is a heuristic device that may be useful: In the first page of the write-up, place the specific research problem (which the reader may or may not find fascinating) in the context of larger, clearly important issues or questions. Consider the example of Senator Jeffords, described earlier. You might begin a research paper on the Senate by recounting the Jeffords case, reminding the reader of the close partisan split in the chamber following the 2000 elections and describing Jeffords's high-profile shift in party alliances. A narrowly focused example? Yes. A dry topic? Not at all. The opening page of this paper could frame larger questions about the role of the Senate in U.S. government. To what extent does party serve as an organizing principle in Congress? How important are constituency or regional factors in shaping the behavior of elected representatives? Your analysis may appear "small," but it will advance our knowledge by illuminating one facet of a larger, more complex question.

Following the introduction, you begin to zero in on the problem at hand. The "theory and process" section describes the logic of the relationships you are studying. Many political phenomena, as you have learned, have competing or alternative explanations. Describe these alternatives, and the tension between them, in this section. Would you expect senators from the South to be more conservative than senators from the Northeast? If so, why? How important is party in explaining congressional voting behavior? Although a complete description of previous research does not appear in this section, you should give appropriate attribution to the most prominent work. These references tie your work to the scholarly community, and they raise the points you will cover in a more detailed review.

Round out the introductory section of your paper with a brief statement of purpose or intent. Think about it from the reader's perspective. Thus far you have made the reader aware of the larger context of the analysis, and you have described the process that may explain the relationships of interest. If this process has merit, then it should submit to an empirical test of some kind. What test do you propose? The "Propositions" page serves this role. Here you set the parameters of the research—informing the reader about the units of analysis, the concepts to be measured, and the type of analysis to be performed.

Previous Research

In this section you provide an intellectual history of the research problem, a description and critique of the published research on which the analysis is based. First you describe these previous analyses in some detail. What data and variables were used? What were the main findings? Did different researchers arrive at different conclusions? Political scientists who share a research interest often agree on many things. Yet knowledge is nourished through criticism, and in reviewing previous work you will notice key points of disagreement—about how concepts should be measured, what are the best data to use, or which variables need to be controlled. In the latter part of this section of the paper, you review these points and perhaps contribute to the debate. Previous studies of congressional voting, for example, have approached the measurement of ideology from different angles. Might not the use of separate measures—a measure of ideology on economic policy and a separate measure on social policy—be superior in some ways? A final, practical point: The frequently asked question "How many articles and books should be reviewed?" has no set answer. It depends on the project. However, here is an estimate: A well-grounded yet manageable review should discuss at least four references.

Data, Hypotheses, and Analysis

Together, the sections "Data and Hypotheses" and "Analysis" form the heart of the project, and they have been the primary concerns of this book. By now you are well versed in how to describe your data and variables and how to frame hypotheses. You also know how to set up a cross-tabulation or mean comparison table, and you can make controlled comparisons and interpret your findings.

In writing these sections, however, bear in mind a few reader-centered considerations. First, assume that the reader might want to replicate your study—collect the data you gathered, define and measure the concepts as you have defined and measured them, manipulate the variables just as you have computed and recoded them, and produce the tables you have reported. By explaining precisely what you did, your write-up should provide a clear guide for such a replication. Second, devote some space to a statistical description of the variables. Often you can add depth and interest to your analysis by briefly presenting the frequency distributions of the variables, particularly the dependent variable. A frequency distribution (or bar chart) of the ADA liberalism scale, for example, might show a distinct bimodal shape, with one group of senators at the liberal end and another at the conservative end. This distribution would make an effective prelude to the region-ideology analysis: Do regional differences help account for this pattern? Finally, exercise care in constructing readable tables. You can select, copy, and paste the tables generated by SPSS directly into a word processor, but they almost always require further editing for readability.

Conclusions and Implications

No section of a research paper can write itself. But the final section comes closest to realizing this optimistic hope. Here you discuss the analysis on three levels. First, you provide a condensed recapitulation. What are the main findings? Are the hypotheses borne out? Were any findings unexpected? Second, you describe where the results fit in the larger fabric of scholarly research on the topic. In what ways are the findings consistent with the work of previous researchers? Does your analysis lend support to one scholarly perspective as opposed to another? Third, research papers often include obligatory "suggestions for further research." Indeed, you might have encountered some methodological problems that still must be worked out, or you might have unearthed a noteworthy substantive relationship that could bear future scrutiny. Describe these new issues or questions. Here, too, you are allowed some room to speculate—to venture beyond the edge of the data and engage in a little "What if?" thinking. After all, the truth is still out there.

NOTES

1. You can browse ICPSR's holdings at www.icpsr.umich.edu.
2. The cases are available from LexisNexis at www.lexis-nexis.com/academic/universe/academic/.
3. Examples include three books published by CQ Press: *Who's Who in Congress,* offered twice a year through 2001; *CQ's Politics in America,* ed. Brian Nutting and H. Amy Stern, published every 2 years; and *Vital Statistics on American Politics,* by Harold W. Stanley and Richard G. Niemi, which also appears every 2 years. *Vital Statistics* is an excellent single-volume general reference on U.S. politics.
4. ADA's homepage is www.adaction.org.
5. SPSS will read data that are crunched together, with no delimiters between values. Fixed-format data, however, can present some complications worth avoiding. If you are entering your own data in a text file, the best practice is to put a space, comma, or tab between the values you are coding.
6. Because party is a potentially important independent variable, you probably want to treat Senator Jeffords (currently coded 3 on party) as a Democrat. Using Recode, create a new party variable for which old value 1 equals new value 1, old value 2 equals new value 2, and old value 3 equals new value 1.
7. For purposes of data augmentation, you can treat the Data Editor's Data View as a spreadsheet. Go to the first blank data column and type the data for each case directly into the Data Editor.
8. If you decide to use Senate2003.sav, you will want to type descriptive variable labels and value labels in the Variable View of the Data Editor. Table 11-1 suggests variable labels that you could use.

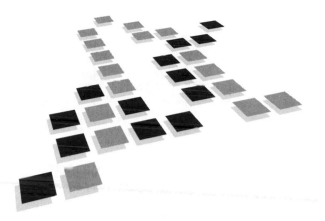

Appendix

Table A-1   Descriptions of Constructed Variables in GSS2002.sav

Variable name and label	Source variables, GSS 1972–2002 cumulative data file	Notes on construction of variable
activism Social activism scale	boycott signpet protest conoffcl givchng	Source variables recoded, number of activist acts summed: 0 (low) through 5 (high). GSS2002.sav variable activsm4 based on activism.
charity Charitable activity past 12 mos	givblood givhmlss givchrty volchrty	Number of charitable acts summed, collapsed: 1 = low; 2 = medium; 3 = high (0–1 act = 1; 2 acts = 2; 3–4 acts = 3).
contact Social contacts via email or meetings?	byemail meetings	Source variables combined: contact = 1 if byemail ≤ 2 and meetings ≤ 2; contact = 2 if byemail > 2 and meetings ≤ 2; contact = 3 if byemail ≤ 2 and meetings > 2; contact = 4 if byemail > 2 and meetings > 2. Final coding: 1 = neither; 2 = mostly email; 3 = mostly face-to-face meetings, 4 = both.
empathy Empathy scale	empathy1 empathy2 empathy3 empathy4 empathy5 empathy6 empathy7	Source variables' 5-point scales recoded in "more empathetic" direction and summed, rescaled: 0 (low) to 28 (high). GSS2002.sav variable empathy3 based on empathy.
fem_role Female role: children, home, politics	fechld fepresch femfam fepol	Source variables recoded in most liberal direction, summed, rescaled: 0 (women domestic) to 12 (women in work, politics). GSS2002.sav variable femrole3 based on fem_role.

Continued

Table A-1 *Continued*

Variable name and label	Source variables, GSS 1972–2002 cumulative data file	Notes on construction of variable
income02 Total family income	income98	GSS uses the name "income98" to identify the coding protocol applied on the 1998, 2000, and 2002 surveys. Author renamed income98 to GSS2002.sav variable income02. GSS2002.sav variable income3 based on income02.
indivism Social responsibility or individual effort?	careself selffrst getahead	Source variables recoded in direction of high individualism, summed and collapsed: 1 = social responsibility; 2 = middle; 3 = individual effort.
pol_int Political interest scale	poldisgn polinfgn	Source variables summed, rescaled: 0 (low) to 6 (high). GSS2002.sav variable pol_int3 based on pol_int.
racial Racial egalitarianism	affrmact blksimp	Source variables' least conservative responses recoded and summed. Scale recoded to 1 = less egalitarian; 2 = middle; 3 = more egalitarian.
rak Random acts of kindness past 12 mos	carried cutahead directns givseat	Source variables' 6-point codes summed, resulting scale collapsed: 1 = many; 2 = some; 3 = few.
soc_cons Social conservatism scale	abany cappun grass homosex pornlaw	Most-conservative codes of source variables summed: 0 (liberal) to 5 (conservative). GSS2002.sav variables soc_con2 and social based on soc_cons.
spend7 Number of programs spending "too little"	natcityy natdrugy nateducy natenviy natfarey nathealy natracey	Source variables recoded, "spending too little" responses summed: 0 (spending "too little" on none) to 7 (spending "too little" on seven). GSS2002.sav variable spend3 based on spend7.
suicide Allow incurable patients to: Die? Commit suicide?	letdie1 suicide1	Source variables recoded, number of "yes" responses summed: 0 = no, neither condition; 1 = yes, one condition; 2 = yes, both conditions.
sz_place Size of place where R resides	xnorcsiz	Source variable recoded using this protocol: (1–2 = 1; 5–7 = 1; 3–4 = 2; 8–10 = 3). sz_place categories: 1 = city; 2 = suburb; 3 = rural.

Table A-1   *Continued*

Variable name and label	Source variables, GSS 1972–2002 cumulative data file	Notes on construction of variable
tolhomo Intolerance of homosexuals	colhomo spkhomo	Source variables recoded and summed. Higher scores more intolerant: 0 = tolerant; 1 = middle; 2 = intolerant. GSS2002.sav variables tolracis, tolath, tolcom, and tolmil constructed in identical fashion.
trst_gov Political trust	confed conjudge conlegis	Source variables summed, resulting scale collapsed using this protocol: (7–9 = 0; 6 = 1; 3–5 = 2). Final variable: 0 = low; 1 = medium; 2 = high.
trst_soc Social trust	helpful fair trust	Source variables recoded, number of trusting responses summed: 0 = low; 1 = med–low; 2 = med–high; 3 = high.
trstmdia Trust in mass media	conpress contv	Source variables summed, resulting scale collapsed: 0 = low; 1 = medium; 2 = high (6 = 0; 5 = 1; 2–4 = 2).
webknow Internet familiarity scale	advsrch mp3 ezines prefsets newsgrps	All source variables recoded in most-familiar direction, summed, rescaled: 0 (low) to 10 (high). GSS2002.sav variable webknow3 based on webknow.

Table A-2 Descriptions of Variables in States.sav

Variable name and label	Description	Source and notes
abortion Abortions per 1000 women	Number of legal abortions per 1,000 women aged 15–44, 1996.	Alan Guttmacher Institute
abortlaw Number of restrictions on abortion	Five variables coded separately and summed: (i) parental (consent = 2, notification = 1, neither = 0); (ii) late term restriction (yes = 2, no = 0); (iii) counseling (and waiting period = 2, counseling only = 1, neither = 0); (iv) state-funded abortions (no = 2, yes = 0); insurance coverage restrictions (several = 2, some = 1, none = 0). Final variable: 0 (least restrictive) to 10 (most restrictive).	Alan Guttmacher Institute, June 2002, www.guttmacher.org Data also available from America's Pregnancy Helpline, www.thehelpline.org www.thehelpline.org/unplanned_pregnancy/abortion/abortionlaws.pdf *Note:* All provisions enacted into law, including legally enjoined provisions, are counted as restrictions.
attend Percent frequent church attenders	Percentage attending religious services "every week" or "almost every week."	Pooled National Election Study, 1988–2002. Percentage coded 1 ("every week") or 2 ("almost every week") on question #vcf0130. *Note:* Thirteen states have fewer than 30 cases and were set to missing values on attend.
battle04 Battleground state	Coded 1 for 2004 battleground states, coded 0 for non–battleground states.	U.S. Department of State, http://usinfo.state.gov/dhr/democracy/elections/battleground_states.html
blkpct Percent black	Percentage of population black.	*State and Metropolitan Data Book,* 1996
bush00 Percent voting for Bush 2000 gore00 Percent voting for Gore 2000 nader00 Percent voting for Nader 2000	Number of votes cast for Bush [Gore, Nader] as a percentage of all votes cast.	Federal Election Commission, www.fec.gov

Table A-2 *Continued*

Variable name and label	Description	Source and notes
bush04 Percent voting for Bush 2004 kerry04 Percent voting for Kerry 2004	Number of votes cast for Bush [Kerry] as a percentage of all votes cast.	Dave Leip's Atlas of U.S. Presidential Elections, http://uselectionatlas.org
carfatal Motor vehicle fatalities (per 100,000 pop)	Motor vehicle fatalities per 100,000 population.	National Safety Council, 2001
christad Percent of pop who are Christian adherents	Percentage of population who are Christian adherents.	*Statistical Abstract of the United States,* 1990
college Percent of pop college grads	Percentage of population who are college graduates.	*State and Metropolitan Data Book,* 1998
cons_hr Conservatism score, US House delegation	Mean American Conservative Union rating of state's delegation to House of Representatives, 2003.	American Conservative Union, http://acuratings.com
defexpen Federal defense expenditures per capita	Federal defense expenditures per capita.	Office of Management and Budget/Census Bureau, 1994
demnat % US House and Senate Democratic	Number of Democratic House and Senate members as a percentage of total House and Senate delegations, 2003.	American Conservative Union, http://acuratings.com
dempct_m Percent mass public Democratic reppct_m Percent mass public Republican indpct_m Percent mass public Independent libpct_m Percent mass public Liberal	Pooled CBS News/*New York Times* poll party identification and ideology estimates, 1977–1999.	Gerald C. Wright, Indiana University. Data used with permission. Robert S. Erikson, Gerald C. Wright, and John P. McIver, *Statehouse Democracy* (Cambridge, U.K.: Cambridge University Press, 1993).

Continued

Table A-2 *Continued*

Variable name and label	Description	Source and notes
modpct_m Percent mass public Moderate		
conpct_m Percent mass public Conservative		
demstate Percent state legislators Democratic	Number of Democratic state house and senate members as a percentage of total house and senate members, 2003.	National Conference of State Legislatures, www.ncsl.org/programs/legman/elect/statevote2002.htm
density Population per square mile	Number of residents per square mile.	*Statistical Abstract of the United States,* 1994
hispanic Percent hispanic	Percentage of population Hispanic.	*State and Metropolitan Data Book,* 1996
hsdip Percent high school graduates	Number of high school graduates as a percentage of adult population.	National Center for Education Statistics, 1990 *Note:* States.sav variable hscat4 based on hsdip.
nobelts Unrestrained motor veh deaths per 100k	Unrestrained motor vehicle deaths per 100,000 population.	National Safety Council, 2001
over64 Percent of pop age 65 or older	Percentage of population aged 65 or older.	*State and Metropolitan Data Book,* 1996
permit Percent public "Always allow" abortion	Percentage responding that abortion should "always" be permitted.	Pooled National Election Study, 1988–2002. Percentage coded 4 on question #vcf0838. *Note:* Ten states have fewer than 30 cases and were set to missing values on permit.
prcapinc Percapita income	Income per capita.	*Statistical Abstract of the United States,* 1994

Table A-2   *Continued*

Variable name and label	Description	Source and notes
seatbelt Seat belt usage: Percent	Estimated percentage of motor vehicle occupants using seat belts.	National Safety Council, 2001
turnout00 turnout04	Number of voters as a percentage of 2000 [2004] voting age population.	Committee for the Study of the American Electorate
under20 Percent of pop age 19 or younger	Percentage of population aged 19 or younger.	*State and Metropolitan Data Book,* 1996
unemploy Unemployment rate	Unemployment rate.	*Statistical Abstract of the United States,* 1996
union Percent workers who are union members	Percentage of workers who are members of a labor union or an employee association similar to a union, 2003.	U. S. Department of Labor, Bureau of Labor Statistics, http://stats.bls.gov/news.release/union2.t05.htm
urban Percent urban pop	Percentage of population in urban areas.	*Statistical Abstract of the United States,* 1996
womleg Percent of state legislators who are women	Percentage of state legislators who are women.	Center for American Women and Politics, 1994

Table A-3   Descriptions of Variables in World.sav

Variable name and label	Compiled by	Source and notes
aids AIDS cases (per 100,000 people), 1997	Norris	*Human Development Report,* 2003, United Nations Development Programme, www.undp.org
civlib Civil liberties score	Author	Freedom House, 1997, www.freedomhouse.org
colony Colony of what country?	Norris	*CIA World Factbook,* www.cia.gov
compulse Compulsory voting used?	Norris	International Institute for Democracy and Electoral Assistance, www.idea.int
democ Is country democratic?	ACLP	Computed by Alvarez, Cheibub, Limongi, and Przeworski, 1990
dem_oth % of other countries in the region that are democracies	ACLP	Computed by Alvarez, Cheibub, Limongi, and Przeworski, 1990
dem_oth3 % of democracies in region: 3 cats	ACLP	Based on dem_oth
divorce divorces (as % of marriages), 1996	Norris	*Human Development Report,* 2003, United Nations Development Programme, www.undp.org
econdev3 Econ devel: 3 cats	Author	*Human Development Report,* 1998, United Nations Development Programme
eth_het Index:Ethno-linguistic heterogeneity (high=more heterogeneous)	ACLP	William Easterly and Ross Levine, 1997
eth_het3 Ethno-linguistic heterogeneity: 3 cats	ACLP	Based on eth_het
fh03rev Freedom House democ rating reversed 2003–2004	Norris	Freedom House, 2004, www.freedomhouse.org

Table A-3   *Continued*

Variable name and label	Compiled by	Source and notes
gdp_1000 GDP per cap ($1000)	ACLP	Heston and Summers, 1991
gdpcap2 GDP percapita: 2 categories	ACLP	Based on gdp_1000
gini Gini coefficient	Norris	*World Bank Development Indicators 2002,* www.worldbank.org
hdi2001 Human development index 2001	Norris	*Human Development Report,* 2003, United Nations Development Programme, www.undp.org
hi_gdp High gdppcap dummy	ACLP	Based on gdpcap2
indy Year of independence	Norris	*CIA World Factbook,* www.cia.gov
legdom Legis dominance of largest party	ACLP	Based on seats
natsize Size of country by population (3 categories)	Norris	*Human Development Report,* 2003, United Nations Development Programme, www.undp.org
oil Did ratio of fuel exports to total exports exceed 50%?	ACLP	International Monetary Fund, 1994
open Imports and exports as a share of GDP	ACLP	Heston and Summers, 1991
party Number of parties: 3 categories	ACLP	Arthur S. Banks, Cross-National Time-Series Data Archive, 1996
pctwom03 % of women in lower house of parliament, 2003	Norris	Inter-Parliamentary Union, *Women in Parliament,* www.ipu.org

Continued

Table A-3   *Continued*

Variable name and label	Compiled by	Source and notes
polrts Political rights score	Author	Freedom House, 1997, www.freedomhouse.org
pop2002 Total population 2002	Norris	*World Bank Development Indicators 2002*, www.worldbank.org
pr_sys PR electoral system?	Norris	International Institute for Democracy and Electoral Assistance, www.idea.int
regime Is country democracy or dictatorship?	ACLP	Computed by Alvarez, Cheibub, Limongi, and Przeworski, 1990
region Region of the world	Norris	Coded by Norris
relcat Type of secular or religious society	Norris	Coded by Norris
rural Rural population (% of total population)	Norris	*World Bank Development Indicators 2002*, www.worldbank.org
seats Percent of seats in lower legis hse held by largest party	ACLP	Arthur S. Banks, Cross-National Time-Series Data Archive, 1996
smoking Cigarette consumption per adult (1970–72=100), 1990–92	Norris	*Human Development Report*, 2003, United Nations Development Programme, www.undp.org
typerel Religious culture	Norris	*CIA World Factbook*, www.cia.gov
unions union density 1995	Norris	International Labour Organization, www.ilo.org
urban Urban population (% of total)	Norris	*World Bank Development Indicators 2002*, www.worldbank.org

Table A-3   *Continued*

Variable name and label	Compiled by	Source and notes
vi_rel % religion 'very' important	Norris	World Values Survey (1995–2000 waves), wvs.isr.umich.edu
votevap Turnout / vap 1990s	Norris	International Institute for Democracy and Electoral Assistance, www.idea.int
womyr_2 Women's suffrage: before/after 1920	Norris	Inter-Parliamentary Union, *Women in Parliament*, www.ipu.org
wrk_rest Elections: Day of work or rest?	Author	LeDuc, Niemi, and Norris, 2002

Notes: Norris = Pippa Norris, Shared Global Database (revised fall 2004), John F. Kennedy School of Government, Harvard University, Cambridge, Mass., www.pippanorris.com. ACLP = Mike Alvarez, Jose Antonio Cheibub, Fernando Limongi, and Adam Przeworski. See Mike Alvarez, Jose Antonio Cheibub, Fernando Limongi, and Adam Przeworski, *Democracy and Development: Political Institutions and Well-Being in the World, 1950–1990* (Cambridge, U.K.: Cambridge University Press, 2000). Easterly and Levine, 1997 = William Easterly and Ross Levine, "Africa's Growth Tragedy: Policies and Ethnic Divisions," *Quarterly Journal of Economics* (November 1997): 1203–1250. Heston and Summers, 1991 = Alan Heston and Robert Summers, "The Penn World Table (Mark 5): An Expanded Set of International Comparisons, 1950–1988," *Quarterly Journal of Economics* (May 1991): 327–368. LeDuc, Niemi, and Norris, 2002 = Lawrence LeDuc, Richard Niemi, and Pippa Norris, "Introduction: Comparing Democratic Elections," in LeDuc, Niemi, and Norris, eds., *Comparing Democracies 2: New Challenges in the Study of Elections and Voting* (Thousand Oaks, CA: Sage, 2002), pp. 1–39, Table 1.3.